PENGUIN BOOKS

IMITATIONS OF IMMORTALITY

Eric Oakley Parrott was born in 1924 in London, well within the sound of Bow Bells and so is technically a Cockney, but was brought up in Shoreham-by-Sea, Sussex, where he attended the local grammar school. After winning that school's most coveted academic award, the Gregory Taylor Scholarship, in 1939, he went to Brighton Technical College, where he studied for a B.Sc. in Mathematics and Geography. He then spent twenty years as a cartographer with the Hydrographic Department of the Ministry of Defence, during which time he edited the Admiralty List of Radio Signals. It was then that he began to write seriously in his spare time – articles, plays and entries in various literary competitions. He has always taken a keen interest in the theatre and was both an amateur actor and producer, becoming an Associate of the Drama Board in 1961. He has had a number of plays produced and has had radio plays performed by the BBC and in Germany, Canada, Australia and New Zealand, among other countries. In 1967 he resigned from the Civil Service, and, after a year at Garnett College, Roehampton, taught English and General Studies at Havering Technical College, Hornchurch, Essex. Here he compiled a number of Units for the Longman's General Studies Project. Failing eyesight has forced him to retire from teaching and he has now begun a third career as a full-time writer. He lives on a converted Dutch sailing barge on the Regent's Canal. He has also edited *How to Become Ridiculously Well-Read in One Evening* and the *Penguin Book of Limericks*.

Compiled and edited by
E. O. PARROTT

Imitations of Immortality

A BOOK OF LITERARY PARODIES

PENGUIN BOOKS

Penguin Books Ltd, Harmondsworth, Middlesex, England
Viking Penguin Inc., 40 West 23rd Street, New York, New York 10010, U.S.A.
Penguin Books Australia Ltd, Ringwood, Victoria, Australia
Penguin Books Canada Ltd, 2801 John Street, Markham, Ontario, Canada L3R 1B4
Penguin Books (N.Z.) Ltd, 182 190 Wairau Road, Auckland 10, New Zealand

First published by Viking 1986
Published in Penguin Books 1987

This collection copyright © E. O. Parrott, 1986

The Acknowledgements on pages 379 83
constitute an extension of this copyright page

All rights reserved

Made and printed in Great Britain by
Richard Clay Ltd, Bungay, Suffolk
Typeset in Baskerville

Except in the United States of America, this book is sold subject
to the condition that it shall not, by way of trade or otherwise, be lent,
re-sold, hired out, or otherwise circulated without the
publisher's prior consent in any form of binding or cover other than
that in which it is published and without a similar condition
including this condition being imposed on the subsequent purchaser

For my son Toby, with love

PREFACE

I would like to express my thanks to the following people, who have assisted me in many ways with the compilation of this anthology: Bernard Palmer of the *Church Times*, Angela Harding of the *New Statesman*, Jonathan Barker of the Arts Council Poetry Library, Russell Lucas and Stanley J. Sharpless for the loan of rare books, Katherine Smith, Michael Woodward, Edward Blishen, Arthur Marshall, R. G. G. Price, Michael J. Rees, Fr Ian Brayley, SJ; John McLaughlin, my agent, for numerous helpful suggestions; Sharron Saint Michael for typing the manuscript.

Particular thanks are due to my wife, Tricia, without whose daily effort the lot of a partially sighted author would be virtually impossible.

E. O. P.

CONTENTS

xxiii

PROLOGUE

READER: Excuse me . . . Excuse me. It was here that I was expecting
to find . . .

EDITOR: A great wodge of unappetizing-looking prose . . . ?

READER: No, no, of course not. Well, yes . . . that is to say – there has
to be an introductory essay – a literary piece, full of nicely
turned phrases – you know the sort of thing . . .

EDITOR: Only too well. With scholarly footnotes, I dare say.

READER: Yes. Then you *do* know what I mean . . .

EDITOR: Of course. Written several in my time.

READER: Then why didn't you put one in here?

EDITOR: So that you could skip it?

READER: Yes, of course . . . that is to say . . . no.

EDITOR: Come now. Be honest! Don't you usually skip introduc-
tions?

READER: No, never. Well, hardly ever . . . that is to say I may just
skim through it . . .

EDITOR: Meaning to come back to it later. Although you never
do.

READER: But it still has to be here. After all, where else can you
delineate the various criteria you have employed in determining
the selection of material for this volume . . . ?

EDITOR: Spoken like a true introduction.

READER: Oh, thank you . . . !

EDITOR: But won't all that be obvious from the book itself?

READER: Well, I suppose it ought to be. But you still need somewhere to explain that anthologies are very much the subjective
choice of their editors and that you have included all the imitative writing that appealed to you personally. That is always
done.

EDITOR: That just wouldn't be true. I could have included ten
times more material than I have and still have had to leave out
items that were worth putting in.

READER: If space was really so short . . .

EDITOR: It really was.

READER: . . . then why put in so much that has been anthologized

I

so often before? Lewis Carroll's parody of Longfellow, 'Hia-watha's Photographing', the A. E. Housman 'Fragment of a Greek Tragedy', the Hugh Kingsmill parodies of Housman. And so on . . .

EDITOR: They are the great classics of literary parody. Leaving them out . . . well, I just couldn't.

READER: And yet you've deliberately omitted all those marvellous parodies of Wordsworth, Isaac Watts and so on in the Alice books.

EDITOR: I felt that the Lewis Carroll versions are better known than the originals. Who reads Isaac Watts nowadays? And, in any case, most people have the Carroll books. And if they haven't, then it's time they did!

READER: Or what about T. S. Eliot? All the Old Possum verses are parodies, you know. Kipling, Macaulay, and so on.

EDITOR: I couldn't get them *all* in, so I thought it better just to mention them in passing.

READER: Yet there are other classics you have had the nerve to cut . . . Even Max Beerbohm. Not to mention Cyril Connolly and Malcolm Bradbury and . . .

EDITOR: Space. Or, rather, the lack of it. And this is a representative collection, not a comprehensive compilation. I wanted as many different authors as possible to be included – both parodists and parodied. In order to leave room for other forms of imitative writing . . .

READER: Other forms? It isn't all parody then?

EDITOR: No. Parody is specifically concerned with mockery of the style of the author – the language, the way it's used, the subject matter. There is pastiche, which is gentler, more affectionate – and there is a large group where the imitation is more concerned with social or other comment on the contemporary scene at the time of writing . . .

READER: But hasn't a lot of that dated?

EDITOR: Of course, but in the pieces I have chosen, it seemed to me that the provenance of the item was still comprehensible, as in the case, say, of the Sagittarius verse about Chamberlain, or Arthur Marshall's Betjeman poem on the end of sweet ration-ing.

READER: This space problem of yours has meant some savage cuts . . .

EDITOR: It wasn't merely a question of space. Sometimes I felt the joke was going on too long. Brevity is the soul of wit, you know. At other times I felt the parody went over the top, and degenerated into burlesque, though perhaps it would be tactful not to specify which these are.

READER: Because I may disagree?

EDITOR: I'm sure everyone will disagree with some of my decisions. That's editing.

READER: I see you've had the cheek to include some of your own parodies.

EDITOR: Others have thought them worth anthologizing, so why indulge in false modesty? Mind you, I have taken the opportunity to tidy them up a bit. And they do all appear under my real name and not under the various pseudonyms I've used in literary competitions.

READER: I've never known why you literary-competition addicts use all those funny names.

EDITOR: Money, mostly. You can win more. Allan M. Laing, the leading literary competitor for many years in the 1930s and 1940s, once confessed that he won over 7,000 prizes in twelve years, using dozens of different names.

READER: Is it still done?

EDITOR: Oh, yes. But not on that scale, so far as I know. Of course, entering under a false name can be just fun, as in the case of Graham Greene parodying himself and winning under an assumed name.

READER: Or not winning?

EDITOR: That's right. On another occasion he was pipped to the post by his brother, Hugh.*

READER: At last. A scholarly footnote. This begins to look like a real introduction.

EDITOR: If it were that, I doubt if you would have got as far as this. You wouldn't want a book with an introduction you've never read, would you?

READER: I own lots of them, actually. Quite a few items that I expected to find are not here at all.

EDITOR: Of course. Some authors are very much parodied – Wordsworth, Browning, Betjeman, Housman and so on. Choosing what to include and what to leave out is a very subjective decision, especially when so much of the material is

* It is rumoured that Graham recognized the entry as his brother's, even though it was written under a pseudonym.

good. And I've had to omit some brilliant parodies of little-known or little-read authors. On the other hand some authors are their own best parodists – McGonagall, for instance.

READER: I don't see much general parody. Of types of popular fiction, for instance. Or of newspapers. That San Seriffe spoof supplement in the *Guardian* . . .

EDITOR: No room! No room!

READER: You sound like the Mad Hatter.

EDITOR: If editors weren't just as mad as that they wouldn't do the job. No, the truth is that my brief was for literary parody. I couldn't do it justice and deal with general parody comprehensively as well.

READER: Maybe another time?

EDITOR: Maybe.

READER: And you'll write a REAL introduction for that one, won't you? You can't shuffle out of your duty. Not for a second time, you know.

EDITOR: No comment.

Aeschylus (*c.* 525–*c.* 456 BC)

Peter Rabbit

(*Enter* MESSENGER.)

MRS RABBIT
In your eyes I see disaster!
What the gods decree for rabbits
Must be known, cannot be hidden.
Tell us, man! Do not keep silent.

MESSENGER
Though my charge beats at my heart's core
I must answer, tell you plainly
Of the god MacGregor's anger.
MacGregor, he we fear and pray to,
MacGregor, with his sullen god-strength,
Black-browed titan of the garden,
Gazed in wrath upon the carnage,
Seeing by the ravaged lettuce
Fearful, mortal Father Rabbit
Crouching in the he-god's lettuce,
Stilled by knowledge of his death-due,
By sudden knowledge of his hubris.

(*The* CHORUS *begins to dance.*)

CHORUS
Thus the gods prepare their pottage,
Thus inflict on mortal rabbits
Wisdom through the death of great ones!

N J. WARBURTON

The Nurse's Tale

(*Enter an old* NURSE.)

CHORUS
Tell us your tidings, O royal nappy-washer.

NURSE
I have written a book.

CHORUS
Relate unto us its contents,
O pusher of the princess's pram!

NURSE
In it I have inscribed
All the tales of Lilibet
And of her sister.

CHORUS
O wonderful day, O far-sighted publisher,
May Zeus bless your paperback sales.
How have I lived all these lonely years
Without such a tome to comfort me?

NURSE
May wise Pallas Athene guide your feet
Unto the wine-dark booksellers.

CHORUS
You read our innermost longings.
We are already on our way.

NURSE
May you have the swiftness of Diana
In your headlong flight.

E. O. PARROTT

Fragment of a Greek Tragedy

ALCMAEON, CHORUS

CHORUS

O suitably-attired-in-leather-boots
Head of a traveller, wherefore seeking whom
Whence by what way how purposed art thou come
To this well-nightingaled vicinity?
My object in enquiring is to know,
But if you happen to be deaf and dumb
And do not understand a word I say,
Then wave your hand, to signify as much.

ALCMAEON

I journeyed hither a Boeotian road.

CHORUS

Sailing on horseback, or with feet for oars?

ALCMAEON

Plying with speed my partnership of legs.

CHORUS

Beneath a shining or a rainy Zeus?

ALCMAEON

Mud's sister, not himself, adorns my shoes.

CHORUS

To learn your name would not displease me much.

ALCMAEON

Not all that men desire do they obtain.

CHORUS

Might I then hear at what your presence shoots?

ALCMAEON

A shepherd's questioned mouth informed me that –

CHORUS

What? for I know not yet what you will say –

Nor will you ever, if you interrupt.

Proceed, and I will hold my speechless tongue.

– This house was Eriphyla's, no one's else.

Nor did he shame his throat with hateful lies.

May I then enter, passing through the door?

Go, chase into the house a lucky foot,
And, O my son, be, on the one hand, good,
And do not, on the other hand, be bad;
For that is very much the safest plan.

I go into the house with heels and speed.

Strophe

    In speculation
I would not willingly acquire a name
    For ill-digested thought;
    But after pondering much
To this conclusion I at last have come:
    Life is uncertain.
    This truth I have written deep
    In my reflective midriff
    On tablets not of wax,
Nor with a pen did I inscribe it there,
For many reasons: *Life, I say, is not*
    A stranger to uncertainty.
Not from the flight of omen-yelling fowls
    This fact did I discover.
Nor did the Delphic tripod bark it out,
    Nor yet Dodona.
Its native ingenuity sufficed
    My self-taught diaphragm.

Why should I mention
The Inachean daughter, loved of Zeus?
    Her whom of old the gods,
    More provident than kind,
Provided with four hoofs, two horns, one tail,
    A gift not asked for,
    And sent her forth to learn
    The unfamiliar science
    Of how to chew the cud.
She therefore, all about the Argive fields,
Went cropping pale green grass and nettle-tops,
    Nor did they disagree with her.
But yet, howe'er nutritious, such repasts
    I do not hanker after:
Never may Cypris for her seat select
    My dappled liver!
Why should I mention Io! Why indeed?
    I have no notion why.

But now does my boding heart,
Unhired, unaccompanied, sing
A strain not meet for the dance.
Yea even the palace appears
To my yoke of circular eyes
(The right, nor omit I the left)
Like a slaughterhouse, so to speak,
Garnished with woolly deaths
And many shipwrecks of cows.
I therefore in a Cissian strain lament;
    And to the rapid,
Loud, linen-tattering thumps upon my chest
    Resounds in concert
The battering of my unlucky head.

ERIPHYLA
(*Within*)
O, I am smitten with a hatchet's jaw;
And that in deed and not in word alone.

9

I thought I heard a sound within the house
Unlike the voice of one that jumps for joy.

ERIPHYLA
He splits my skull, not in a friendly way,
One more; he purposes to kill me dead.

CHORUS
I would not be reputed rash, but yet
I doubt if all be gay within the house.

ERIPHYLA
O! O! another stroke! that makes the third.
He stabs me to the heart against my wish.

CHORUS
If that be so, thy state of health is poor;
But thine arithmetic is quite correct.

A. E. HOUSMAN

Aristotle (384–322 BC)

from Concerning Golf

Translation of an Aristotelian fragment in the Bodleian

Now it is possible to play in several ways: for perhaps they strike indeed, yet not as is necessary, nor where, nor when; as the man who played in the Parks and wounded the infant: for this was good for him, yet not absolutely, nor for the infant. Wherefore here as in other things we should aim at the mean between excess and defect. For the player in excess hits the ball too often, as they do at cricket; and the deficient man cannot hit it at all, except by accident [κατὰ συμβεβηκός]: as it is related of the man who kicked his caddie, as they do at football. For the beginning is to hit it: and the virtue of a good golfer is to hit well and according to reason and as the professional would hit. And to speak briefly, to play Golf is either the part of a man of genius or a madman, as has been said in the *Poetics*.

And because it is better to hit few times than many – for the good is finite, but the man who goes round in three hundred strokes stretches out in the direction of the infinite – some have said that here too we ought to remember the saying of Hesiod, 'The half is better than the whole,' thinking not rightly, according at least to my opinion: for in relation to your adversary it is much better to win the Hole than the Half. And Homer is a good master both in other respects and also here: for he alone has taught us how to lie as is necessary, both as to the hole [καθόλου], and otherwise.

Again, every art and every method, and likewise every action and intention aims at the good. Some, therefore, making a syllogism, aim at a Professor: for Professors, they say, are good (because dry things are good for men, as has been said in the *Ethics*), and this is a Professor: but perhaps they make a wrong use of the major premiss. At any rate, having hit him, it is better to act in some such way as this, not as tragedians seek a recognition [ἀναγνώρισις]; for this is most unpleasant [μιαρόν], and perhaps leads to a catastrophe. It is doubted, whether the man who killed his tutor with a golf-ball acted voluntarily or involuntarily; for on the one hand he did not do it deliberately, since no one deliberates about the results of chance, as, for instance, whether one will hit the ball this time at any rate or not: yet he wished to kill him, and was glad having done it: and probably on the whole it was a mixed action.

At any rate, it has been discussed sufficiently among the topics of swearing. But it is a question whether a caddie can be called happy, and most probably he cannot; those who seem to be so are congratulated on account of their hope [διὰ τὴν ἐλπίδα μακαρίζονται].

A. D. GODLEY

Anon (Chinese)

Our Head-waiter

The snow-flakes do not fall like petals upon our Head-waiter
Nor has the wealthy Lao Pei remembered him in his will.
It is not that the Spirits of the Middle Air are offended,
Or that our Head-waiter
Is deficient in the Four Virtues.
It is that the snow-flakes
Are abashed in the presence of the grill-room fire,
And that the honourable Lao Pei
Is not aware of our Head-waiter's existence.

L. E. JONES

The Girl of So Ho

When I was a girl I sat with the old men,
Or watching my cherry blossom
I would play with your *ts'ing*.*
When the birds flew westward
I came to the Province of So Ho
Where no cherry is to be found.
But the old men turned up.
They rose like carp to the feeding hand.
Now after too many months I sit alone.
I mark the days on my calendar.
When you read these words
Clasp your *ts'ing* and come.

GERARD BENSON

* *Ts'ing*: an instrument, similar to a *d'ong*, but smaller (translator's note).

Kindness to the Starfish

Kindness to the starfish is as wind
In the desert of Kobo;
I will sit among the rice,
Strumming my *Yenize*,
Till you cry,
'Dost thou bring a bagpipe
To one with earache,
O honourable pest?'
Under the hat all is human,
And he is a fool who speaks to the tortoise
Of lightning.
Therefore, at the feast of cherry-blossom,
I will hang my lantern
At the door of another.
He is a persistent dog who knows
The boots of the householders.

J. B. MORTON ('BEACHCOMBER')

Anon (Early English)

Ancient Music

Winter is icummen in,
Lhude sing Goddamm,
Raineth drop and staineth slop,
And how the wind doth ramm!
        Sing: Goddamm.

Skiddeth bus and sloppeth us,
An ague hath my ham.
Freezeth river, turneth liver,
   Damn you, sing: Goddamm.
Goddamm, Goddamm, 'tis why I am, Goddamm,
   So 'gainst the winter's balm.
Sing goddamm, damm, sing Goddamm,
Sing goddamm, sing goddamm, DAMM.

EZRA POUND

An Antient Poem

Wynter ys i-cumen in;
Lhoudly syng *tish-ù*!
Wyndës blo and snoeth sno,
  And all ys icë nu.
    (Syng *tish-ù*!)

Leggës trembel after bath,
  And fingrës turneth blu,
Wisker freseth, nosë sneseth –
  Merie syng *tish-ú-*
    -tish-ù-
    -tish-ù-
Wel singest thou *tish-ù*;
Ne stop thou never nu!

FRANK SIDGWICK

Geoffrey Chaucer (*c.* 1343–1400)

Imitation of Chaucer

Women ben full of Ragerie,
Yet swinken not sans secresie
Thilke Moral shall ye understand,
From Schoole-boy's Tale of fayre Irelond:
Which to the Fennes hath him betake,
To filch the gray Ducke fro the Lake.
Right then, there passen by the Way
His Aunt, and eke her Daughters tway.
Ducke in his Trowses hath he hent,
Not to be spied of Ladies gent.
'But ho! our Nephew,' (crieth one)
'Ho,' quoth another, 'Cozen John';
And stoppen, and laugh, and callen out, –
This sely Clerk full low doth lout:
They asken that, and talken this,
'Lo here is Coz, and here is Miss.'
But, as he glozeth with Speeches soote,
The Ducke sore tickleth his Erse-root:
Fore-piece and buttons all-to-brest,
Forth thrust a white neck, and red crest.
'Te-he,' cry'd Ladies; Clerke nought spake:
Miss star'd; and gray Ducke crieth Quake.
'O Moder, Moder' (quoth the daughter)
'Be thilke same thing Maids longen a'ter?
'Bette is to pyne on coals and chalke,
'Then trust on Mon, whose yerde can talke.'

ALEXANDER POPE

The Probatioun Officere's Tale

The lede guiterriste was a craftie ladde,
Wel koude he luren chickes to his padde
To dyg the sownes of Clapton or The Stones
And share a joynte and turn on for the nones,
Till met he wyth a drogge squadde maiden fayre
Who yaf him think she was a Frenssche au pair,
That whan at last he caused hir sens to feynte
And subtilly to frote hir at the queynte,
And whyspere sucred words, and strook her sore,
'Lay on!' she cried, 'my rammysh prikasour!'
For she was nothing loth to amorous sport
So be she got hir Pusheres into court.

GERARD BENSON

The Hicche-hykere

This yonge fresshe wenche, wel loking honey-swete,
Hir thumbe up-haf and gan a lifte entrete,
Wherat eftsone oon sely wight dide stoppe
And curteislie, I-wis, bade hir in hoppe.
Quod he, Gode morwe, whider wendestow?
Thanne quod this murie jade, til Marlborrowe
Thereto he syde that she moghte with hym steye
Til Gildforde, wher his destinacioun leye.
Bur whan hem neghen dide to Gildforde toun
She til hir verray queynte up-drow hir goun,
And swoor to crye out Ravyne! and Harrow!
So mote he bere hir ful to Marlborrowe.

W. F. N. WATSON

Anon (Border Ballad)

The New Ballad of Sir Patrick Spens

The King sits in Dunfermline toun
  Drinking the blude-red wine:
'O, wha will rear me an equilateral triangle
  Upon a given straight line?'

O, up and spake an eldern knight
  Sat at the King's right knee –
'Of a' the clerks by Granta side
  Sir Patrick bears the gree.

' 'Tis he was taught by the Tod-huntere
  Tho' not at the tod-hunting;
Yet gif that he be given a line
  He'll do as brave a thing.'

Our King has written a braid letter
  To Cambrigge or thereby
And there it found Sir Patrick Spens
  Evaluating π.

He hadna worked his quotient
  A point but barely three,
There stepped to him a little foot-page
  And louted on his knee.

The first word that Sir Patrick read
  '*Plus* x' was a' he said:
The neist word that Sir Patrick read
  'Twas '*plus* expenses paid'.

The last word that Sir Patrick read
  The tear blinded his e'e:
'The pound I most admire is not
  In Scottish currencie.'

Stately stepped he east the wa',
   And stately stepped he north;
He fetched a compass frae his ha'
   And stood beside the Forth.

Then gurly grew the waves of Forth
   And gurlier by-and-by –
'O, never yet was sic a storm
   Yet it isna sic as I!'

Syne he had crossed the Firth o'Forth
   Untill Dunfermline toun
And tho' he came with a kittle wame
   Fu' low he louted down.

'A line, a line, a gude straight line,
   O King, purvey me quick!
And see it be of thilka kind
   That's neither braid nor thick.'

'Nor thick nor braid?' King Jamie said,
   'I'll eat my gude hat-band
If arra line as ye define
   Be found in our Scotland.'

'Tho' there be nane in a' thy rule
   It sall be ruled by me';
And lichtly with his little pencil
   He's ruled the line AB.

Stately stepped he east the wa',
   And stately stepped he west;
'Ye touch the button,' Sir Patrick said,
   'And I sall do the rest.'

And he has set his compass foot
   Untill the centre A,
From A to B he's stretched it out –
   'Ye Scottish carles, give way!'

Syne he has moved his compass foot
   Untill the centre B,
From B to A he's stretched it out.
   And drawn it viz-a-vee.

The ane circle was BCD,
   And ACE the tither.
'I rede ye well,' Sir Patrick said,
   'They interseck ilk ither.

'See here, and where they interseck –
   To wit with yon point C –
Ye'll just obsairve that I conneck
   The twa points A and B.

'And there ye have a little triangle
   As bonny as e'er was seen;
The whilk is not isosceles,
   Nor yet is it scalene.'

'The proof! the proof!' King Jamie cried:
   'The how and eke the why!'
Sir Patrick laughed within his beard –
   ' 'Tis *ex hypothesi* –

'When I ligg'd in my mither's wame
   I learn'd it frae my mither,
That things was equal to the same
   Was equal ane to t'ither.

'Sith in the circle first I drew
   The lines BA, BC,
Be radii true, I wit to you
   The baith maun equal be.

'Likewise and in the second circle
   Whilk I drew widdershins
It is nae skaith the radii baith
   AB, AC, be twins.

'And sith of three a pair agree
   That ilk suld equal ane,
By certes they maun equal be
   Ilk unto ilk by-lane.'

'Now by my faith!' King Jamie saith,
  'What *plane* geometrie!
If only Potts had written in Scots,
  How loocid Potts would be!'

'Now, wow's my life!' saith Jamie the King,
  And the Scots lords said the same,
For but it was that envious knicht
  Sir Hughie o' the Graeme.

'Flim-flam, flim-flam!' and 'Ho-indeed?'
  Quod Hughie o' the Graeme;
' 'Tis I could better upon my heid
  This prabblin prablem-game.'

Sir Patrick Spens was nothing laith
  When as he heard 'flim-flam',
But syne he's ta'en a silken claith
  And wiped his diagram.

'Gif my small feat may bettered be,
  Sir Hugh, by thy big head,
What I hae done with an A B C
  Do thou with X Y Z.

Then sairly sairly swore Sir Hew,
  And loudly laught the King;
But Sir Patrick tuk the pipes and blew,
  And played that eldritch thing!

He's played it reel, he's played it jig,
  And the baith alternative;
And he's danced Sir Hew to the Asses' Brigg
  That's Proposeetion Five.

And there they've met and there they've fet,
  Forenenst the Asses' Brigg,
And waefu' waefu' was the fate
  That gar'd them there to ligg.

For there Sir Patrick's slain Sir Hew
　　And Sir Hew, Sir Patrick Spens.
Now was that not a fine to do
　　For Euclid's Elemens?

But let us sing Long live the King!
　　And his foes the Deil attend 'em:
For he has gotten his little triangle,
　　Quod erat faciendum!

SIR ARTHUR QUILLER-COUCH

Francis Bacon (1561–1626)

from Of Donnes

Of the Reason for Donnes, then, I give this Account; That it is by some Approved; But by others not. And, of which the views be wiser, I say not; Though I know well.

Now there be full many kindes of Donnes; Whereof some be very Loathesome; But others less. And, at the Firste, I entend to Speake of Them, which have the Preheminence in Wisedome. These be, for the greater Parte, Antiques and Babornes; But like rather to be called Eccentricks. And yet, for the Difference, it pusleth Alle, who should strive to Discerne it. And they bee full often Evill favoured; And care not to be bravely Attired. And others of their kinde they holde in Utmost Aversation; And assaile Them in Bookes; with much tribunitious Choler. But so soone as they die, they become at once Plausible; And receive abundant Laudatives from their Adversaries; And not seldome a Statua; Being Dead.

And other Donnes there bee, of an exceeding difficilnesse. For these be mainly interessed in the Reiglement of Colleges; And the Sustentation of Laws. Alle manner of Bruit they utterly Abhorre; And will not listen to any excusation thereof; Though it be very

Cunning. With such I am Distasted; For Zelants be alwaies Absurd.

But of others againe the Nature is faire Opposite; So that they bee of a certaine Towardnesse; And meeke Humilitie; Desiring always to Avoid the Eyes of Menne; With such I would have you to Deale tenderly; For though they be Donnes, they be Conscient of their Shame.

But it is of this Plie in Donnes that I doe chiefly Complayn; That they can, at no Time, rid them of their Advocation. So that, and if you shall Falle upon a Donne of whom you shall not at Once be able to Pronownce; *This is a Donne*; Then you may sing *Nunc Dimittis* (the Sweetest, beleeve me, of all Canticles) with a thankfulle Hart. For of such an one, it is True, which Master Shakespeare hath written; (Or it may be I myselfe);

> *We shall not look upon his Like againe.*

G. F. FORREST

Christopher Marlowe (1564–1593)

Another Passionate Shepherd

Come, live with me and be my Ms.
And earn a princely bonus, *viz*:
The charm of my society,
Whose scintillant variety
Will momently reveal why I
Am just the sort of modest guy
Who, (serious but never solemn)
Employs the *Statesman*'s 'Personal Column'
To itemize his giant ego
(Constructed out of psychic Lego);
Then sits and broods and wonders why
No dolly ever *dare* reply . . .

MARTIN FAGG

William Shakespeare (1564–1616)

from Savonarola Brown

ACT II
Scene: Lucrezia's Laboratory. Retorts, test-tubes, etc. On small Renaissance table, up centre, is a great poison-bowl, the contents of which are being stirred by the FIRST APPRENTICE. *The* SECOND APPRENTICE *stands by, watching him.*

                    SECOND APPRENTICE
For whom is the brew destin'd?

                         FIRST APPRENTICE
                              I know not.
Lady Lucrezia did but lay on me
Injunctions as regards the making of 't,
The which I have obey'd. It is compounded
Of a malignant and a deadly weed
Found not save in the Gulf of Spezia,
And one small phial of 't, I am advis'd,
Were more than 'nough to slay a regiment
Of Messer Malatesta's condottieri
In all their armour.

                    SECOND APPRENTICE
                    I can well believe it.
Mark how the purple bubbles froth upon
The evil surface of its nether slime!

(*Enter* LUCREZIA BORGIA.)

                    LUCREZIA
                    (*To* FIRST APPRENTICE)
Is't done, Sir Sluggard?

                    FIRST APPRENTICE
                    Madam, to a turn.

Had it not been so, I with mine own hand
Would have outpour'd it down thy gullet, knave.
See, here's a ring of cunningly-wrought gold
That I, on a dark night, did purchase from
A goldsmith on the Ponte Vecchio.
Small was his shop, and hoar of visage he.
I did bemark that from the ceiling's beams
Spiders had spun their webs for many a year,
The which hung erst like swathes of gossamer
Seen in the shadows of a fairy glade,
But now most woefully were weighted o'er
With gather'd dust. Look well now at the ring!
Touch'd here, behold, it opes a cavity
Capacious of three drops of yon fell stuff.
Dost heed? Whoso then puts it on his finger
Dies, and his soul is from his body rapt
To Hell or Heaven as the case may be.
Take thou this toy and pour the three drops in.

(*Hands ring to* FIRST APPRENTICE *and comes down centre.*)

So, Sav'narola, thou shalt learn that I
Utter no threats but I do make them good.
Ere this day's sun hath wester'd from the view
Thou art to preach from out the Loggia
Dei Lanzi to the cits in the Piazza.
I, thy Lucrezia, will be upon the steps
To offer thee with phrases seeming-fair
That which shall seal thine eloquence for ever.
O mighty lips that held the world in spell
But would not meet these little lips of mine
In the sweet way that lovers use – O thin,
Cold, tight-drawn, bloodless lips, which natheless I
Deem of all lips the most magnifical
In this our city –

(*Enter the Borgias'* FOOL.)

Well, Fool, what's thy latest?

FOOL

Aristotle's or Zeno's, Lady – 'tis neither latest nor last. For, marry, if
the cobbler stuck to his last, then were his latest his last *in rebus*

ambulantibus. Argal, I stick at nothing but cobble-stones, which, by
the same token, are stuck to the road by men's fingers.

LUCREZIA

How many crows may nest in a grocer's jerkin?

FOOL

A full dozen at cock-crow, and something less under the dog-star, by
reason of the dew, which lies heavy on men taken by the scurvy.

LUCREZIA
(*To* FIRST APPRENTICE)
Methinks the Fool is a fool.

FOOL

And therefore, by auricular deduction, am I own twin to the Lady
Lucrezia!

(*Sings*)
> When pears hang green on the garden wall
> > With a nid, and a nod, and a niddy-niddy-o
> Then prank you, lads and lasses all
> > With a yea and a nay and a niddy-o.

> But when the thrush flies out o' the frost
> > With a nid, *etc*.
> 'Tis time for loons to count the cost,
> > With a yea *etc*.

(*Enter the* PORTER.)

PORTER

O my dear Mistress, there is one below
Demanding to have instant word of thee.
I told him that your Ladyship was not
At home. Vain perjury! He would not take
Nay for an answer.

LUCREZIA
Ah? What manner of man
Is he?

PORTER
A personage the like of whom
Is wholly unfamiliar to my gaze.
Cowl'd is he. But I saw his great eyes glare

From their deep sockets in such wise as leopards
Glare from their caverns, crouching ere they spring
On their reluctant prey.

> LUCREZIA
>
> And what name gave he?

> PORTER
> (*After a pause*)

Something-arola.

> LUCREZIA
>
> Savon – ?

(PORTER *nods.*)

> Show him up.

(*Exit* PORTER.)

> FOOL

If he be right astronomically, Mistress, then is he the greater dunce
in respect of true learning, the which goes by the globe. Argal,
'twere better he widened his wind-pipe.

> (*Sings*)
> Fly home, sweet self,
> Nothing's for weeping,
> Hemp was not made
> For lovers' keeping,
>   Lovers' keeping,
> Cheerly, cheerly, fly away.
>
> Hew no more wood
> While ash is glowing,
> The longest grass
> Is lovers' mowing,
>   Lovers' mowing,
> Cheerly, *etc.*

(*Re-enter* PORTER, *followed by* SAVONAROLA. *Exeunt* PORTER,
FOOL, *and* FIRST *and* SECOND APPRENTICES.)

> SAVONAROLA

I am no more a monk, I am a man
O' the world.

(*Throws off cowl and frock, and stands forth in the costume of a Renaissance
nobleman.* LUCREZIA *looks him up and down.*)

LUCREZIA

Thou cutst a sorry figure.

SAVONAROLA

That
Is neither here nor there. I love you, Madam.

LUCREZIA

And this, methinks, is neither there nor here,
For that my love of thee hath vanishèd,
Seeing thee thus beprankt. Go pad thy calves!
Thus mightst thou, just conceivably, with luck
Capture the fancy of some serving-wench.

SAVONAROLA

And this is all thou hast to say to me?

LUCREZIA

It is.

SAVONAROLA

I am dismiss'd?

LUCREZIA

Thou art.

SAVONAROLA

'Tis well.

(*Resumes frock and cowl.*)
Savonarola is himself once more.

LUCREZIA

And all my love for him returns to me
A thousandfold!

SAVONAROLA

Too late! My pride of manhood
Is wounded irremediably. I'll
To the Piazza, where my flock awaits me.
Thus do we see that men make great mistakes
But may amend them when the conscience wakes.

(*Exit.*)

LUCREZIA

I'm half avengèd now, but only half;
'Tis with the ring I'll have the final laugh!

Tho' love be sweet, revenge is sweeter far.
To the Piazza! Ha, ha, ha, har!

(*Seizes ring, and exit. Through open door are heard, as the Curtain falls, sounds of a terrific hubbub in the Piazza.*)

SIR MAX BEERBOHM

King Canute

The coast near Southampton. Enter, from royal barge, CANUTE, COURTIERS, *and* FOOL.

FOOL

'Tis clear, Great Dane, thy barque's worse than thy bite.

CANUTE

Once more unto the beach, dear friends, once more –

FOOL

A line, methinks, too good to throw away,
'Twill soon be echoed in another play.

CANUTE

– For now I needs must show these slavering curs
That e'en Canute cannot roll back the sea.

FOOL

Canute cannot? Cannot Canute? For shame!

CANUTE

Cease, fool. We at the mighty ocean's marge,
Exchanging throne for deckchair for the nonce,
Shall thus disport, paddling our royal feet.

FOOL

Nay, if it please thee, paddle thine own, Canute,
And get thy breeches wet into the bargain.
But why not summon statecraft to thine aid
And make a secret compact with the moon?
Sit tight until the tide is on the turn,

Then it would seem as though thy royal command,
'Back, waters, back', had wrought a miracle.

CANUTE

Verily, my boy, thou'rt on the ball.

FOOL

On land or sea, good sire, timing is all.

CANUTE

Henceforth I'll hear no ill spoken of fools.

FOOL

Thou rul'st the waves; my task's to waive the rules.

STANLEY J. SHARPLESS

All's Well

CHARMIAN

What hast thou there?

CLEOPATRA

The certain instrument of my undoing.
(*Undoes bra.*)
Now shalt thou see the serpent of old Nile
Another serpent to her bosom take;
A mother once, a mummy soon to be.
(*Applies asp to breast.*)

CHARMIAN

What dreadful jest is this?

CLEOPATRA

When I am dead, good wench, thou canst explain
How on this very couch was Cleo lain.

CHARMIAN

Nay, nay – I have a sov'reign remedy.

CLEOPATRA

'Tis very apt. A sov'reign remedy. Ha!

A simple, madam, highly spoken of,
Made to an old Egyptian recipe,
With locusts, bitter herbs and camel dung,
One guaranteed to cure all mortal ills,
Snake bites and boils and other royal distempers,
Jaundice, pimples, the plague – thou namest it.
(*Applies serum to affected area.*)

CLEOPATRA

'Tis magic, sure; the sting abates already.
So shall I live to fight another day.
And – the gods willing – in another play.

STANLEY J. SHARPLESS

Once More unto the Peace

'*Mr. Chamberlain always travels with a pocket Shakespeare.*' –
Daily Telegraph, *23 February 1939*

Once more unto the peace, dear friends, once more,
And wean aggressors with our English gold!
Costly our armament as purse can buy,
For, while we are in silken dalliance led,
Come the Dictators of the world in arms,
And they will shock us; they will shock this England,
This precious stone set in a sea of troubles.
Let me with cyphers for this great accompt
On your imaginary terrors work,
While armourers are closing up the gaps
With note of aimless preparation.
You all know this umbrella: I remember
When first I flew with it to Berchtesgaden,
The day I overthrew democracy,
For thine especial safety. Follow it!
It beckons you, a most miraculous organ,
And none so Left but does it reverence.
See these few precepts we in memory keep.

Give every man our voice but few our aid:
Be ever strong upon the stronger side:
This above all – to our own class be true;
And it must follow, as the boom the slump,
We cannot then astonish any man.
Methinks I am a prophet new-inspired!
Friends, Britons, countrymen, lend me your cash;
Cry 'Jitterbug!' and pay the price of peace
To profiteers, gaping for increment.

SAGITTARIUS

By All Accounts

Barclays Bank gave its male staff crash courses in beauty treatment, so that they could present a more attractive image to the public.

I know a bank where tellers paint their toes,
And clients wink: 'I think he's one of those',
Where the branch manager may reign supreme
Among the jars of moisturizing cream:
There serve the cashiers, bushy-tailed and bright,
Whose lacquered hair is all for your delight;
And there the local grocer paying in
Will wish he had so delicate a skin,
And borrowers trust private enterprise
Less than the promise of mascara'd eyes.
Take heart, you seekers of an overdraft,
From products of the cosmetician's craft;
And even while you talk of shares and scrips,
Admire the fullness of those Cupid lips,
The rich apparel that proclaims the man,
The magic of that artificial tan.
Compare the puckers in your pocketbook
With his unwrinkled, ever-youthful look,
And should, with age, your facial muscles sag,
Draw comfort from the deputy in drag.
Astringent lotion can do more than bread

To clear accounts forever in the red,
And if you suffer blemishes and boils,
Let beauty care replace your natural oils,
Let make-up mask the system's fall from grace
And hide its spotty and unpleasant face.

ROGER WODDIS

Enter Puck

*Greenwich Council organized a Midsummer Night hunt for the ghost of an
amorous seventeenth-century squire. Most of the tickets were bought by women.*

Now the lovelorn ladies queue,
    Hoping to be led astray
By Sir William Langhorne who
    Got his noble end away.

Now the unrequited heart
    Hankers for the ghostly mouth,
Puckered and with lips apart,
    Breathing hard in London South.

Now all Greenwich is alight,
    Burning with forbidden fire;
Through the darkness of the night
    Comes the priapistic squire.

Servicing this friendly town,
    Someone spectral stands and waits;
If the swooning girls go down,
    Up will go the local rates.

Now the happy housewives boast,
    Pumpkin-plump or willow-slim,
How they laid the Charlton ghost,
    And what is more, were laid by him.

ROGER WODDIS

This Railway Station

This squalid dome of soot-obscurèd glass,
This larger lavatory or spittoon,
This vault of echoes, rudely amplified,
This meeting place of draughts, whose smut-filled air
Strikes chill upon the stoutest traveller's chest,
This worried trippers' haunt, this dunghill world
Whence porter-cocks crow false civilities,
This traffic jam, stirred in a thousand jars,
Which serves as hypodermic for the times,
Inoculating tourists 'gainst the press
Of progress and the piercing shrieks of speed,
This dark and dank depression of the soul,
This builder's blot, this curse, this Railway Station.

ALLAN M. LAING

When Icicles

When icicles encrust the bath,
   And wheels churn madly in the snow,
And glaciers line the garden path,
   And everywhere's too far to go.
When lights go out, and gas runs short,
Then daily do the Boards exhort:
'Switch off, conserve, economize!'
For winter takes them by surprise.

When plumbers' boots thud through the hall,
   And frozen privies close the schools,
And trains bog down and buses crawl,
   And Drake and Lawton guess the Pools,
When coal is low and taps run dry,
The Boards repeat their plaintive cry:
'Switch off, economize, conserve!'
May God forgive their bloody nerve!

PETER VEALE

33

W. S. at his Mirror

To me, dear friend, you never looked so old:
Like as the curling waves desert the shore
And leave a promontory bare and cold
So do these traitor locks that clung before
Creep from the parent brow with stealthy pace,
Edging their treacherous ebb with streaks of white.
Must I acknowledge this autumnal face,
Which once knew summer's pride and spring's delight?
The mole of care my fading features mines:
There mark his crevices, and here his hills;
What bygone lover, looking on these lines,
Could from his heart declare them to be *Will's*?
Then let my heirs this glassy image break
And of smooth marble my memorial make.

MARY HOLTBY

When to the Sessions

When to the sessions of group therapy
You summon up those traumas of your past,
Like being in your mother's pregnancy
While your father kept coming hard and fast.
You learned your penis envy there and then
But consciously you did not know that fact,
Nor that you loved your sire above all men
With top billing in the Electra act;
Until analysis did well define
That you craved sexual lewdness with your dad;
As far as your libido goes that's fine:
Your son could be your brother and that's bad.
When Mister Sigmund Freud was very Jung
That's when the doctor's neck should have been wrung.

RONN MARVIN

34

Anon (Elizabethan Dramatist)

'Tis Pity He's a Stockfish

VOLUMINA

... O pretty youth, O super-dainty youth!
His arched brows, his hawking eye, his curls
Are meat for lusty bawds. By God, I'll have him.

SLENDER

Save you, fair lady. Keep you comfortable.

VOLUMINA

Marry, so I mean, sweet Joseph, in thy bed.
Myself am moved to woo thee for my husband.

SLENDER

Now, by Dian, I am too young for you.

VOLUMINA

Out, whey-face! You are as a tallow candle,
The better part burnt out. Virginity
Is but the cowish terror of thy spirit
That dares not undertake. Your self-abuse
Is the initiate fear that wants hard use.

MADAM TRULL

Whip thee, gosling. 'Tis a cold thing, a very stockfish.

VOLUMINA

I must needs have him with a codpiece then ...
Nay, by the Mass, he's fled.

TROOPER JONES

from The Critic

Enter TILBURINA *stark mad in white satin, and her* CONFIDANT *stark mad in white linen.*

TILBURINA
The wind whistles – the moon rises – see,
They have kill'd my squirrel in his cage:
Is this a grasshopper? – Ha! no, it is my
Whiskerandos – you shall not keep him –
I know you have him in your pocket –
An oyster may be cross'd in love! – who says
A whale's a bird? – Ha! did you call, my love?
He's here! he's there! – He's everywhere!
Ah me! he's nowhere!
(*Exit.*)

RICHARD BRINSLEY SHERIDAN

Robert Herrick (1591–1674)

Upon Julia's Clothes

'*Toy dogs with coats to match their owners' furs were a feature of the recent show at the Horticultural Hall.*' – Daily Press.

Whenas in furs my Julia goes,
Of slaughtered vermin, goodness knows
What tails depend upon her clothes!

Next, when I cast my eyes and see
The living whelp she lugs to tea,
Oh, how their likeness taketh me!

E. V. KNOX

Upon Julia's Clothes

Whenas in slacks my Julia goes,
Then, then, methinks, how adipose
Her tissue grows.

Next, when I cast mine eyes and see
That undulation, each way free;
O how that movement taketh me!

MICHAEL BARSLEY

John Milton (1608–1674)

Ode to Conservation

Abandon'd offspring of Decay,
Improvidence and Waste, away!
Despoilers of the rural view,
Hie thee to Hell – thy litter too!
But come, due Care, and bring with thee
Good Housewif'ry and Husbandry.
In tidy habit, frugal Thrift,

Come, collect, and sort and shift.

Cast not away the scrumpled bag,
The cardboard box, the ancient mag.
Into neat sheaves the papers bind;
Thus saved, recycled and refined,
Reports of yesterday's defeats
Can be tomorrow's fairer sheets,
Where Clio, on the virgin page,
May yet record a wiser age.

JOYCE JOHNSON

Paradise Lost 2–0

Their tumult ceased awhile, th'encircling throng,
Agape with keen anticipation, see,
Like coloured marbles roll'd on the green sward
By young Olympians, th'opposing Teams
Now scatter as the Contest starts. Flies now,
As if some insect were caught in the Game
The Gods play with mere men, a speckl'd sphere;
Nor does it come to rest in either net,
Though those who watch implore their several Gods
It should be; some one end, t'other some,
But wait awhile! When th'allotted Time's
Not half way done, Vict'ry attends one man:
Nor is't in vain! At last the argent Cup,
Spite foul attacks, is held up by his Chief.
Then, breaking loose, the herded hordes run free:
Relieve themselves, drink deep, and savage all
Who in their path might accident'ly stray.

MARGARET ROGERS

Richard Lovelace (1618–1658)

To My Lady Nicotine

Tell me not, sweet, I am remiss,
 That from the sanctuary
Of thy most aromatic charms,
 To abstinence I flee.

The soothing balsams of thy breath
 I oft, erstwhile, have sung;
And, in thy thrall, have sacrificed
 A heart, a throat, a lung.

This sad renouncement is not one
 That thou wilt all deplore:
I could not love thee half as much
 Loved I not living more.

MARTIN FAGG

Alibi

Blame me not, Sweet, if here and there
 My wayward self inclines
To note that others, too, are fair,
 To bow at lesser shrines.

What though with eye or tongue I praise
 Iona's gentle wile,
Camilla's happy turn of phrase,
 Or Celia's winning smile?

My constancy shall be thy boast
   From now to Kingdom Come.
How could I love thee, Dear, the most,
   Loved I not others some?

Andrew Marvell (1621–1678)

To his Coarse Mistress

Had we but privacy tonight
This coarseness, lady, were all right.
For just three minutes we'd converse;
I'd praise your beauty, you my verse;
And after that we'd copulate,
Nor would I love at slower rate,
For, Lady, when alone with me
And softly moving, knee to knee
And breast to breast you are unique,
But it all changes when you speak;
For we are in a public place
And how I wish you'd shut your face,
For at my back I always hear
At your each word, a colleague's sneer,
And yonder all before us lie
Aeons of brash banality.
Since seven double gins can buy
That fictional virginity,
Come on, my amorous bird of play,
You've had fifteen, let's hit the hay.

GERARD BENSON

40

John Aubrey (1626–1697)

Memories of 1966

Being hard-prest for a debt of 200 *li*, I was prevayled upon to take parte in a publick discussione got up for the Televizione. Old Oxonian Freinds have counselled me often to doe this, they having founde it a most excellent way for a scholarely man to make moneye. I met with a Mr Andrewes, who took me somewhat aback by saying he would not have me talke of historikal matters, or of bookes and learnynge, since those watching the Entertaynment would be more disposed to lyke Joakes of a lewde nature, though Mr Andrewes himselfe confesst he was not of that minde.

I consented with some apprehention to appeare, though I was much chagrined to hear it put about that I was a famous Gossipe. At the studioe I came upon others that were to joyne in the Conversations, among them persons of Tytle, who amazed me with their behaviour, appearing to be no little in drinke; also a raskal with long haire, a singer of sortes, with an Estate among the richest in England.

I was myselfe given royal entertaynment, and on the conversation starting I tolde a storye or two, which pleased some mightilye but drewe harsh words from Mrs Whyte House, who is sett up to judge what is good for the People; also Mr Andrewes, I feare, somewhat out of humour with me.

PETER VEALE

41

Dean Jonathan Swift (1667–1745)

Voyage to Cynosuria

Cynosuria: A land populated by intelligent dogs

... When I was recovered of my well-deserved biting, my master, that placid and dignified St. Bernard, promised me that if I behaved well and showed myself docile and of clean house habits, he would presently enlarge me from the kennel where I lay into the freedom of his own dwelling. 'For,' said he (and by now I began to comprehend the Wowff speech very well) 'though you Lacktails are puppishly conceited and quarrelsome, you are not without a measure of intelligence, when suitably encouraged.'

In halting and humble speech, I thanked him, promising in return for his kindness to a miserable two-footed animal that I would try to emulate my master in all things, such as making a better use of my nose than blowing it, endeavouring to walk like a rational being on four legs, and praying (since my unaided efforts were of no avail) for hair to cover my nakedness and a tail to lend me dignity.

I fear, however, from the look in my master's eye, that this speech only confirmed him in his belief in my conceit. None the less, he kept his word, and in about a fortnight, he gave me the run of his own well-appointed mansion, where I soon became the inseparable pet of his housemaid, a jolly, spotted Dalmatian. She liked nothing better than to roll me over on my back and tickle my belly with her cool nose till I wriggled with pleasure. I was fed on the juiciest and tenderest bones, and a special hearth rug was tacitly appropriated to my exclusive use. Here I would lie while Dalmatia was busy with the housework and (somewhat ungratefully) dream of the England I would never see again.

ALLAN M. LAING

Alexander Pope (1688–1744)

On 'Who's Who'

Behold a volume, cover'd all in red,
Thick as a clod and ponderous as lead,
Within whose pages is inscrib'd the name
Of ev'ryone of quality or fame;
The chosen of the nation, great and less,
Each carrying the stigma of success.
'Tis certain that in life he cannot fail
Whose father makes his fortune brewing ale;
So Joseph Bloggs is now a magistrate
And sits in judgment on th' inebriate.
Here is the Earl whose ancestors of old
Purloin'd and pilfer'd, cozen'd and cajol'd,
Till riches made them safe from reckoning
And earn'd the favour of a grateful King.
Their scion now enjoys his lofty place,
The tenth transmitter of a foolish face.

H. A. C. EVANS

A Limerick Rewritten

There was an old lady of Chertsey,
Who made a remarkable curtsey;
  She twirled round and round
  Till she sank underground
Which distressed all the people of Chertsey.

EDWARD LEAR

For Chertsey people sing a mournful lay,
For ever have they cause to rue the day
When Royalty, whom graciousness adorns,
Received their homage on their sylvan lawns.
Here gentry and nobility, arrayed
In their resplendent finery, Parade:
See an old lady from the throng advance,
And for a formal curtsey take her stance;
With skilful motion give her dress a twirl,
And with it, suddenly, begin to whirl
Around, around with ever greater speed –
And vanish rapidly beneath the mead!
Some rush to aid, but come, alas, too late;
The dame is deep, still spinning to her fate!
A piteous cry goes up from all around,
As Pluto claims his victim underground.

J. H. FRANK

Samuel Richardson (1689–1761)

from Shamela

LETTER TEN

Shamela Andrews to Henrietta Maria Honora Andrews

. . . I had not been long in my chamber before Mrs. Jewkes came to me, and told me, my master would not see me any more that evening, that is, if he can help it; for, added she, I easily perceive the great ascendant you have over him, and to confess the truth, I don't doubt but you will shortly be my mistress.

What, says I, dear Mrs. Jewkes, what do you say? Don't flatter a poor girl; it is impossible his Honour can have any honourable design upon me. And so we talked of honourable designs till supper-time. And Mrs. Jewkes and I supped together upon a hot buttered apple-pie; and about ten o'clock we went to bed.

We had not been a-bed half an hour, when my master came pit-a-pat into the room in his shirt as before; I pretended not to hear him, and Mrs. Jewkes laid hold of one arm, and he pulled down the bed-clothes and came into bed on the other side, and took my other arm and laid it under him, and fell a-kissing one of my breasts as if he would have devoured it; I was then forced to awake, and began to struggle with him; Mrs. Jewkes crying Why don't you do it? I have one arm secure, if you can't deal with the rest I am sorry for you. He was as rude as possible to me; but I remembered, Mama, the in-structions you gave me to avoid being ravished, and followed them, which soon brought him to terms, and he promised me, on quitting my hold, that he would leave the bed.

O Parson Williams, how little are all the men in the world compared to thee!

My master was as good as his word; upon which Mrs. Jewkes said, O sir, I see you know very little of our *sect*, by parting so easily from the blessing when you was so near it. No, Mrs. Jewkes, answered he, I am very glad no more hath happened; I would not have injured Shamela for the world. And to-morrow morning perhaps she may hear of something to her advantage. This she may be certain of, that I will never take her by force; and then he left the room.

What think you now, Mrs. Shamela? says Mrs. Jewkes; are you not yet persuaded my master hath honourable designs? I think he hath given no great proof of them to-night, said I. Your experience I find is not great, says she, but I am convinced you will shortly be my mistress, and then what will become of poor me?

With such sort of discourse we both fell asleep. Next morning early my master sent for me, and after kissing me, gave a paper into my hand which he bid me read; I did so, and found it to be a proposal for settling 250*l.* a year on me, besides several other advantageous offers, as presents of money and other things. Well, Shamela, said he, what answer do you make me to this? Sir, said I, I value my vartue more than all the world, and I had rather be the poorest man's wife than the richest man's whore. You are a simpleton, said he; that may be, and yet I may have as much wit as some folks, cried I; meaning me, I suppose, said he; every man knows himself best,

says I. Hussy, says he, get out of the room, and let me see your saucy
face no more, for I find I am in more danger than you are, and
therefore it shall be my business to avoid you as much as I can; and
it shall be mine, thinks I, at every turn to throw myself in your way.
So I went out, and as I parted, I heard him sigh and say he was
bewitched.

Mrs. Jewkes hath been with me since, and she assures me she is
convinced I shall shortly be mistress of the family, and she really
behaves to me as if she already thought me so. I am resolved now to
aim at it. I thought once of making a little fortune by my person. I
now intend to make a great one by my vartue. So asking pardon for
this long scroll, I am,

Your dutiful Daughter,
SHAMELA

HENRY FIELDING

Thomas Gray (1716–1771)

If Gray had had to Write his Elegy in the Cemetery at Spoon River instead of in that of Stoke Poges

The curfew tolls the knell of parting day,
  The whippoorwill salutes the rising moon,
And wanly glimmer in her gentle ray,
  The sinuous windings of the turbid Spoon.

Here where the flattering and mendacious swarm
  Of lying epitaphs their secrets keep,
At last incapable of further harm
  The lewd forefathers of the village sleep.

The earliest drug of half-awakened morn,
    Cocaine or hashish, strychnine, poppy-seeds
Or fiery produce of fermented corn
    No more shall start them on the day's misdeeds.

For them no more the whetstone's cheerful noise,
    No more the sun upon his daily course
Shall watch them savouring the genial joys,
    Of murder, bigamy, arson and divorce.

Here they all lie; and, as the hour is late,
    O stranger, o'er their tombstones cease to stoop,
But bow thine ear to me and contemplate
    The unexpurgated annals of the group.

There are two hundred only: yet of these
    Some thirty died of drowning in the river,
Sixteen went mad, ten others had D.T.'s
    And twenty-eight cirrhosis of the liver.

Several by absent-minded friends were shot,
    Still more blew out their own exhausted brains,
One died of a mysterious inward rot,
    Three fell off roofs, and five were hit by trains.

One was harpooned, one gored by a bull-moose,
    Four on the Fourth fell victims to lock-jaw,
Ten in electric chair or hempen noose
    Suffered the last exaction of the law.

Stranger, you quail, and seem inclined to run;
    But, timid stranger, do not be unnerved;
I can assure you that there was not one
    Who got a tithe of what he had deserved.

Full many a vice is born to thrive unseen,
    Full many a crime the world does not discuss,
Full many a pervert lives to reach a green
    Replete old age, and so it was with us.

Here lies a parson who would often make
   Clandestine rendezvous with Claflin's Moll,
And 'neath the druggist's counter creep to take
   A sip of surreptitious alcohol.

And here a doctor, who had seven wives,
   And, fearing this *ménage* might seem grotesque,
Persuaded six of them to spend their lives
   Locked in a drawer of his private desk.

And others here there sleep who, given scope,
   Had writ their names large on the Scrolls of Crime,
Men who, with half a chance, might haply cope,
   With the first miscreants of recorded time.

Doubtless in this neglected spot is laid
   Some village Nero who has missed his due,
Some Bluebeard who dissected many a maid,
   And all for naught, since no one ever knew.

Some poor bucolic Borgia here may rest
   Whose poisons sent whole families to their doom,
Some hayseed Herod who, within his breast,
   Concealed the sites of many an infant's tomb.

Types that the Muse of Masefield might have stirred,
   Or waked to ecstasy Gaboriau,
Each in his narrow cell at last interred,
   All, all are sleeping peacefully below.

Enough, enough! But, stranger, ere we part,
   Glancing farewell to each nefarious bier,
This warning I would beg you take to heart,
   'There is an end even to the worst career.'

SIR JOHN SQUIRE

Christopher Smart (1722-1771)

To his Mirror

Mad is the poet men call Kit;
Mad is his thought, and mad his wit,
  And madness, sure, he writes:
Mad as the pig when he is stuck;
Mad as the bull that runs amuck,
  Or rabid dog that bites.

Mad as his eyes are rimmed with black;
Mad as his stare is lustre-lack;
  Mad as his prayers are long:
Mad as his wig is shrunk and torn;
Mad as his shoes are long outworn;
  Mad as his faith is strong.

STANLEY SHAW

Oliver Goldsmith (?1730-1774)

When Lovely Woman

When lovely woman wants a favour,
  And finds, too late, that man won't bend,
What earthly circumstance can save her
  From disappointment in the end?

The only way to bring him over,
    The last experiment to try,
Whether a husband or a lover,
    If he have feeling, is, to cry!

PHOEBE CAREY

James Boswell (1740–1795)

Two Hitherto Unpublished Extracts from his Life of Dr Johnson

Returning from our weekly visit to the Stews, the Doctor was in an excellent humour. I was in a deep melancholy, usual on such occasions, and hummed a little tune to raise my spirits. *Johnson:* 'That was a very pretty *Lay.*' *Boswell:* 'Some little thing from Ossian, I believe'. *Johnson:* 'Spoken like a true Scot. I had not even considered the provenance of the lady.' Whereupon I saw he was in one of his *carnal* moods. *Johnson:* 'I noticed———' (naming a prominent Whig) 'slipping out of the chamber as I entered. Necessity makes strange bedfellows.' *Boswell:* 'It is a necessity of which I am ashamed.' *Johnson:* 'Who are we to question the ordinances of the Almighty? Doubtless God could have devised other ways of propagating the species. Praise be that he did not choose to do so. We are uxorious and philoprogenitive by divine decree; to gainsay it were a kind of blasphemy. Truly the bed is a great *Leveller.* The prophet, the poet and the prostitute are all equal in bed. Sir, I would rate the inventor of the bed alongside the inventor of the wheel.' He nudged me with his elbow. 'Only six more days, Bozzie; six more days.'

STANLEY J. SHARPLESS

On hearing from Mrs Thrale, that Johnson had removed himself to Grosvenor Street, I took the liberty of paying my respects to him, early the following morning. As I reached the door, I had some misgivings about the immoderate hour of my visit and my confusion was completed, when Mrs Thrale received me in her undergarments. She did not betray the slightest embarrassment however, and I followed her into the house, where, to my utter astonishment, I discovered Johnson dressed in a linen vest and short cotton drawers.

'You need not fear for her modesty sir,' Johnson said, immediately sensible of the apprehension in my eyes. 'I am not a lecher, whatever you may be. We are engaged in certain innocent prescriptions, of which you shall soon be witness.'

'I will go sir,' I ventured, 'and return at a more convenient hour.'

'You will stay sir,' Johnson thundered, 'and understand the nature of our exertions.'

So saying, he fastened one extremity of a long knotted rope to a hook on the wall and required me to hold the other end. He then instructed me to turn it in a quick circular motion, whereupon both Mrs Thrale and he skipped over the moving rope, with great judgment and speed. As they jumped, they chanted some words, which I have taken pains to remember and record. They were . . . Salt . . . Pepper . . . Vinegar . . . Mustard . . .

RUSSELL LUCAS

Robert Burns (1759–1796)

For A' That and A' That

More luck to honest poverty,
  It claims respect, and a' that;
But honest wealth's a better thing,
  We dare be rich for a' that.

For a' that, and a' that,
    And spooney cant and a' that,
A man may have a ten-pun note,
    And be a brick for a' that.

What though on soup and fish we dine,
    Wear evening togs and a' that,
A man may like good meat and wine,
    Nor be a knave for a' that.
        For a' that, and a' that,
            Their fustian talk and a' that,
        A gentleman, however clean,
            May have a heart for a' that.

You see yon prater called a Beales,
    Who bawls and brays and a' that,
Tho' hundreds cheer his blatant bosh,
    He's but a goose for a' that.
        For a' that, and a' that,
            His Bubblyjocks, and a' that,
        A man with twenty grains of sense,
            He looks and laughs at a' that.

A prince can make a belted knight,
    A marquis, duke, and a' that,
And if the title's earned, all right,
    Old England's fond of a' that.
        For a' that, and a' that,
            Beales' balderdash, and a' that,
        A name that tells of service done
            Is worth the wear, for a' that.

Then let us pray that come it may
    And come it will for a' that,
That common sense may take the place
    Of common cant and a' that.
        For a' that, and a' that,
            Who cackles trash and a' that,
        Or be he lord, or be he low,
            The man's an ass for a' that.

C. W. SHIRLEY BROOKS

The Queys are Mooping

The queys are mooping' i' the mirk,
An' gin ye thole ahin' the kirk,
I'll gar ye tocher hame fra' work,
    Sae straught an' primsie;
In vain the lavrock leaves the snaw,
The sonsie cowslips blithely blaw,
The elbucks wheep adoon the shaw,
    Or warl a whimsy.

The cootie muircocks crously craw,
The maukins tak' their fud fu' braw,
I gie their wames a random paw,
    For a' they're skilpy;
For wha' sae glaikit, gleg an' din,
To but the ben, or loup the linn,
Or scraw aboon the tirlin'-pin
    Sae frae an' gilpie?

CHORUS
Och, snood the sporran roun' ma lap,
The cairngorm clap in ilka cap,
    Och, hand me o'er
    Ma long claymore,
    Twa bannocks an' a bap,
        Wha hoo!
    Twa bannocks an' a bap!

HARRY GRAHAM

Justice to Scotland

An unpublished poem by Burns. (Communicated by the Edinburgh Society for Promoting Civilization in England.)

O mickle yeuks the keckle doup,
 An' a' unsicker girns the graith,
For wae and wae! the crowdies loup
 O'er jouk an' hallan, braw an' baith.

Where ance the coggie hirpled fair,
 And blithesome poortith toomed the loof,
There's nae a burnie giglet rare
 But blaws in ilka jinking coof.

The routhie bield that gars the gear
 Is gane where glint and pawky een,
And aye the stound is birkin lear
 Where sconnered yowies wheeped yestreen.

The creeshie rax wi' skelpin kaes
 Nae mair the howdie bicker whangs,
Nor weanies in their wee bit claes
 Glour licht as lammies wi' their sangs.

Yet leeze me on my bonnie byke!
 My drappie aiblins blinks the noo,
An' leesome luve has lapt the dyke
 Forgatherin' just a wee bit fou.

And Scotia! while thy rantin' lunt
 Is mirk and moop with gowans fine,
I'll stowlins pit my unco brunt,
 An' cleek my duds for auld land syne.

C. W. SHIRLEY BROOKS

Rigid Body Sings

Gin a body meet a body
  Flyin' through the air,
Gin a body hit a body,
  Will it fly? and where?
Ilka impact has its measure,
  Ne'er a' ane hae I,
Yet a' the lads they measure me,
  Or, at least, they try.

Gin a body meet a body
  Altogether free,
How they travel afterwards
  We do not always see.
Ilka problem has its method
  By analytics high;
For me, I ken na ane o' them,
  But what the waur am I?

JAMES CLERK MAXWELL

William Wordsworth (1770–1850)

A Sonnet

Two voices are there: one is of the deep;
It learns the storm-cloud's thunderous melody,
Now roars, now murmurs with the changing sea,
Now bird-like pipes, now closes soft in sleep:
And one is of an old half-witted sheep
Which bleats articulate monotony,

And indicates that two and one are three,
That grass is green, lakes damp, and mountains steep:
And, Wordsworth, both are thine: at certain times
Forth from the heart of thy melodious rhymes,
The form and pressure of high thoughts will burst:
At other times – good Lord! I'd rather be
Quite unacquainted with the ABC
Than write such hopeless rubbish as thy worst.

J. K. STEPHEN

On First Hearing that Wordsworth had an Illegitimate Child

Byron! Thou shouldst be living at this hour,
    We need thy verse, thy venom and thy wit
    To castigate the ancient hypocrite.
We need thy pith, thy passion and thy power –
How often did that prim old face turn sour
    Even at the mention of thy honoured name,
    How oft those prudish lips have muttered 'shame'
In jealous envy of thy golden lyre.
In words worth reading hadst thou told the tale
    Of what the lakeland bard was really at
When on those long excursions he set sail.
    For now there echoes through his tedious chat
Another voice, the third, a phantom wail
    Or peevish prattle of a bastard brat.

JOHN JULIUS NORWICH

Epilogue

There's something in a stupid ass;
And something in a heavy dunce;
But never since I went to school
I saw or heard so damned a fool
As William Wordsworth is for once.

And now I've seen so great a fool
As William Wordsworth is for once,
I really wish that Peter Bell
And he who wrote it were in hell,
For writing nonsense for the nonce.

I saw the 'light in ninety-eight',
Sweet Babe of one and twenty years!
And then he gave it to the nation,
And deems himself of Shakespeare's peers.
He gives the perfect works to light!
William Wordsworth – if I might advise,
Content you with the praise you get
From Sir George Beaumont, Baronet,
And with your place in the excise.

GEORGE GORDON, LORD BYRON

The Wordsworths

We wondered – nay, we said out loud,
'Oh happy, happy daffodils!'
Alas, but we had not allowed
For him who haunts these gloomy hills,
His muffler flapping in the breeze,
Muttering and stumbling through the trees.

Lugubrious as the sheep that pine
And sulk behind each boulder damp,
He stands, disconsolate, for a time,
Underneath his dripping gamp.
While all about the rain drops fall;
We wish to God he wouldn't call.

We wish to hell he'd wander on,
We've never been so sorely tried.
A daffodil thus gazed upon,
Might well consider suicide.
He stares and stares, 'How rude!' We sing,
'What blank despair to us you bring.'

For oft, as in this bog we lie,
In vacant, or in pensive mood,
He looms upon that inward eye,
Which is the curse of solitude;
And then our hearts of pleasure drain,
To see that dreary bard again.

WILLIAM BEALBY-WRIGHT

It's Those Daffodils Again

I wandered, as a sheep content
That crops the grass on dales and hills.
Then all at once I caught the scent
That brings hay fever – daffodils!
All around my feet, and everywhere
Casting their pollen on the air.

And oft when on my couch I lie
In dark and apprehensive mood,
They bring the tear into the eye
And spoil the bliss of all my food.
And then my nose with moisture fills
And drips for those damn daffodils!

LANCE A. HAWARD

A Fragment

There is a river clear and fair,
    'Tis neither broad nor narrow;
It winds a little here and there –
It winds about like any hare;
And then it takes as straight a course
As on the turnpike road a horse,
    Or through the air an arrow.

The trees that grow upon the shore,
Have grown a hundred years or more;
    So long there is no knowing.
Old Daniel Dobson does not know
When first those trees began to grow;
But still they grew, and grew, and grew,
As if they'd nothing else to do,
    But ever to be growing.

The impulses of air and sky
Have reared their stately stems so high,
    And clothed their boughs with green;
Their leaves the dews of evening quaff, –
    And when the wind blows loud and keen,
I've seen the jolly timbers laugh,
    And shake their sides with merry glee –
    Wagging their heads in mockery.

Fix'd are their feet in solid earth,
    Where winds can never blow;
But visitings of deeper birth
    Have reached their roots below.
For they have gained the river's brink,
And of the living waters drink.

There's little Will, a five years' child –
    He is my youngest boy;
To look on eyes so fair and wild,
    It is a very joy: –
He hath conversed with sun and shower,
And dwelt with every idle flower,
    As fresh and gay as them.
He loiters with the briar rose –
The blue bells are his play-fellows,
    That dance upon their slender stem.

And I have said, my little Will,
Why should not he continue still
    A thing of Nature's rearing?
A thing beyond the world's control –
A living vegetable soul, –
    No human sorrow fearing.

It were a blessed sight to see
That child become a willow-tree,
    His brother trees among.
He'd be four times as tall as me,
    And live three times as long.

CATHERINE FANSHAWE

The Hardened Brat

I met a little cottage brat,
Her petticoat was red.
She had some contradiction flat
For everything I said.

I took the tombstone next to her,
She gave a dirty grin,
And stirred her little porringer
That had no porridge in.

I told her that I had been sent
To teach the unemployed
The blessings of this Government . . .
She only seemed annoyed.

I said: 'We keep food prices high
And subsidize the land,
Lest it should chance the food supply
Might equal the demand.'

Of levies on imported meat
I then began to speak.
She said: 'We live and dress and eat
On one pound eight per week.'

I asked: 'How many may you be
That gratis we maintain?'
She answered: 'Ma and Pa and me,
Since we lost John and Jane.'

Our recent budgetary gain
I next enlarged upon.
She said: 'You're sitting down on Jane,
I'm sitting down on John.'

I said: 'Our records we affix
To hoardings in the town.'
She said: 'John died at three-and-six
And Jane at half-a-crown.'

I praised our charity about
The means test and the cuts.
She said: 'Young John and Jane passed out
Because they'd got no guts.

'And furthermore, till Pa is dead,
He'll never get a job.
But if I die for it,' she said,
'I'll live to fifteen bob!'

I left the tombstone next to her,
She gave a dirty grin,
And stirred her little porringer
That had no porridge in.

SAGITTARIUS

He Lived amidst th' Untrodden Ways

He lived amidst th' untrodden ways
  To Rydal Lake that lead;
A bard whom there were none to praise,
  And very few to read.

Behind a cloud his mystic sense,
  Deep hidden, who can spy?
Bright as the night when not a star
  Is shining in the sky.

Unread his works – his 'Milk White Doe'
  With dust is dark and dim;
It's still in Longman's shop, and oh!
  The difference to him!

HARTLEY COLERIDGE

Samuel Taylor Coleridge (1772–1834)

On a Ruined House in a Romantic Country

   And this reft house is that the which he built
Lamented Jack! And here his malt he pil'd,
Cautious in vain! These rats that squeak so wild,
Squeak, not unconscious of their father's guilt.
Did ye not see her gleaming thro' the glade?
Belike, 'twas she, the maiden all forlorn.
What though she milk no cow with crumpled horn,
Yet *aye* she haunts the dale where *erst* she stray'd;
And *aye* beside her stalks her amorous knight!
Still on his thighs their wonted brogues are worn,
And thro' those brogues, still tatter'd and betorn,
His hindward charms gleam an unearthly white;
As when thro' broken clouds at night's high noon
Peeps in fair fragments forth the full-orb'd harvest-moon.

SAMUEL TAYLOR COLERIDGE

The Ancient Mariner
(The Wedding Guest's Version of the Affair)

It is an ancient Mariner,
   And he stoppeth one of three –
In fact he coolly took my arm –
   'There was a ship,' quoth he.

'Bother your ships!' said I, 'is this
   The time a yarn to spin?
This is a wedding, don't you see,
   And I am next of kin.

'The wedding breakfast has begun,
    We're hungry as can be –
Hold off! Unhand me, longshore man!'
    With that his hand dropt he.

But there was something in his eye,
    That made me sick and ill,
Yet forced to listen to his yarn –
    The Mariner'd had his will.

While Tom and Harry went their way
    I sat upon a stone –
So queer on Fanny's wedding day
    Me sitting there alone!

Then he began, that Mariner,
    To rove from pole to pole,
In one long-winded, lengthened-out,
    Eternal rigmarole,

About a ship in which he'd sailed,
    Though whither, goodness knows,
Where 'ice will split with a thunder-fit',
    And every day it snows.

And then about a precious bird
    Of some sort or another,
That – was such nonsense ever heard? –
    Used to control the weather!

Now, at this bird the Mariner
    Resolved to have a shy,
And laid it low with his cross-bow –
    And then the larks! My eye!

For loss of that uncommon fowl,
    They couldn't get a breeze;
And there they stuck, all out of luck,
    And rotted on the seas.

The crew all died, or seemed to die,
    And he was left alone
With that queer bird. You never heard
    What games were carried on!

At last one day he stood and watched
    The fishes in the sea,
And said, 'I'm blest!' and so the ship
    Was from the spell set free.

And it began to rain and blow,
    And as it rained and blew,
The dead got up and worked the ship –
    That was a likely crew!

However, somehow he escaped,
    And got again to land,
But mad as any hatter, say,
    From Cornhill to the Strand.

For he believes that certain folks
    Are singled out by fate,
To whom this cock-and-bull affair
    Of his he must relate,

Describing all the incidents,
    And painting all the scenes,
As sailors will do in the tales
    They tell to the Marines.

Confound the Ancient Mariner!
    I knew I should be late;
And so it was; the wedding guests
    Had all declined to wait.

Another had my place, and gave
    My toast; and sister Fan
Said, ''Twas a shame. What could you want
    With that seafaring man?'

I felt like one that had been stunned
  Through all this wrong and scorn;
A sadder and a later man
  I rose the morrow morn.

ANON

Robert Southey (1774–1843)

Epitaph on a Well-known Poet

Beneath these poppies buried deep,
  The bones of Bob the bard lie hid;
Peace to his manes; and may he sleep
  As soundly as his readers did!

Through every sort of verse meandering,
  Bob went without a hitch or fall,
Through epic, Sapphic, Alexandrine,
  To verse that was no verse at all;

Till fiction having done enough,
  To make a bard at least absurd,
And give his readers *quantum suff.*,
  He took to praising George the Third,

And now, in virtue of his crown,
  Dooms us, poor Whigs, at once to slaughter;
Like Donellan of bad renown,
  Poisoning us all with laurel-water.

And yet at times some awful qualms he
  Felt about leaving honour's track;
And though he's got a butt of Malmsey,
  It may not save him from a sack.

Death, weary of so dull a writer,
  Put to his books a *finis* thus.
Oh! may the earth on him lie lighter
  Than did his quartos upon us!

THOMAS MOORE

Jane Austen (1775–1817)

Pride and Porringers

Elizabeth laid aside her diary. Her recollection of the scene was sharper than the few inadequate sentences which she had penned the same evening.

'See, Mr Bear,' her mother had said, surveying the dining-room, 'there have been callers in our absence, and not a servant to receive them, and we all out walking. I cannot think why, since I abominate the pursuit, especially in woods. They are so tedious. The quantity of trees makes for considerable monotony.'

'It must be the new tenants of Polar Hall,' she went on, with growing apprehension. 'The shame of it, when I have begged and prayed to you, Mr Bear, to call there, for at least a week.'

Mr Bear observed that it had seemed to him a much longer period.

'Mr Bruin, a wealthy young man with an independent income from stocks, and a very plain sister, so Lady Grizzly informs me.'

Mrs Bear did not say whether the sister was regarded as an enhancement or as an impediment to the aforementioned fortune.

'For I am sure,' she went on, 'that all our old neighbours would know our "at home" days.'

'Mama, one bowl of porridge has been quite eaten up!'

'And so I should have presumed, Elizabeth, for I am sure I make very good porridge, quite the nicest to be found in any of the better houses in these parts – unlike Lady Grizzly's, which has always such obtrusive lumps. Yes, it must have been the Bruins who called, so mortifying when our neighbourhood so lacks eligible bachelors for Lizzie.'

'I am sure, Mama,' said Elizabeth gravely, 'I could not regard a man as a prospective husband until I had met him and found him to be agreeable in ways unconnected with his fortune.'

'What an obstinate, talkative minx you are becoming, Miss!' exclaimed Mrs Bear with some annoyance.

'Perhaps you should withdraw to your room, Lizzie,' said her father. 'This may not be the moment for such opinions.'

He was regarding the wreckage of a small chair. 'It would appear,' he went on, after Elizabeth had left the room, 'that gentility does not necessarily go hand-in-hand with gentleness in the matter of furniture, at least.'

'I daresay the Bruins are accustomed to such superior chairs that they found our old ones insufficient for them. I am positively ashamed of . . .'

Her disenchantment with her household belongings was interrupted by a loud cry and a scrambling sound.

'That was Lizzie's voice,' said Mr Bear. 'But, look!'

He drew his spouse's attention to a fair-haired girl who, at that moment, dropped lightly upon the lawn and rapidly retreated into the concealing shelter of the trees.

'So it was not the Bruins who partook of our comestibles, Mrs Bear.'

'I am sure that it was not your fault that it wasn't,' said Mrs Bear. 'Now, you must call on them before such an incident as we have imagined does occur. Mr Bruin might suit Lizzie very well. I cannot think what has happened to the girl, I am sure. She has become such a chatterbox. Though, of course, marriage may cure her, or not, as the case may be.'

Mr Bear observed that to his certain knowledge, entering into wedlock had very little or no effect upon such matters.

E. O. PARROTT

Pride and Punishment

'Are not you happy in Hertfordshire, Mr Raskolnikov?' said Elizabeth.

Raskolnikov looked into her beautiful dark eyes. His own shone with feverish brilliance.

'Would you be happy,' he said, 'if you had killed a miserable pawnbroker?'

Elizabeth turned away to hide a smile. 'I hope I am not so deficient in sense and feeling as either to be capable of the attempt, or to remain in spirits when the crime was accomplished,' said she. 'But they are not within the range of my acquaintance – pawnbrokers are safe from me.'

'She was only a louse, a miserable insect,' murmured Raskolnikov. 'But I was wrong to kill her – and to kill Lizaveta too.'

'How easily may a bad habit be formed!' cried Elizabeth; and with this in mind, though she hoped he was not in earnest, she very soon afterwards took leave of him.

GWEN FOYLE

Mansfield Mill

If Jane Austen had come from a Lancashire mill town . . .

'Such a genteel young man, even for a foreman,' said Miss Yates, deftly blowing her nose upon her mob-cap. 'And so understanding. Never a word on how long we mill-hands spend in our toilets or things of that sort.'

There was general approval for the finer feelings of Mr Longbotham.

'I do hear,' said the elder Miss Pudden, 'that his sister owns no fewer than three pairs of clogs in her own right and a pair of shawls inherited from an aunt who actually owned a very refined whelk-stall down by the Canal.'

'I can vouch for all that,' nodded Miss Yates, wringing out her cap and replacing it upon her head. ''Tis long since we had such an heiress here in Oldham.'

At that moment the personable young foreman made his appearance, and the ladies scuttled back to their shuttles. Fanny noted the handsome little whip which he carried. What an honour it would be, she thought, to be beaten by such a whip held in such a hand!

E. O. PARROTT

from Sense and Centenaries

Written to commemorate the bicentenary of Jane Austen's birth

That Sir Walter Elliott, of Kellynch Hall, in Somersetshire, should never rest his eye upon any other entry in *Who Was Who* than his own is not to be supposed.

'I never thought highly of Ellenborough,' he had been heard to observe to his elder daughter Elizabeth; 'your attorneys too readily engage themselves in the affairs of others to be altogether gentleman-like.'

On a different occasion a fitful draught so far disturbed his choice of reading that he found himself contemplating, with wrinkled lip, the careers of several Elphinstones, until a sense of what was owing to himself restored his attention to a more familiar and more welcome creation.

No such predispositions, however, confined the enjoyment of his younger daughter Anne. She did not scruple to turn the pages of the great book as fancy or inclination dictated, nor did she feel herself ill-used if it fell open as far afield as Lord Acton or the Bishop of Zululand. It was Anne who, on receiving the volume from Sir Walter when he had satisfied himself with a third or fourth reading of his own history, quietly withdrew her eyes from a page that, through her father's self-indulgence, had long excited her disgust and was soon agreeably refreshing her jaded spirits with other names, other histories.

Experience had taught Anne that sensible conversation, a sympathetic concern with people, problems, the world that lay outside their own narrow circle of acquaintance, were not to be expected from her father or Elizabeth. But now, as she bent her head over the pages, she made a discovery which her lively mind and generous wish to please prompted her, despite every discouragement, to share with her companions.

'Austen, Jane,' cried Anne. 'Born December the 16th, 1775. No very prolonged reflection is needed to convince me that she would have been two hundred years old this Christmas.'

'Austen?' replied Sir Walter with a shrug. 'I have no one of my acquaintance with that name. There was at one time a Sir Austen, I believe, who dabbled in the offensive trade of politics.'

'Did not his father Joseph manufacture screws in Birmingham?' put in Elizabeth coolly.

Anne was not to be so easily put down by their ill-bred disdain.

'You do not entirely comprehend me,' said she. 'The lady who at present commands my interest is a Miss Austen, the daughter of a respectable clergyman, of Steventon in the county of Hampshire. Do not you know that she is the author of some six or seven romances praised on every hand for their neatness of expression, propriety of diction and refined delineation of character?'

'Novels!' rejoined Sir Walter, looking his indignation. 'I am by no means disposed to countenance the mention in my house of so objectionable a mode of writing. Romances,' turning to Elizabeth, 'as your sister presumes to call them, excite my contempt on a number of counts. In the first place –'

Whatever were the grounds upon which Sir Walter based his dismissal of Miss Austen's pretensions, they were not now to be heard. The sound of wheels on the gravel, followed soon after by the announcement of a party of callers, brought his opening periods abruptly to a conclusion and he retired to a far corner of the room in no more contented a frame of mind than is commonly the lot of persons who, with nothing of consequence to say, feel all the mortification and indignity of being deprived of an opportunity to say it.

Their unexpected visitors proved, to Anne's pleasure at least, to be all old friends, and in the bustle and animation of arrival, greetings exchanged, inquiries to be made, everybody delighted, nothing so agreeable as a surprise, Anne had time only to observe that the party included Mr Knightley, Miss Bates, Mr Woodhouse and his daughter Emma, Frank Churchill, Mr Bennet with his daughter Elizabeth, Mr Collins, Mr Henry Dashwood and the Misses Dashwood, Mrs Norris, Mr Edmund Bertram looking grave, General Tilney, and Miss Mary Crawford with a number of young men in attendance, before her attention was claimed by Mrs Elton, who pushed herself forward with –

'Is not this a good scheme? My brother's barouche-landau – my brother, Mr Suckling of Maple Grove, you know – happened to be not required and it was very soon spoken for, I assure you. "Let us make a plan," said I. Mr Bennet heard me. "Let us make up a party," I said – Did not I, Mr Bennet? "Let us all call upon Sir Walter and family, to wish them the compliments of the season," I said. And here we are! Was not that well thought of?'

'You must have been a little crushed, I fear.'

'Oh no, indeed. My brother's barouche-landau –'

'Mrs Elton is not easily crushed,' said Mr Bennet.

H. F. ELLIS

Thomas Moore (1779–1852)

'Twas Ever Thus

I never rear'd a young gazelle,
  (Because, you see, I never tried);
But had it known and loved me well,
  No doubt the creature would have died.
My rich and aged Uncle John
  Has known me long and loves me well
But still persists in living on –
  I would he were a young gazelle.

I never loved a tree or flower;
  But, if I had, I beg to say,
The blight, the wind, the sun, or shower
  Would soon have withered it away.
I've dearly loved my Uncle John,
  From childhood to the present hour,
And yet he will go living on –
  I would he were a tree or flower!

HENRY S. LEIGH

George Gordon, Lord Byron (1788–1824)

From Beer

O Beer! O Hodgson, Guinness, Allsopp, Bass!
   Names that should be on every infant's tongue!
Shall days and months and years and centuries pass,
   And still your merits be unrecked, unsung?
Oh! I have gazed into my foaming glass,
   And wished that lyre could yet again be strung
Which once rang prophet-like through Greece, and taught her
Misguided sons that 'the best drink was water'.

How would he now recant that wild opinion,
   And sing – as would that I could sing – of you!
I was not born (alas!) the 'Muses' minion',
   I'm not poetical, not even blue:
And he (we know) but strives with waxen pinion,
   Whoe'er he is that entertains the view
Of emulating Pindar, and will be
Sponsor at last to some now nameless sea.

Oh! when the green slopes of Arcadia burned
   With all the lustre of the dying day,
And on Cithaeron's brow the reaper turned,
   (Humming, of course, in his delightful way,
How Lycidas was dead, and how concerned
   The Nymphs were when they saw his lifeless clay;
And how rock told to rock the dreadful story
That poor young Lycidas was gone to glory:)

What would that lone and labouring soul have given,
   At that soft moment, for a pewter pot!
How had the mists that dimmed his eye been riven,
   And Lycidas and sorrow all forgot!

If his own grandmother had died unshriven,
      In two short seconds he'd have recked it not;
Such power hath Beer. The heart which Grief hath canker'd
Hath one unfailing remedy – the Tankard.

Coffee is good, and so no doubt is cocoa;
      Tea did for Johnson and the Chinamen:
When 'Dulce est desipere in loco'
      Was written, real Falernian winged the pen.
When a rapt audience has encored 'Fra Poco'
      Or 'Casta Diva,' I have heard that then
The Prima Donna, smiling herself out,
Recruits her flagging powers with bottled stout.

C. S. CALVERLEY

The Poet Sees Himself

He turned and caught his features in a mirror –
And found a cherub utterly debauched,
From whom all goodly matrons fled in terror,
In case their reputations should be torched
By one whose stamina in moral error
Had many a haunt of haughty virtue scorched.
'What can there be', he brooded, 'in my phiz
To throw so many harpies in a tizz?'

Its ruin marked the progress of an odyssey
Begun in youth: for he was just a stripling
The day he fumbled his first bodice. He
Went on to other pleasures: gaming, tippling,
Incest, sodomy. But what is odd is he,
Despite these sins his days so starkly stippling,
The sombre truth could never start to swallow –
That no one ages faster than Apollo.

MARTIN FAGG

A Grievance

Dear Mr Editor: I wish to say –
  If you will not be angry at my writing it –
But I've been used, since childhood's happy day,
  When I have thought of something, to inditing it:
I seldom think of things: and, by the way,
  Although this metre may not be exciting, it
Enables one to be extremely terse,
Which is not what one always is in verse.

I used to know a man, – such things befall
  The observant wayfarer through Fate's domain:
He was a man, take him for all in all,
  We shall not look upon his like again:
I know that statement's not original:
  What statement is, since Shakspere? or, since Cain,
What murder? I believe 'twas Shakspere said it, or
Perhaps it may have been your Fighting Editor.

Though why an Editor should fight, or why
  A Fighter should abase himself to edit,
Are problems far too difficult and high
  For me to solve with any sort of credit:
Some greatly more accomplished man than I
  Must tackle them: let's say then Shakspere said it:
And, if he did not, Lewis Morris may
(Or even if he did). Some other day,

When I have nothing pressing to impart,
  I should not mind dilating on this matter:
I feel its import both in head and heart,
  And always did, – especially the latter:
I could discuss it in the busy mart
  Or on the lonely housetop: hold! this chatter
Diverts me from my purpose. To the point:
The time, as Hamlet said, is out of joint,

And I perhaps was born to set it right;
  A fact I greet with perfect equanimity;

I do not put it down to 'cursed spite':
    I don't see any cause for cursing in it: I
Have always taken very great delight
    In such pursuits since first I read divinity:
Whoever will may write a nation's songs
As long as I'm allowed to right its wrongs.

What's Eton but a nursery of wrong-righters,
    A mighty mother of effective men,
A training-ground for amateur reciters,
    A sharpener of the sword as of the pen,
A factory of orators and fighters,
    A forcing-house of genius? Now and then,
The world at large shrinks back, abashed and beaten,
Unable to endure the glare of Eton.

I think I said I knew a man: what then?
    I don't suppose such knowledge is forbid:
We nearly all do, more or less, know men, –
    Or think we do: nor will a man get rid
Of that delusion, while he wields a pen:
    But who this man was, what, if aught, he did,
Nor why I mentioned him, I do not know:
Nor what I 'wished to say' a while ago.

J. K. STEPHEN

James Fenimore Cooper (1789–1851)

from Muck-a-Muck

CHAPTER V

The moon rose cheerfully above Donner Lake. On its placid bosom
a dug-out canoe glided rapidly, containing Natty Bumpo and
Genevra Tompkins.

Both were silent. The same thought possessed each, and perhaps there was sweet companionship even in the unbroken quiet. Genevra bit the handle of her parasol and blushed. Natty Bumpo took a fresh chew of tobacco. At length Genevra said, as if in half-spoken revery: –

'The soft shining of the moon and the peaceful ripple of the waves seem to say to us various things of an instructive and moral tendency.'

'You may bet yer pile on that, Miss,' said her companion, gravely. 'It's all the preachin' and psalm singin' I've heern since I was a boy.'

'Noble being!' said Miss Tompkins to herself, glancing at the stately Pike as he bent over his paddle to conceal his emotion. 'Reared in this wild seclusion, yet he has become penetrated with visible consciousness of a Great First Cause.' Then, collecting herself, she said aloud: 'Methinks 'twere pleasant to glide ever thus down the stream of life, hand in hand with the one being whom the soul claims as its affinity. But what am I saying?' – and the delicate-minded girl hid her face in her hands.

A long silence ensued, which was at length broken by her companion.

'If you mean you're on the marry,' he said, thoughtfully, 'I ain't in no wise partikler!'

'My husband,' faltered the blushing girl; and she fell into his arms. In ten minutes more the loving couple had landed at Judge Tompkins's.

CHAPTER VI

A year has passed away. Natty Bumpo was returning from Gold Hill, where he had been to purchase provisions. On his way to Donner Lake, rumours of an Indian uprising met his ears. 'Dern their pesky skins, ef they dare to touch my Jenny,' he muttered between his clenched teeth.

It was dark when he reached the borders of the lake. Around a glittering fire he dimly discerned dusky figures dancing. They were in war paint. Conspicuous among them was the renowned Muck-a-Muck. But why did the fingers of Natty Bumpo tighten convulsively around his rifle?

The chief held in his hand long tufts of raven hair. The heart of the pioneer sickened as he recognized the clustering curls of Genevra. In a moment his rifle was at his shoulder, and with a sharp 'ping'

Muck-a-Muck leaped into the air a corpse. To knock out the brains of the remaining savages, tear the tresses from the stiffening hand of Muck-a-Muck, and dash rapidly forward to the cottage of Judge Tompkins, was the work of a moment.

He burst open the door. Why did he stand transfixed with open mouth and distended eyeballs? Was the sight too horrible to be borne? On the contrary, before him, in her peerless beauty, stood Genevra Tompkins, leaning on her father's arm.

'Ye'r not scalped, then!' gasped her lover.

'No. I have no hesitation in saying that I am not; but why this abruptness?' responded Genevra.

Bumpo could not speak, but frantically produced the silken tresses. Genevra turned her face aside.

'Why, that's her waterfall!' said the Judge.

Bumpo sank fainting to the floor.

The famous Pike chieftain never recovered from the deceit, and refused to marry Genevra, who died, twenty years afterwards, of a broken heart. Judge Tompkins lost his fortune in Wild Cat. The stage passes twice a week the deserted cottage at Donner Lake. Thus was the death of Muck-a-Muck avenged.

BRET HARTE

Percy Bysshe Shelley (1792–1822)

Ozymandias Revisited

I met a traveller from an antique land
Who said: Two vast and trunkless legs of stone
Stand in the desert. Near them on the sand
Half sunk, a shatter'd visage lies, whose frown
And wrinkled lip and sneer of cold command
Tell that its sculptor well those passions read
Which still survive, stamp'd on these lifeless things,
The hand that mocked them and the heart that fed;

And on the pedestal these words appear:
'My name is Ozymandias, king of kings!
Look on my works, ye Mighty and despair!'
Also the names of Emory P. Gray,
Mr and Mrs Dukes, and Oscar Baer,
Of 17 West 4th Street, Oyster Bay.

MORRIS BISHOP

John Keats (1795–1821)

A Grecian Urn Reconsidered

Into my room of peaceful quietude,
Unwished-for and mistrusted Grecian gift,
Thou com'st, a pseudo-attic shape, whose crude
Cheap gaudiness Time's workings cannot shift
Since, hourly, thou dost more unlovely grow.
From what small gifte-shoppe by the sad sea shore
(O Devil's mass-produced!), what Churchly sale,
What bargain-counter in a chainèd store,
Or stall in dusty market did'st thou hail?
Alas! – thou must be seen to be believed,
A tablet marked 'reduced' clings yet to thee,
And on the side in letters gold-relieved
These words, 'A PRESENT FROM THERMOPYLAE',
Tell all we know of thee or need to know.

NANCY GUNTER

Ode to Another Nightingale

My head aches, and my drowsy eyelids fain
Would close in soothing, care-dispelling sleep
Yet thou conspirest to increase my pain
And, like an evil spirit, here dost keep
Thy noisy vigil. Fools have praised thy song
That so disturbs the flower-scented peace
Of this enchanted garden, that I long
For Summer's end when all thy notes shall cease.

How oft my thoughts in rapturous dreams would fly,
Into the magic realms of poesy.
But slumber needs a sweeter lullaby
Than piping strains of such monotony.
Away! away! and in some other bower
Of leafy darkness hide from human sight
Thy dismal plumage, chanting hour by hour
Thy melancholy anthem to the night.

A. SHERIDAN

Ode to a Slug

My head aches, and a drowsy numbness fogs
    My sense, because of Tetley's I have drunk
(Though emptied my full bladder in the outside bogs
    One minute past). Now pathwards I have sunk.
O for a beaker full of a cold drug,
    Full of the effervescent Pepsi
        With bursting bubbles fizzing on the clack,
            For one long soothing slug!
    To drink and lapse into a narcolepsy
        And with thee lie all day upon my back.

Thou wast not born for death (just yet) oh gastropod,
  Though gardening generations tread thee flat.
The slime I tread this soggy morn was trod
  In recent nights by bogeyman and cat.
Perhaps the selfsame trail that lit the path
  Of pottering Fungus, when, dying for a steep,
    He stood on tarmac by the wrong hut,
      The same that oftimes hath
  Tripped the early bird who, straight from sleep,
    Slipping in thy deposit, hath bust a gut.

Gut! the very word is like a bell
  To toll inside my skull from lug to lug.
Adieu! the fancy did not cheat so well
  That I could lie all day with you, dear slug.
Adieu! adieu! thy slimey trail draws thin
  Past green lettuces, through the dark trees,
    By the house-side: and now 'tis buried deep
      In the empties by the dustbin.
  Was it a vision, or the onset of D.T.'s?
    Fled is the mollusc: – do I wake or sleep?

ANDREW STIBBS

Thomas Hood (1799–1845)

Elegy

O spare a tear for poor Tom Hood,
Who, dazed by death, here lies;
His days abridged, he sighs across
The Bridge of Utmost Size.

His *penchant* was for punning rhymes
(Some lengthy, others – shorties);
But though his *forte* was his life,
He died within his forties.

The Muses cried: 'To you we give
The crown of rhymester's bay, Thos.'
Thos mused and thought that it might pay
To ladle out the pay-thos.

He spun the gold yet tangled yarn
Of sad Miss Kilmansegg;
And told how destiny contrived
To take her down a peg.

But now the weary toils of death
Have closed his rhyming toil,
And charged this very vital spark
To jump his mortal coil.

MARTIN FAGG

Ben Barley

Ben Barley was a barman stout
  Who drank both day and night,
Which made him heavy, dull and fat
  Though all he drank was Light.

He slowly drank himself to death,
  And at his wake so drear,
Although 'twas he who'd passed away,
  The guests laid on the beer.

His ghost came in and asked for gin
  In accents strange and far.
The landlord said, 'Clear off; we don't
  Serve spirits in this bar.'

GERARD BENSON

Elizabeth Barrett Browning (1806–1861)

Sonnet

How do I hate you? Let me count the ways:
I hate your greying hair, now almost white,
Your blotchy skin, a most repellent sight,
The eyes that stare back in a sort of daze,
The turned-up nose, the hollow that betrays
The missing dentures, taken out at night,
Receding chin, whose contour isn't quite
Masked by the scraggy beard – in a phrase,
I hate the sight of you, as every morn,
We meet each other in our favourite place,
And casually, as to the manner born,
You make your all too customary grimace,
Something between disgust, boredom and scorn;
God, how I loathe you, shaving-mirror face.

STANLEY J. SHARPLESS

Henry Wadsworth Longfellow (1807–1882)

Hiawatha's Photographing

From his shoulder Hiawatha
Took the camera of rose-wood,
Made of sliding, folding rose-wood;
Neatly put it all together,

In its case it lay compactly,
Folded into nearly nothing;
But he opened out the hinges,
Pushed and pulled the joints and hinges,
Till it looked all squares and oblongs,
Like a complicated figure
In the second book of Euclid.

This he perched upon a tripod,
And the family in order
Sat before him for their pictures.
Mystic, awful was the process.

First a piece of glass he coated
With Collodion, and plunged it
In a bath of Lunar Caustic
Carefully dissolved in water:
There he left it certain minutes.

Secondly, my Hiawatha
Made with cunning hand a mixture
Of the acid Pyro-gallic,
And of Glacial Acetic,
And of Alcohol and water:
This developed all the picture.

Finally, he fixed each picture
With a saturate solution
Of a certain salt of Soda –
Chemists call it Hyposulphite.
(Very difficult the name is
For a metre like the present,
But periphrasis has done it.)

All the family in order
Sat before him for their pictures.
Each in turn, as he was taken,
Volunteered his own suggestions,
His invaluable suggestions.

First the Governor, the Father:
He suggested velvet curtains
Looped about a massy pillar;
And the corner of a table,
Of a rose-wood dining table.
He would hold a scroll of something,
Hold it firmly in his left hand;

He would keep his right hand buried
(Like Napoleon) in his waistcoat;
He would contemplate the distance
With a look of pensive meaning,
As of ducks that die in tempests.
   Grand, heroic was the notion:
Yet the picture failed entirely:
Failed, because he moved a little,
Moved, because he couldn't help it.
   Next, his better half took courage;
She would have her picture taken:
She came dressed beyond description,
Dressed in jewels and in satin
Far too gorgeous for an empress.
Gracefully she sat down sideways,
With a simper scarcely human,
Holding in her hand a nosegay
Rather larger than a cabbage.
All the while that she was taking,
Still the lady chattered, chattered,
Like a monkey in the forest.
'Am I sitting still?' she asked him.
'Is my face enough in profile?
Shall I hold the nosegay higher?
Will it come into the picture?'
And the picture failed completely.
   Next the Son, the Stunning-Cantab:
He suggested curves of beauty,
Curves pervading all his figure,
Which the eye might follow onward,
Till they centred in the breast-pin,
Centred in the golden breast-pin.
He had learnt it all from Ruskin
(Author of 'The Stones of Venice',
'Seven Lamps of Architecture',
'Modern Painters', and some others);
And perhaps he had not fully
Understood his author's meaning;
But, whatever was the reason,
All was fruitless, as the picture
Ended in an utter failure.

Next to him the eldest daughter:
She suggested very little;
Only asked if he would take her
With her look of 'passive beauty'.

Her idea of passive beauty
Was a squinting of the left-eye,
Was a drooping of the right-eye,
Was a smile that went up sideways
To the corner of the nostrils.

Hiawatha, when she asked him,
Took no notice of the question,
Looked as if he hadn't heard it;
But, when pointedly appealed to,
Smiled in his peculiar manner,
Coughed and said it 'didn't matter',
Bit his lip and changed the subject.

Nor in this was he mistaken,
As the picture failed completely.

So in turn the other sisters.
Last, the youngest son was taken:
Very rough and thick his hair was,
Very round and red his face was,
Very dusty was his jacket,
Very fidgety his manner.
And his overbearing sisters
Called him names he disapproved of:
Called him Johnny, 'Daddy's Darling',
Called him Jacky, 'Scrubby School-boy'.
And, so awful was the picture,
In comparison the others
Might be thought to have succeeded,
To have partially succeeded.

Finally my Hiawatha
Tumbled all the tribe together,
'Grouped' is not the right expression,
And, as happy chance would have it,
Did at last obtain a picture
Where the faces all succeeded:
Each came out a perfect likeness.

Then they joined and all abused it,
Unrestrainedly abused it,

As 'the worst and ugliest picture
They could possibly have dreamed of.
Giving one such strange expressions!
Sulkiness, conceit, and meanness!
Really any one would take us
(Any one that did not know us)
For the most unpleasant people!'
(Hiawatha seemed to think so,
Seemed to think it not unlikely.)
All together rang their voices,
Angry, loud, discordant voices,
As of dogs that howl in concert,
As of cats that wail in chorus.

But my Hiawatha's patience,
His politeness and his patience,
Unaccountably had vanished,
And he left that happy party,
Neither did he leave them slowly,
With that calm deliberation,
That intense deliberation
Which photographers aspire to
But he left them in a hurry,
Left them in a mighty hurry,
Vowing that he would not stand it.

Hurriedly the porter trundled
On a barrow all his boxes;
Hurriedly he took his ticket,
Hurriedly the train received him:
Thus departed Hiawatha.

LEWIS CARROLL

What I Think of Hiawatha

Do you ask me what I think of
This new song of Hiawatha,
With its legends and traditions,
And its frequent repetitions
Of hard names which make the jaw ache,

And of words most unpoetic?
I should answer, I should tell you
I esteem it wild and wayward,
Slipshod metre, scanty sense,
Honour paid to Mudjekeewis,
But no honour to the muse.

J. W. MORRIS

The Modern Hiawatha

When he killed the Mudjokivis,
Of the skin he made him mittens,
Made them with the fur side inside,
Made them with the skin side outside,
He, to get the warm side inside,
Put the inside skin side outside;
He, to get the cold side outside,
Put the warm side fur side inside.
That's why he put fur side inside,
Why he put the skin side outside,
Why he turned them inside outside.

GEORGE A. STRONG

The Village Burglar

Under a spreading gooseberry bush the village burglar lies,
The burglar is a hairy man with whiskers round his eyes
And the muscles of his brawny arms keep off the little flies.

He goes on Sunday to the church to hear the Parson shout.
He puts a penny in the plate and takes a pound note out
And drops a conscience-stricken tear in case he is found out.

ANON

J. G. Whittier (1807–1892)

The Ballad of Hiram Hover

Where the Moosatockmaguntic
Pours its waters in the Skuntic,
  Met, along the forest-side,
  Hiram Hover, Huldah Hyde.

She, a maiden fair and dapper,
He, a red-haired, stalwart trapper,
  Hunting beaver, mink, and skunk,
  In the woodlands of Squeedunk.

She, Pentucket's pensive daughter,
Walked beside the Skuntic water,
  Gathering, in her apron wet,
  Snakeroot, mint, and bouncing-bet.

'Why,' he murmured, loath to leave her,
'Gather yarbs for chills and fever,
  When a lovyer, bold and true,
  Only waits to gather you?'

'Go,' she answered, 'I'm not hasty;
I prefer a man more tasty:
  Leastways, one to please me well
  Should not have a beasty smell.'

'Haughty Huldah!' Hiram answered;
'Mind and heart alike are cancered:
  Jest look here! these peltries give
  Cash, wherefrom a pair may live.

'I, you think, am but a vagrant,
Trapping beasts by no means fragrant:
  Yet – I'm sure it's worth a thank –
  I've a handsome sum in bank.'

Turned and vanished Hiram Hover
And, before the year was over,
   Huldah, with the yarbs she sold,
   Bought a cape, against the cold.

Black and thick the furry cape was;
Of a stylish cut the shape was,
   And the girls, in all the town,
   Envied Huldah up and down.

Then, at last, one winter morning,
Hiram came, without a warning:
   'Either,' said he, 'you are blind,
   Huldah, or you've changed your mind.

'Me you snub for trapping varmints,
Yet you take the skins for garments:
   Since you wear the skunk and mink,
   There's no harm in me, I think.'

'Well,' she said, 'we will not quarrel,
Hiram: I accept the moral,
   Now the fashion's so, I guess
   I can't hardly do no less.'

Thus the trouble all was over
Of the love of Hiram Hover;
   Thus he made sweet Huldah Hyde
   Huldah Hover as his bride.

Love employs, with equal favour,
Things of good and evil savour;
   That, which first appeared to part,
   Warmed, at last, the maiden's heart.

Under one impartial banner,
Life, the hunter, Love, the tamer,
   Draw, from every beast they snare
   Comfort for a wedded pair.

BAYARD TAYLOR

Alfred, Lord Tennyson (1809–1892)

The Laureate

> Who would not be
> The Laureate bold,
> With his butt of sherry
> To keep him merry,
> And nothing to do but to pocket his gold?

'Tis I would be the Laureate bold!
When the days are hot, and the sun is strong,
I'd lounge in the gateway all the day long
With her Majesty's footmen in crimson and gold.
I'd care not a pin for the waiting-lord,
But I'd lie on my back on the smooth greensward
With a straw in my mouth, and an open vest,
And the cool wind blowing upon my breast,
And I'd vacantly stare at the clear blue sky,
And watch the clouds that are listless as I,
    Lazily, lazily!

And I'd pick the moss and the daisies white,
And chew their stalks with a nibbling bite;
And I'd let my fancies roam abroad
In search of a hint for a birthday ode,
    Crazily, crazily!

Oh, that would be the life for me,
With plenty to get and nothing to do,
But to deck a pet poodle with ribbons of blue,
And whistle all day to the Queen's cockatoo,
    Trance-somely, trance-somely!

Then the chambermaids, that clean the rooms,
Would come to the windows and rest on their brooms,
With their saucy caps and their crispèd hair,

And they'd toss their heads in the fragrant air,
And say to each other – 'Just look down there,
At the nice young man, so tidy and small,
Who is paid for writing on nothing at all,
    Handsomely, handsomely!'

They would pelt me with matches and sweet pastilles,
And crumpled-up balls of the royal bills,
Giggling and laughing, and screaming with fun,
As they'd see me start, with a leap and a run,
From the broad of my back to the points of my toes,
When a pellet of paper hit my nose,
    Teasingly, sneezingly!

Then I'd fling them bunches of garden flowers,
And hyacinths plucked from the Castle bowers;
And I'd challenge them all to come down to me,
And I'd kiss them all till they kissed me,
    Laughingly, laughingly.

Oh, would not that be a merry life,
Apart from care and apart from strife,
With the Laureate's wine, and the Laureate's pay,
And no deductions at quarter-day?
Oh, that would be the post for me!
With plenty to get and nothing to do,
But to deck a pet poodle with ribbons of blue,
And whistle a tune to the Queen's cockatoo,
And scribble of verses remarkably few,
And empty at evening a bottle or two,
    Quaffingly, quaffingly!

      'Tis I would be
      The Laureate bold,
      With my butt of sherry
      To keep me merry,
    And nothing to do but to pocket my gold!

WILLIAM AYTOUN

The Higher Pantheism in a Nutshell

One, who is not, we see: but one, whom we see not, is;
Surely this is not that: but that is assuredly this.

What, and wherefore, and whence? for under is over and under;
If thunder could be without lightning, lightning could be without
   thunder.

Doubt is faith in the main: but faith, on the whole, is doubt;
We cannot believe by proof: but could we believe without?

Why, and whither, and how? for barley and rye are not clover;
Neither are straight lines curves: yet over is under and over.

Two and two may be four; but four and four are not eight;
Fate and God may be twain: but God is the same thing as fate.

Ask a man what he thinks, and get from a man what he feels;
God, once caught in the fact, shews you a fair pair of heels.

Body and spirit are twins: God only knows which is which;
The soul squats down in the flesh, like a tinker drunk in a ditch.

One and two are not one: but one and nothing is two;
Truth can hardly be false, if falsehood cannot be true.

Once the mastodon was: pterodactyls were common as cocks;
Then the mammoth was God: now is He a prize ox.

Parallels all things are: yet many of these are askew:
You are certainly I: but certainly I am not you.

Springs the rock from the plain, shoots the stream from the rock;
Cocks exist for the hen; but hens exist for the cock.

God, whom we see not, is: and God, who is not, we see;
Fiddle, we know, is diddle: and diddle, we take it, is dee.

ALGERNON CHARLES SWINBURNE

The Charge of the Bread Brigade

From *The poems of Alfred Venison, the Poet of Titchfield Street*

Half a loaf, half a loaf,
Half a loaf? Um-hum?
Down through the vale of gloom
Slouched the ten million,
 Onward th' 'ungry blokes,
 Crackin' their smutty jokes!
We'll send 'em mouchin' 'ome,
Damn the ten million!

There goes the night brigade,
They got no steady trade,
Several old so'jers know
 Monty has blunder'd.
Theirs not to reason why,
Theirs but to buy the pie,
Slouching and mouching,
 Lousy ten million!

Plenty to right of 'em,
Plenty to left of 'em,
 Yes, wot is left of 'em,
Damn the ten million.
Stormed at by press and all,
How shall we dress 'em all?
 Glooming and mouching!

See 'em go slouching there,
With cowed and crouching air
 Dundering dullards!
How the whole nation shook
While Milord Beaverbrook
 Fed 'em with hogwash!

EZRA POUND

94

What the Ghost Told Hamlet

It fell upon a jasper afternoon
Whose very music was a somnolence
Of plaining pigs in purgatorial plight
And whizzing of inevitable wasps.
I lay, I slept and lent the distant quire
My nasal diapason. So he came,
The evil Claudius, his cheek as wan
As ever maiden who the mandrake heard
Dragged screeching at the sinking of the moon.
He bent and drew his dire ampulla forth
To drip its foul intinction in mine ear,
To set a creeping horror in my flesh,
To drive me forth unbenisoned, to stray
Until, an aeon hence, I shall attain
That blessed strand beyond the sunset marge
Where I shall meet my Guide, and learn of peace.

RHODA TUCK POOK

Maud

Keep out of the garden, Maud,
  Till your primal urge has flown;
Keep out of the garden, Maud,
  For I'm here in the house alone
And my masculinity's gone by the board
  And the fuse of love is blown.

All night have the moonlit rooftops high
  Echoed the prowling feet
As the hunting tabbies' hungry cry
  Has wakened the sleeping street
But the silent tom has known to fly
  To his secret dark retreat.

She is coming, my doom, my fate!
    I know that purposeful tread!
My breath is beginning to bate
    And the migraine flies to my head,
My mouth is whispering, 'Wait, O Wait!'
    As I cower beneath the bed.

DOUGLAS HAWSON

The Modern Brook

I come from dregs of old and brown
    And drips from ancient motors;
I trickle through the busy town
    And horrify the voters.

The local works contribute sludge,
    The local girls detergent;
The local lads do not begrudge
    Their mite, when need is urgent.

I'm kept alive by showers of rain
    With atmospheric smog in;
I've here and there a cycle chain,
    And here and there a dog in.

They block my flow till I'm so slow
    I'll never reach the river;
For brooks may come and brooks may go,
    But men go on for ever.

PAUL GRIFFIN

Edgar Allan Poe (1809–1849)

Nevermore

Once upon a midnight dreary, eerie, scary,
I was wary, I was weary, full of worry, thinking of my lost Lenore,
Of my cheery, airy, faery, fiery Dearie – (Nothing more).
I was napping, when a tapping on the overlapping coping, woke me
   grapping, yapping, groping ... toward the rapping. I went
   hopping, leaping ... hoping that the rapping on the coping
Was my little lost Lenore,
That on opening the shutter to admit the latter critter, in she'd
   flutter from the gutter with her bitter eyes a-glitter;
So I opened the wide door, what was there? The dark weir and the
   drear moor, – or I'm a liar – the dark mire, the drear moor, the
   mere door and nothing more!

Then in stepped a stately raven, shaven like the bard of Avon; yes, a
   rovin' grievin' Raven, seeking haven at my door.
Yes, that shaven, rovin' Raven had been movin' (Get me Stephen)
   for the warm and lovin' haven of my stove an' oven door –
Oven door and nothing more.

Ah, distinctly I remember, every ember that December turned from
   amber to burnt umber;
I was burning limber lumber in my chamber that December, and it
   left an amber ember.
With a silken, sad, uncertain flirtin' of a certain curtain,
That old Raven, cold and callous, perched upon the bust of Pallas,
   Just above my chamber door;
(A lusty, trusty, bust, thrust just
  Above my chamber door.)

Had that callous cuss shown malice? Or sought solace, there on
   Pallas?
   (You may tell us, Alice Wallace.)
Tell this soul with sorrow laden, hidden in the shade an' broodin', –

If a maiden out of Eden sent this sudden bird invadin'
My poor chamber; and protrudin' half an inch above my door.
Tell this broodin' soul (he's breedin' bats by too much sodden'
   readin' – readin' Snowden's ode to Odin)
Tell this soul by nightmares ridden, if (no kiddin') on a sudden
He shall clasp a radiant maiden born in Aidenn or in Leyden, or
   indeed in Baden Baden –
Will he grab this buddin' maiden, gaddin' in forbidden Eden,
Whom the angels named Lenore?
Then that bird said: 'Nevermore.'

'Prophet,' said I, 'thing of evil, navel, novel, or boll weevil,
You shall travel, on the level! Scratch the gravel now and travel!
Leave my hovel, I implore,'
And that Raven never flitting, never knitting, never tatting, never
   spouting 'Nevermore,'
Still is sitting (out this ballad) on the solid bust (and pallid) – on the
   solid, valid, pallid bust above my chamber door:
And my soul is in the shadow, which lies floating on the floor,
Fleeting, floating, yachting, boating on the fluting of the matting, –
   Matting on my chamber floor.

C. L. EDSON

Edward FitzGerald (1809–1883)

from Strugnell's Rubáiyát

1.
Awake! for Morning on the Pitch of Night
Has whistled and has put the Stars to Flight.
The incandescent football in the East
Has brought the splendour of Tulse Hill to Light.

7.
Another Pint! Come, loosen up, have Fun!
Fling off your Hang-Ups and enjoy the Sun:
Time's Spacecraft all too soon will carry you
Away – and Lo! the Countdown has begun.

11.
Here with a Bag of Crisps beneath the Bough,
A Can of Beer, a Radio – and Thou
Beside me half asleep in Brockwell Park
And Brockwell Park is Paradise enow.

12.
Some Men to everlasting Bliss aspire,
Their Lives, Auditions for the heavenly Choir:
Oh, use your Credit Card and waive the Rest –
Brave Music of a distant Amplifier!

26.
Oh, come with Strugnell – Argument's no Tonic.
One thing's certain: Life flies supersonic.
One thing's certain, Man's Evasion chronic –
The Flower that's blown can never be bionic.

51.
The Moving Telex writes, and having writ,
Moves on; nor all thy Therapy nor Wit
Shall lure it back to cancel half a Line
Nor Tide nor Daz wash out a word of it.

WENDY COPE

Charles Dickens (1812–1870)

Christmas Afternoon

What an afternoon! Mr. Gummidge said that, in his estimation, there never had *been* such an afternoon since the world began, a sentiment which was heartily endorsed by Mrs. Gummidge and all the little Gummidges, not to mention the relatives who had come over from Jersey for the day.

In the first place, there was the *ennui*. And such *ennui* as it was! A heavy, overpowering *ennui*, such as results from a participation in eight courses of steaming, gravied food, topping off with salted nuts which the little old spinster Gummidge from Oak Hill said she never knew when to stop eating – and true enough she didn't – a dragging, devitalising *ennui*, which left its victims strewn about the living room in various attitudes of prostration suggestive of those of the petrified occupants in a newly unearthed Pompeian dwelling; an *ennui* which carried with it a retinue of yawns, snarls and thinly veiled insults, and which ended in ruptures in the clan spirit serious enough to last throughout the glad new year.

Then there were the toys! Three and a quarter dozen toys to be divided among seven children. Surely enough, you or I might say, to satisfy the little tots. But that would be because we didn't know the tots. In came Baby Lester Gummidge, Lillian's boy, dragging an electric grain-elevator which happened to be the only toy in the entire collection that appealed to little Norman, five-year-old son of Luther, who lived in Rahway. In came curly-headed Effie in frantic and throaty disputation with Arthur, Jr., over the possession of an articulated zebra. In came Everett, bearing a mechanical negro which would no longer dance, owing to a previous forcible feeding by the baby of a marshmallow into its only available aperture. In came Fonlansbee, teeth buried in the hand of little Ormond, who bore a popular but battered remnant of what had once been the proud false bosom of a hussar's uniform. In they all came, one after another, some crying, some snapping, some pulling, some pushing – all appealing to their respective parents for aid in their intramural warfare.

And the cigar smoke! Mrs. Gummidge said that she didn't mind the smoke from a good cigarette, but would they mind if she opened the windows for just a minute in order to clear the room of the heavy aroma of used cigars? Mr. Gummidge stoutly maintained that they were good cigars. His brother, George Gummidge, said that he, likewise, would say that they were. At which colloquial sally both Gummidge brothers laughed testily, thereby breaking the laughter record for the afternoon.

Aunt Libbie, who lived with George, remarked from the dark corner of the room that it seemed just like Sunday to her. An amendment was offered to this statement by the cousin, who was in the insurance business, stating that it was worse than Sunday. Murmurings indicative of as hearty agreement with this sentiment as their lethargy would allow came from the other members of the family circle, causing Mr. Gummidge to suggest a walk in the air to settle their dinner.

And then arose such a chorus of protestations as has seldom been heard. It was too cloudy to walk. It was too raw. It looked like snow. It looked like rain. Luther Gummidge said that he must be starting along home soon, anyway, bringing forth the acid query from Mrs. Gummidge as to whether or not he was bored. Lillian said that she felt a cold coming on, and added that something they had had for dinner must have been undercooked. And so it went, back and forth, forth and back, up and down, and in and out, until Mr. Gummidge's suggestion of a walk in the air was reduced to a tattered impossibility and the entire company glowed with ill-feeling.

In the meantime, we must not forget the children. No one else could. Aunt Libbie said that she didn't think there was anything like children to make a Christmas; to which Uncle Ray, the one with the Masonic fob, said, 'No, thank God!' Although Christmas is supposed to be the season of good cheer, you (or I, for that matter) couldn't have told, from listening to the little ones, but what it was the children's Armageddon season, when Nature had decreed that only the fittest should survive, in order that the race might be carried on by the strongest, the most predatory and those possessing the best protective colouring. Although there were constant admonitions to Fonlansbee to 'Let Ormond have that whistle now; it's his,' and to Arthur, Jr., not to be selfish, but to 'give the kiddie-car to Effie; she's smaller than you are,' the net result was always that Fonlansbee kept the whistle and Arthur, Jr., rode in permanent, albeit disputed, possession of the kiddie-car. Oh, that we mortals should set ourselves up against the inscrutable workings of Nature!

Hallo! A great deal of commotion! That was Uncle George stumbling over the electric train which had early in the afternoon ceased to function and which had been left directly across the threshold. A great deal of crying! That was Arthur, Jr., bewailing the destruction of his already useless train, about which he had forgotten until the present moment. A great deal of recrimination! That was Arthur, Sr., and George fixing it up. And finally a great crashing! That was Baby Lester pulling over the tree on top of himself, necessitating the bringing to bear of all of Uncle Ray's knowledge of forestry to extricate him from the wreckage.

And finally, Mrs. Gummidge passed the Christmas candy around. Mr. Gummidge afterwards admitted that this was a tactical error on the part of his spouse. I no more believe that Mrs. Gummidge thought they wanted that Christmas candy than I believe she thought they wanted the cold turkey which she later suggested. My opinion is that she wanted to drive them home. At any rate, that is what she succeeded in doing. Such cries as there were of 'Ugh! Don't let me see another thing to eat!' and 'Take it away!' Then came hurried scramblings in the coat-closet for overshoes. There were the rasping sounds made by cross parents when putting wraps on children. There were insincere exhortations to 'come and see us soon' and to 'get together for lunch sometime'. And, finally, there were slammings of doors and the silence of utter exhaustion, while Mrs. Gummidge went about picking up stray sheets of wrapping paper.

And, as Tiny Tim might say in speaking of Christmas afternoon as an institution, 'God help us, every one.'

ROBERT BENCHLEY

More Hard Times

It was not the Department of Snipping and Chopping, nor yet the Department of Lopping and Severing, nor even the Bureau of Natural Wastage and Redundancy, but the Office of Cuts itself (that all-sufficient central cog of educational administration) to which Thaddaeus Skimple aspired. A primary school in Cleveland desired crayons, sardonic laughter was heard in the corridors of the Office of Cuts; a Birmingham headmaster died, the fact was filed in the Office of Cuts, with great rubbing of dry hands and cracking of calcified knuckles; work halted on an EPA school building, an annexe was appended to the Office of Cuts.

'Though governments come and governments depart,' he observed philosophically, 'the Office of Cuts forever accrues floorspace and personnel. Oh that I might number myself among the latter! If only! The axings! The closures! The *sympathetic* denials!' (His voice soared passionately.) 'I should be the blissfullest bureaucrat alive!'

GERARD BENSON

Edward Lear (1812–1888)

The Cottonwool Tour

They went on a Cottonwool Tour, they did,
    On a Cottonwool Tour for two!
With a scrupulous nurse and a maundy purse
And a reegle-me-ree and a Dumble-bee
And an Oofah-fox in a washable box
    And a bottle of crawfy Goo.

And all the Cottonwool people say:
'Oh, runcible couple! Hooray! Hooray!
They make us Dames and they teach us Games
    And they wave and smile all day!
For they come from the land of the Dimble-folk,
Good-gracious lady and popular bloke,
They open the fête and present the prize,
Oh, we never will sunder our Cottonwool ties!'

So they gave them a silver snorkel
And a parachute made of clay
And a sporty bonnet of Corgi tails
    To save for a rainy day,
As the sun set low on the Oompah
    And they sadly sailed away.

TROOPER JONES

Robert Browning (1812–1889)

A Girtonian Funeral

The Academy reports that the students of Girton College have dissolved their 'Browning Society', and expended its remaining funds, two shillings and twopence, upon chocolate creams.

Let us begin and portion out these sweets,
    Sitting together.
Leave we our deep debates, our sage conceits, –
    Wherefore? and whether?
Thus with a fine that fits the work begun
    Our labours crowning,
For we, in sooth, our duty well have done
    By Robert Browning.
Have we not wrought at essay and critique,
    Scorning supine ease?
Wrestled with clauses crabbed as Bito's Greek,
    Baffling as Chinese?
Out the Inn Album's mystic heart we took,
    Lucid of soul, and

Threaded the mazes of the Ring and Book;
        Cleared up Childe Roland.
We settled Fifine's business – let her be –
        (Strangest of lasses;)
Watched by the hour some thick-veiled truth to see
        Where Pippa passes.
(Though, dare we own, secure in victor's gains,
        Ample to shield us?
Red Cotton Night-cap Country for our pains
        Little would yield us.)
What then to do? Our culture-feast drag out
        E'en to satiety?
Oft such the fate that findeth, nothing doubt,
        Such a Society.
Oh, the dull meetings! Some one yawns an *aye*,
        One gapes again a *yea*,
We girls determined not to yawn, but buy
        Chocolate Menier.
Fry's creams are cheap, but Cadbury's excel,
        (Quick, Maud, for none wait)
Nay, now, 'tis Menier bears the bell,
        Sold by the ton-weight.
So, with unburdened brains and spirits light,
        Blithe did we troop hence,
All our funds voted for this closing rite,–
        Just two-and-two-pence.
Do – make in scorn, old Croesus, proud and glum,
        Peaked eyebrow lift eye;
Put case one stick's a halfpenny; work the sum;
        Full two and fifty.
Off with the twine! who scans each smooth brown slab
        Yet not supposeth
What soft, sweet, cold, pure whiteness, bound in drab,
        Tooth's bite discloseth?
Are they not grand? (you may think it odd)
        Some power alchemic
Turns, as we munch, to Zeus-assenting nod
        Sneers Academic.
Till, when one cries: ''Ware hours that fleet like clouds,
        Time, deft escaper!'
We answer bold: 'Leave Time to Dons and Dowds;

(Grace, pass the paper)
Say, boots it aught to evermore affect
        Raptures high-flying?
Though *we* choose chocolate, will the world suspect
        Genius undying?'

ANON

Sincere Flattery of R.B.

Birthdays? yes, in a general way;
For the most if not for the best men:
You were born (I suppose) on a certain day:
So was I: or perhaps in the night: what then?

Only this: or at least, if more.
You must know, not think it, and learn, not speak:
There is truth to be found on the unknown shore,
And many will find where few will seek.

For many are called and few are chosen,
And the few grow many as ages lapse:
But when will the many grow few: what dozen
Is fused into one by Time's hammer-taps?

A bare brown stone in a babbling brook: –
It was wanton to hurl it there, you say:
And the moss, which clung in the sheltered nook
(Yet the stream runs cooler), is washed away.

That begs the question: many a prater
Thinks such a suggestion a sound 'stop thief!'
Which, may I ask, do you think the greater,
Sergeant-at-arms or a Robber Chief?

And if it were not so? still you doubt?
Ah! yours is a birthday indeed if so.

That were something to write a poem about,
If one thought a little. I only know.

P.S.

There's a Me Society down at Cambridge,
Where my works, *cum notis variorum*,
Are talked about; well, I require the same bridge
That Euclid took toll at as *Asinorum*:

And, as they have got through several ditties
I thought were as stiff as a brick-built wall,
I've composed the above, and a stiff one *it* is,
A bridge to stop asses at, once for all.

J. K. STEPHEN

How I Brought the Good News from Aix to Ghent, or Vice Versa

I sprang to the rollocks and Jorrocks and me,
And I galloped, you galloped, we galloped all three.
Not a word to each other: we kept changing place,
Neck to neck, back to front, ear to ear, face to face:
And we yelled once or twice, when we heard a clock chime,
'Would you kindly oblige us, *is that the right time?*'
As I galloped, you galloped, he galloped, we galloped, ye galloped,
  they two shall have galloped: *let us trot.*

I unsaddled the saddle, unbuckled the bit,
Unshackled the bridle (the thing didn't fit)
And ungalloped, ungalloped, ungalloped, ungalloped a bit.
Then I cast off my buff coat, let my bowler hat fall,
Took off both my boots and my trousers and all –
Drank off my stirrup-cup, felt a bit tight,
And unbridled the saddle: it still wasn't right.

Then all I remember is, things reeling round,
As I sat with my head 'twixt my ears on the ground –
For imagine my shame when they asked what I meant
And I had to confess that I'd been, gone and went
And *forgotten* the news I was bringing to Ghent,
Though I'd galloped and galloped and galloped and galloped
   and galloped
And galloped and galloped and galloped. (Had I not would have
   been galloped?)

ENVOI

So I sprang to a taxi and shouted 'To Aix!'
And he blew on his horn and he threw off his brakes,
And all the way back till my money was spent
We rattled and rattled and rattled and rattled and rattled
And rattled and rattled –
And eventually sent a telegram.

WALTER CARRUTHERS SELLAR *and*
ROBERT JULIAN YEATMAN

How They Brought the Bad News

British Rail boosted its fines for railway offences.

I nipped down the platform, and Doris, and he;
I sprinted, Dick sprinted, we sprinted all three;
'Good God!' cried a passenger, mother of two;
'Get back!' said a bloke who was head of the queue.
We elbowed two nuns, a right couple of bags,
And in the compartment we lit up our fags.

We roughed up a Pakki and chucked out his case,
And blimey! the look on the poor bleeder's face.
I'd have written 'Punks Rule' if I knew how to write,
So I ripped up the seating and set it alight.
Dick looked out and pointed: 'Ain't that a great tit?'
But then he was always a bit of a wit.

Then I took off my jacket and let my belt fall,
And Doris, she wasn't half willing and all;
But when I got started some berk sitting near
Said: 'Oh! how disgusting! – you can't do that here.'
And I wouldn't be stuck with this fifty quid fine,
If I could have figured the 'No Smoking' sign.

ROGER WODDIS

The Last Ride Together (from her point of view)

When I had firmly answered 'No',
And he allowed that that was so,
I really thought I should be free
For good and all from Mr B.,
   And that he would soberly acquiesce:
I said that it would be discreet
That for a while we should not meet;
I promised I would always feel
A kindly interest in his weal;
I thanked him for his amorous zeal;
   In short, I said all I could but 'yes'.

I said what I'm accustomed to,
I acted as I always do;
I promised he should find in me
A friend, – a sister, if that might be:
   But he was still dissatisfied:
He certainly was most polite;
He said exactly what was right,
He acted very properly,
Except indeed for this, that he
Insisted on inviting me
   To come with him for 'one more last ride'.

A little while in doubt I stood:
A ride, no doubt, would do me good:
I had a habit and a hat
Extremely well worth looking at:
    The weather was distinctly fine:
My horse too wanted exercise,
And time, when one is riding, flies:
Besides it really seemed, you see,
The only way of ridding me
Of pertinacious Mr B.;
    So my head I graciously incline.

I won't say much of what happened next:
I own I was extremely vexed:
Indeed I should have been aghast
If anyone had seen what passed:
    But nobody need ever know
That, as I leaned forward to stir the fire,
He advanced before I could well retire,
And I suddenly felt, to my great alarm,
The grasp of a warm unlicensed arm,
An embrace in which I found no charm;
    I was awfully glad when he let me go.

Then we began to ride: my steed
Was rather fresh, too fresh indeed,
And at first I thought of little, save
The way to escape an early grave,
    As the dust rose up on either side.
My stern companion jogged along
On a brown old cob both broad and strong:
He looked as he does when he's writing verse,
Or endeavouring not to swear and curse,
Or wondering where he has left his purse,
    Indeed it was a sombre ride.

I spoke of the weather to Mr B.:
But he neither listened nor spoke to me;
I praised his horse, and I smiled the smile
Which was wont to move him once on a while;
   I said I was wearing his favourite flowers:
But I wasted my words on the desert air,
For he rode with a fixed and gloomy stare:
I wonder what he was thinking about:
As I don't read verse, I shan't find out:
It was something subtle and deep, no doubt,
   A theme to detain a man for hours.

Ah! there was the corner where Mr S.
So nearly induced me to whisper 'yes':
And here it was that the next but one
Proposed on horseback, or would have done,
   Had his horse not most opportunely shied;
Which perhaps was due to the unseen flick
He received from my whip: 'twas a scurvy trick,
But I never could do with that young man:
I hope his present young woman can.
Well, I must say, never, since time began,
   Did I go for a duller or longer ride.

He never smiles and he never speaks:
He might go on like this for weeks:
He rolls a slightly frenzied eye
Towards the blue and burning sky,
   And the cob bounds on with tireless stride.
If we aren't at home for lunch at two
I don't know what Papa will do;
But I know full well he will say to me
'I never approved of Mr B.:
It's the very devil that you and he
   Ride, ride together, for ever ride.'

J. K. STEPHEN

Home Truths from Abroad

Oh, to be in England
Now that April's there,
And whoever wakes in England
Sees some morning, in despair,
There's a horrible fog i' the heart o' the town,
And the greasy pavement is damp and brown;
While the rain-drop falls from the laden bough,
In England – now!

And after April when May follows,
How foolish seem the returning swallows.
Hark! how the east wind sweeps along the street,
And how we give one universal sneeze!
The hapless lambs at thought of mint-sauce bleat,
And ducks are conscious of the coming peas.

Lest you should think the Spring is really present,
A biting frost will come to make things pleasant,
And though the reckless flowers begin to blow,
They'd better far have nestled down below;
And English spring sets men and women frowning,
Despite the rhapsodies of Robert Browning.

ANON

My First Abstract

That's my first Abstract hanging on the wall,
Looking like a Mondrian; I call
That piece a wonder, now: my eager hands
Worked busily a session – there it stands.
Will't please you sit and look at it? I said
'My eager hands' by design, for never read
Strangers like you that cunning dissonance,
The depth of passion of its utterance,

But to myself they turned (since none puts by
The curtain I have drawn for you but I)
And seemed as they would ask me, if they durst,
How came I by such skill; so, not the first
Are you to turn and ask thus. Sir, 'twas not
My teacher's presence only called that spot
Of colour into lovely being; perhaps
It were immodest to say, 'My genius taps
A spring where Mondrian drank. Nay, let it go
– Yet, I fancy . . . Note the purple, though!
Leave it that genius is a rarity,
And Evening Classes brought it out in me.

T. GRIFFITHS

From a Spanish Cloister

Grrr – what's that? A dog? A poet?
  Uttering his damnations thus –
If hate killed things, Brother Browning,
  God's Word, would not hate kill us?

If we ever meet together,
  Salve tibi! I might hear
How you know poor monks are really
  So much worse than they appear.

There's a great text in Corinthians
  Hinting that our faith entails
Something else, that never faileth,
  Yet in you, perhaps, it fails.

But if *plena gratia* chokes you,
  You at least can teach us how
To converse in wordless noises,
  Hy, zi; hullo! – Grrr – Bow-wow!

G. K. CHESTERTON

Charlotte Brontë (1816–1855)

from Miss Mix

CHAPTER II

Blunderbore Hall, the seat of James Rawjester, Esq., was encompassed by dark pines and funereal hemlocks on all sides. The wind sang weirdly in the turrets and moaned through the long-drawn avenues of the park. As I approached the house I saw several mysterious figures flit before the windows, and a yell of demoniac laughter answered my summons at the bell. While I strove to repress my gloomy forebodings, the housekeeper, a timid, scared-looking old woman, showed me into the library.

I entered, overcome with conflicting emotions. I was dressed in a narrow gown of dark serge, trimmed with black bugles. A thick green shawl was pinned across my breast. My hands were encased with black half-mittens worked with steel beads; on my feet were large pattens, originally the property of my deceased grandmother. I carried a blue cotton umbrella. As I passed before a mirror, I could not help glancing at it, nor could I disguise from myself the fact that I was not handsome.

Drawing a chair into a recess, I sat down with folded hands, calmly awaiting the arrival of my master. Once or twice a fearful yell rang through the house, or the rattling of chains, and curses uttered in a deep, manly voice broke upon the oppressive stillness. I began to feel my soul rising with the emergency of the moment.

'You look alarmed, miss. You don't hear anything, my dear, do you?' asked the housekeeper nervously.

'Nothing whatever,' I remarked calmly, as a terrible scream, followed by the dragging of chairs and tables in the room above, drowned for a moment my reply. 'It is the silence, on the contrary, which has made me foolishly nervous.'

The housekeeper looked at me approvingly, and instantly made some tea for me.

I drank seven cups; as I was beginning the eighth, I heard a crash, and the next moment a man leaped into the room through the broken window.

114

The crash startled me from my self-control. The housekeeper bent toward me and whispered:

'Don't be excited. It's Mr Rawjester – he prefers to come in sometimes in this way. It's his playfulness, ha! ha! ha!'

'I perceive,' I said calmly. 'It's the unfettered impulse of a lofty soul breaking the tyrannizing bonds of custom,' and I turned toward him.

He had never once looked at me. He stood with his back to the fire, which set off the Herculean breadth of his shoulders. His face was dark and expressive; his under-jaw squarely formed, and re-markably heavy. I was struck with his remarkable likeness to a Gorilla.

As he absently tied the poker into hard knots with his nervous fingers, I watched him with some interest. Suddenly he turned toward me:

'Do you think I'm handsome, young woman?'

'Not classically beautiful,' I returned calmly; 'but you have, if I may so express myself, an abstract manliness – a sincere and wholesome barbarity which, involving as it does the naturalness' – but I stopped, for he yawned at that moment – an action which singularly developed the immense breadth of his lower jaw – and I saw he had forgotten me. Presently he turned to the housekeeper:

'Leave us.'

The old woman withdrew with a curtsy.

Mr. Rawjester deliberately turned his back upon me and remained silent for twenty minutes. I drew my shawl the more closely around my shoulders and closed my eyes.

'You are the governess?' at length he said.

'I am, sir.'

'A creature who teaches geography, arithmetic, and the use of the globes – ha! – a wretched remnant of femininity – a skimp pattern of girlhood with a premature flavour of tea-leaves and morality. Ugh!'

I bowed my head silently.

'Listen to me, girl!' he said sternly; 'this child you have come to teach – my ward – is not legitimate. She is the offspring of my mistress – a common harlot. Ah! Miss Mix, what do you think of me now?'

'I admire', I replied, calmly, 'your sincerity. A mawkish regard for delicacy might have kept this disclosure to yourself. I only recognize in your frankness that perfect community of thought and sentiment which should exist between original natures.'

I looked up; he had already forgotten my presence, and was engaged in pulling off his boots and coat. This done, he sank down in an armchair before the fire, and ran the poker wearily through his hair. I could not help pitying him.

The wind howled fearfully without, and the rain beat furiously against the windows. I crept toward him and seated myself on a low stool beside his chair.

Presently he turned, without seeing me, and placed his foot absently in my lap. I affected not to notice it. But he started and looked down.

'You here yet, Carrothead? Ah, I forgot. Do you speak French?'

'*Oui, Monsieur.*'

'*Taisez-vous!*' he said sharply, with singular purity of accent. I complied. The wind moaned fearfully in the chimney, and the light burned dim. I shuddered in spite of myself. 'Ah, you tremble, girl!'

'It is a fearful night.'

'Fearful! Call you this fearful – ha! ha! ha! Look! you wretched little atom, look!' and he dashed forward, and, leaping out of the window, stood like a statue in the pelting storm, with folded arms. He did not stay long, but in a few minutes he returned by way of the hall chimney. I saw from the way that he wiped his feet on my dress that he had again forgotten my presence.

'You are a governess. What can you teach?' he asked, suddenly and fiercely thrusting his face in mine.

'Manners!' I replied calmly.

'Ha! teach *me*!'

'You mistake yourself,' I said adjusting my mittens. 'Your manners require not the artificial restraint of society. You are radically polite; this impetuosity and ferociousness is simply the sincerity which is the basis of a proper deportment. Your instincts are moral; your better nature, I see, is religious. As St Paul justly remarks – see chap. 6, 8, 9 and 10 –'

He seized a heavy candlestick, and threw it at me. I dodged it submissively, but firmly.

'Excuse me,' he remarked, as his under-jaw slowly relaxed. 'Excuse me, Miss Mix – but I can't stand St Paul. Enough – you are engaged.'

BRET HARTE

Walt Whitman (1819–1892)

Camarados

Everywhere, everywhere, following me;
Taking me by the buttonhole, pulling off my boots, hustling me
    with the elbows;
Sitting down with me to clams and the chowder-kettle;
Plunging naked at my side into the sleek, irascible surges;
Soothing me with the strain that I neither permit nor prohibit;
Flocking this way and that, reverent, eager, orotund, irrepressible;
Denser than sycamore leaves when the north-winds are scouring
    Paumanok;
What can I do to restrain them? Nothing, verily nothing.
Everywhere, everywhere, crying aloud for me;
Crying, I hear; and I satisfy them out of my nature;
And he that comes at the end of the feast shall find something
    over.
Whatever they want I give; though it be something else, they shall
    have it.
Drunkard, leper, Tammanyite, small-pox and cholera patient,
    shoddy and codfish millionaire,
And the beautiful young men, and the beautiful young women,
    all the same,
Crowding, hundreds of thousands, cosmical multitudes,
Buss me and hang on my hips and lean up to my shoulders,
Everywhere listening to my yawp and glad whenever they hear it;
Everywhere saying, say it, Walt, we believe it:
Everywhere, everywhere.

BAYARD TAYLOR

Sincere Flattery of W.W. (Americanus)

The clear cool note of the cuckoo which has ousted the legitimate
    nest-holder,
The whistle of the railway guard dispatching the train to the
    inevitable collision,
The maiden's monosyllabic reply to a polysyllabic proposal,
The fundamental note of the last trump, which is presumably D
    natural;
All of these are sounds to rejoice in, yea to let your very ribs
    re-echo with:
But better than all of them is the absolutely last chord of the
    apparently inexhaustible pianoforte player.

J. K. STEPHEN

A Classic Waits for Me

*With apologies to Walt Whitman, plus a trial membership in the classics
club*

A classic waits for me, it contains all, nothing is lacking,
Yet all were lacking if taste were lacking, or if the endorsement of
    the right man were lacking.
O clublife, and the pleasures of membership,
O volumes for sheer fascination unrivalled.
Into an armchair endlessly rocking,
Walter J. Black my president,
I, freely invited, cordially welcomed to membership,
My arm around John Kieran, Pearl S. Buck,
My taste in books guarded by the spirits of William Lyon Phelps,
    Hendrik Willem Van Loon,
(From your memories, sad brothers, from the fitful risings and
    callings I heard),
I to the classics devoted, brother of rough mechanics, beauty-
    parlor technicians, spot welders, radio-program directors

(It is not necessary to have a higher education to appreciate these books),

I, connoisseur of good reading, friend of connoisseurs of good reading everywhere,

I, not obligated to take any specific number of books, free to reject any volume, perfectly free to reject Montaigne, Erasmus, Milton,

I, in perfect health except for a slight cold, pressed for time, having only a few more years to live,

Now celebrate this opportunity.

Come, I will make the club indissoluble,

I will read the most splendid books the sun ever shone upon,

I will start divine magnetic groups,

    With the love of comrades,

    With the life-long love of distinguished committees.

I strike up for an Old Book.

Long the best-read figure in America, my dues paid, sitter in armchairs everywhere, wanderer in populous cities, weeping with Hecuba and with the late William Lyon Phelps,

Free to cancel my membership whenever I wish,

Turbulent, fleshy, sensible,

Never tiring of clublife,

Always ready to read another masterpiece provided it has the approval of my president, Walter J. Black,

Me imperturbe, standing at ease among writers,

Rais'd by a perfect mother and now belonging to a perfect book club,

Bearded, sunburnt, gray-neck'd, astigmatic,

Loving the masters and the masters only

(I am mad for them to be in contact with me),

My arm around Pearl S. Buck, only American woman to receive the Nobel Prize for Literature,

I celebrate this opportunity.

And I will not read a book not the least part of a book but has the approval of the Committee,

For all is useless without that which you may guess at many times and not hit, that which they hinted at,

All is useless without readability.

By God! I will accept nothing which all cannot have their counterpart of on the same terms (89¢ for the Regular Edition or $1.39 for the DeLuxe Edition, plus a few cents postage).

I will make inseparable readers with their arms around each other's necks,

By the love of classics,
By the manly love of classics.

E. B. WHITE

Charles Kingsley (1819–1875)

Two Extracts from The Unexpurgated Water Babies

Tom was rather disappointed with his gorse-and-thistle shirt. At first it was lovely and prickly and tickly and tormenting but, saturated with sea-water, it grew less and less itchy and irritating – which, of course, made poor Tom more and more irrita*ted*! However, there was always the weekly visit of Mrs Be-done-by-as-you-did – and her thrillingly swishy birch-rod! – to look forward to. For, truth to tell, Tom not only enjoyed being naughty but, in a queer sort of way, enjoyed being punished for his naughtiness. So this week he took pains to be *really* bad, cramming extra large stones as false dinners into the poor anemones' mouths, and tickling the corals almost to death. By behaving thus, Tom knew he would be assured of a really sound whipping and of a nice warm tingly bottom, whose roseate blush he could admire in his own little mother-of-pearl sea-mirror . . .

MARTIN FAGG

Under the snow-white coverlet, upon the snow-white pillow, lay the most beautiful little girl Tom had ever seen. Tom glanced back at the grim reflection in the mirror. Should he wash first? But no: it was the soot in the creases that smarted so deliciously. He tiptoed across to the bed.

Falling on his knees (for you must know, children, that poor Tom being only a poor little heathen, knew no better use for them), he looked up at the picture of the Man in the long garments, and it seemed to him that the Man smiled at him approving. Stretching out a hand he touched her, as low as he dared.

Up jumped the little lady in her bed, and, seeing Tom, screamed as shrill as any peacock.

'Don't be frightened!' pleaded poor Tom: 'I don't want to hurt you. I want *you* to hurt *me*.'

E. M. E. WOOD

Arthur Hugh Clough (1819–1861)

The Most Famous Poem of J. Strugnell

Say not the Strugnell nought availeth,
   The biro and the beer are vain,
Poetic craft wherein he baileth
   Lost on the vast illit'rate main!

If odes are dupes, verse plays are liars,
   Where meaning lies in tropes concealed,
The High Sublime is looking pious
   And something silly is revealed.

For while the poets, proudly reading,
   Don't entice the prettiest girls,
Faber and Faber, both, are speeding
   To smother them in gold and pearls.

And not by magazine sales only
   Or playing trumpets, all that jazz,
Shall Strugnell cease from feeling lonely –
   Slim volumes give him what he has!

GAVIN EWART

Jean Ingelow (1820–1897)

Lovers, and a Reflection

In moss-prankt dells which the sunbeams flatter
   (And Heaven it knoweth what that may mean;
Meaning, however, is no great matter)
   Where woods are a-tremble, with rifts atween:

Thro' God's own heather we wonned together,
   I and my Willie (O love, my love):
I need hardly remark it was glorious weather,
   And flitterbats wavered alow, above:

Boats were curtseying, rising, bowing,
   (Boats in that climate are so polite),
And sands were a ribbon of green endowing
   And O, the sundazzle on bark and bight!

Through the rare red heather we danced together,
   (O love, my Willie!) and smelt for flowers:
I must mention again it was glorious weather,
   Rhymes are so scarce in this world of ours: –

By rises that flushed with their purple favours,
   Through becks that brattled o'er grasses sheen,
We walked and waded, we two young shavers,
   Thanking our stars we were both so green.

We journeyed in parallels, I and Willie,
   In fortunate parallels! Butterflies,
Hid in weltering shadows of daffodilly
   Or marjoram, kept making peacock eyes:

Songbirds darted about, some inky
   As coal, some snowy (I ween) as curds;
Or rosy as pinks, or as roses pinky –
   They reck of no eerie To-come, those birds!

But they skim over bents which the mill stream washes,
    Or hang in the lift 'neath a white cloud's hem;
They need no parasols, no goloshes;
    And good Mrs. Trimmer she feedeth them.

Then we thrid God's cowslips (as erst His heather)
    That endowed the wan grass with their golden blooms
And snapt – (it was perfectly charming weather)
    Our fingers at Fate and her goddess-glooms:

And Willie 'gan sing (O, his notes were fluty;
    Wafts fluttered them out to the white-winged sea) –
Something made up of rhymes that have done much duty
    Rhymes (better to put it) of 'ancientry':

Bowers of flowers encounter'd showers
    In William's carol – (O love, my Willie!)
Then he bade sorrow borrow from blithe to-morrow
    I quite forget what – say a daffodilly:

A nest in a hollow, 'with buds to follow',
    I think occurred next in his nimble strain;
And clay that was 'kneaden' of course in Eden –
    A rhyme most novel, I do maintain:

Mists, bones, the singer himself, love-stories,
    And all least furlable things got 'furled';
Not with any designs to conceal their 'glories'
    But simply and solely to rhyme with 'world'.

O, if billows and pillows and hours and flowers,
    And all the brave rhymes of an elder day,
Could be furled together this genial weather,
    And carted or carried on 'wafts' away,
Nor ever again trotted out – ah me!
How much fewer volumes of verse there'd be!

C. S. CALVERLEY

Fyodor Dostoevsky (1821–1881)

The Gollies Karamazov

According to a new publishing company, Enfance Publishing, 'every leading author has at least one children's book in him'.

On a bitterly cold morning towards the end of November, 18— a pale young man left his little room at the top of a toadstool in one of the meaner tree-roots of the province of Toyland, and began to descend the dark and freezing stairs.

He was praying that he would not meet his landlady. Her burrow gave directly on to the corridor, and he had to pass it every time he went in or out. The door was usually open, and he would have to run past to avoid seeing Mrs Rabbitoyeva, and when he did so he would experience a sensation of terror which left him shaking and sick to his stomach. Sometimes he would be physically sick. Other times, he would become possessed of a hacking and terrible cough, and his thin little body would grow luminous with sweat.

It was not merely that he was behind with his rent, living as he did in wretched poverty: it was simply that he had of late a horrible fear of meeting anybody, of engaging them in the lightest of conversations, of remarking upon the weather. This fear had itself become a sickness. Mrs Rabbitoyeva, if she saw him, would wipe her paws on her apron (an action which itself brought an uncontrollable trembling to the young man's emaciated limbs, and set the pattern on his threadbare herringbone overcoat twitching like a nest of spiders), and smile, and nod and say:

'Good morning, Noddy Noddeyovich! I have a nice worm ragout cooking on the stove for your lunch.'

Or:

'You should have a young lady, Noddy Noddeyovich! It is not right for a fine young man to spend so much time in the company of gnomes.'

At this, the young man would fall to the ground and kiss the hem of her garment.

But on this occasion, Mrs Rabbitoyeva called Noddy Noddeyovich into her kitchen, and, despite the fearful trembling of his limbs which set the bell upon his cap tinkling like some derisory omen of imminent doom, he followed her. He counted his steps, as he always did – eleven, twelve, thirteen, to the table, fourteen, fifteen, to the workbench, where the knives were, and the big meat chopper. The kitchen smelt of boiled sedge, and old ferret offal, and the grey, fatty soup that Mrs Rabbitoyeva always kept simmering for the pitiful little civil servants who inhabited her dark, cold building.

'Noddy Noddeyovich,' said Mrs Rabbitoyeva, 'I wish to talk with you about the Gollies Karamazov.'

His trembling worsened. The Gollies Karamazov had recently moved in to the room next to Noddy Noddeyovich, and they came from the Big Wood, and their faces were black as round holes in the white winter ice. Whenever Noddy Noddeyovich saw them, he began to shake all over, and often he was sick down the stairwell, and sometimes he fainted altogether. He did not want to talk about the Gollies Karamazov. He listened for a while to the sound of Mrs Rabbitoyeva, and it was of no sense, a heavy buzz, like the flies upon the far steppes when spring wakes the eggs.

And then he picked up the big meat chopper, and he brought it down on Mrs Rabbitoyeva's old head, and she looked very surprised, and when the blood was all over his hands, their trembling stopped.

'I should not be here,' said Noddy Noddeyovich, possibly aloud. 'Soon Plod Plodnikov of the State Police will be here for his morning glass of tea, and he may engage me in some philosophical discussion about guilt, with reference to the words of Morotny, and it would be better if I were to get in my little car and go Beep! Beep! and seek the advice of Bigears Bigearsnitkin . . .'

ALAN COREN

Dante Gabriel Rossetti (1828–1882)

After 'Dilettante Concetti'

'Why do you wear your hair like a man,
      Sister Helen?
This week is the third since you began.'
'I'm writing a ballad; be still if you can,
      Little brother.
    (*O Mother Carey, mother!*
What chickens are these between sea and heaven!)'

'But why does your figure appear so lean,
      Sister Helen?
And why do you dress in sage, sage green?'
'Children should never be heard, if seen,
      Little brother!
    (*O Mother Carey, mother!*
What fowls are a-wing in the stormy heaven!)'

'But why is your face so yellowy white,
      Sister Helen?
And why are your skirts so funnily tight?'
'Be quiet, you torment, or how can I write,
      Little brother?
    (*O Mother Carey, mother!*
How gathers thy train to the sea from the heaven!)'

'And who's Mother Carey, and what is her train,
      Sister Helen?
And why do you call her again and again?'
'You troublesome boy, why that's the refrain,
      Little brother.
    (*O Mother Carey, mother!*
What work is toward in the startled heaven?)'

'And what's a refrain? What a curious word,
        Sister Helen!
Is the ballad you're writing about a sea-bird?'
'Not at all; why should it be? Don't be absurd,
        Little brother.
    (*O Mother Carey, mother!*
Thy brood flies lower as lowers the heaven.)'

(*A big brother speaketh:*)

'The refrain you've studied a meaning had,
        Sister Helen!
It gave strange force to a weird ballad.
But refrains have become a ridiculous "fad",
        Little brother.
    And *Mother Carey, mother,*
Has a bearing on nothing in earth or heaven.

'But the finical fashion has had its day,
        Sister Helen.
And let's try in the style of a different lay
To bid it adieu in poetical way,
        Little brother.
    So Mother Carey, mother!
Collect your chickens and go to – heaven.'

(*A pause. Then the big brother singeth, accompanying himself in a plaintive*
wise on the triangle:)

    'Look in my face. My name is Used-to-was;
    I am also called Played-out and Done-to-death,
    And It-will-wash-no-more. Awakeneth
Slowly, but sure awakening it has,
The common sense of man; and I, also!
    The ballad-burden trick, now known too well,
    Am turned to scorn, and grown contemptible –
A too transparent artifice to pass.'

H. D. TRAILL

Soul Severance

Because the cithole hath a thousand tones
    Inwrought with many subtile harmonies
    Of lute and flute wherein sweet music dies,
Yea, all the bitter-sweet that love disowns,
Mournful are they and full of heavy moans
    And tears and interpenetrative sighs,
    Soul-stirred with ultimate immensities,
And incommunicable antiphones!
So is the soul fulfilled of saddest things,
    Of multitudinous sighs and more sad than they
    Whereof Earth hears no sound, yet nothing may
Drown the deep murmur of its echoings:
Even so of soul and soul the poet sings
    And what on earth he means can no man say.

ST JOHN HANKIN

George Meredith (1828–1909)

The Charlady at Patterne Hall

Mrs. Huggins, feather-duster skyward, seeking Arachne, or pursuing such motes and particles of Mother Earth as, interpenetrating matter one might incline to conjecture knowing Mrs. Montague's hawk-eye for the speck, lurked prey for dustpan, invaded the Library, con-queror-wise, and went down to carpet, not unmechanically, her peripheral senses but lightly tickled by the motions of a too familiar task, while the nerve-centre of her being, as with all her kind, turned inward to the spiritually absorbing, but on the molecular plane just the reverse subcutaneous flux in that region which, proverbially denied to a royal lady of Spain, is a tea-cup topic to be tossed to and fro, with head-shakings for the lethal, by her humbler sisters of the slop-pail.

'One sees she has a leg,' said Mrs. Mountstuart.

L. E. JONES

The Charwoman

Of the category of draggletails, she. The questing eye travels upward from wrinkled stockings, down-at-heel, slashed slippers eloquent of the vulgarly obtrusive bunion, to shabby, shapeless garments, dirt-coloured, secured equatorially over abundance of unimaginable petticoats. The hands, of the earth earthy, and sodden with the imperfectly desiccated residue of floor-washings, convulsively clutch a bag, satchel or species of hold-all, distended product of successful cringing. What of the face? Charity averts kindly eye from thin lips prisoning ivory decayed, of negligible quantity and irregular distribution, rests a saddening moment on bulbous nose, open-pored, flabby, permanently damp, on fish-like eyes pricked for easy lachrymation, and finally settles with smiles on small, sequin-studded velvet bonnet, string-tied, perched on a bird's-nest hair. 'Honest labour bears a lovely face,' saith the poet. Then must grave suspicions of Mrs. B.'s integrity in the performance of those tasks advertised with such unsavoury insistence on her rag-bag person.

ALLAN M. LAING

Emily Dickinson (1830–1886)

Morning Disturbance

The cock that splits my slumber
  Is a very raffish bird
Who has had my number
  Ever since he heard

That I would rather be,
  By a lengthy sight,
Ravished into morning
  Than jilted out of night.

The lord of light is brazen;
  I see his lance come nigh
When at last I open
  The aspic of my eye.

PETER DE VRIES

She Sees Another Door Opening

My fortitude is all awry
To sit upon this chair
And, idly lifting up my eye,
To glimpse the door ajar there.

Through that door could come what bother
In what undreamed of pelts –
A cat, a dog, or God the Father,
Or – gulp – somebody else!

FIRMAN HOUGHTON

T. E. Brown (1830–1897)

My Garden

A garden is a loathsome thing, God wot! –
A veritable blot
Made up of weed and broken flowerpot,
Squat gnome and blighted apricot,
Trampled forget-me-not,
Rank lily, wasp, inedible shallot.
That geezer should be shot
What wrote that lot
Of Palgrave's Golden Tommy-rot,
That T. E. Brown, he seems to have forgot:
Left to itself a garden goes to pot.
Not that I don't enjoy a neat, well-ordered plot,
A nice secluded spot;
I do, but when it rains it's not
Much cop, and when it's hot
I'd rather sun myself on Uncle's yacht.

GERARD BENSON

Louisa May Alcott (1832–1888)

Little Liberated Women

'These are capital boots, so boyish and comfortable,' cried Jo. 'What did Marmee say about your new mini-dress, Meg?'

Meg's cheeks grew rosy as she answered thoughtfully, 'Mother said it was neat and well made, but she wondered if I was wise to use a kingsize crochet hook.'

'It would look nicely over my body stocking,' said Jo. 'You might have it, but it's laddered. Mercy, what are you painting, Amy?'

'A psychopathic experience I had at the party last night,' returned Amy with dignity.

'If you mean psychedelic, I'd say so,' advised Jo, laughing, while Meg looked at the little picture and said gently, 'If that's his beard, dear, it was auburn, not red.'

'Mercy, I must fly,' exclaimed Jo. 'I'm meeting Laurie for a demonstration.'

'Let me come too,' coaxed Amy. 'I'd dearly love to see him pull a policeman off a horse.'

'Stop bothering,' scolded Jo. 'You'll be frightened of the crowds, Laurie will have to put his arm round you and protect you, and that will spoil our fun. How happy Beth looks!'

'She's hearing heavenly music,' said Amy.

'Christopher Columbus, look at the cats!'

'She shares her LSD with them,' whispered Meg, 'the little saint.'

GWEN FOYLE

William Morris (1834–1896)

Ballad

PART I

The auld wife sat at her ivied door,
  (*Butter and eggs and a pound of cheese*)
A thing she had frequently done before;
  And her spectacles lay on her aproned knees.

The piper he piped on the hill-top high,
   (*Butter and eggs and a pound of cheese*)
Till the cow said: 'I die,' and the goose asked: 'Why?'
   And the dog said nothing, but searched for fleas.

The farmer he strode through the square farmyard;
   (*Butter and eggs and a pound of cheese*)
His last brew of ale was a trifle hard –
   The connection of which with the plot one sees.

The farmer's daughter hath frank blue eyes;
   (*Butter and eggs and a pound of cheese*)
She hears the rooks caw in the windy skies,
   As she sits at her lattice and shells her peas.

The farmer's daughter hath ripe red lips;
   (*Butter and eggs and a pound of cheese*)
If you try to approach her, away she skips
   Over tables and chairs with apparent ease.

The farmer's daughter hath soft brown hair;
   (*Butter and eggs and a pound of cheese*)
And I met with a ballad, I can't say where,
   Which wholly consisted of lines like these.

PART II

She sat, with her hands 'neath her dimpled cheeks,
   (*Butter and eggs and a pound of cheese*)
And spake not a word. While a lady speaks
   There is hope, but she didn't even sneeze.

She sat, with her hands 'neath her crimson cheeks,
   (*Butter and eggs and a pound of cheese*)
She gave up mending her father's breeks,
   And let the cat roll in her new chemise.

She sat, with her hands 'neath her burning cheeks,
   (*Butter and eggs and a pound of cheese*)
And gazed at the piper for thirteen weeks;
   Then she followed him out o'er the misty leas.

Her sheep followed her, as their tails did them.
   (*Butter and eggs and a pound of cheese*)
And this song is considered a perfect gem,
   And as to the meaning, it's what you please.

C. S. CALVERLEY

Rondel

Behold the works of William Morris,
   Epics, and here and there wall-papery,
   Mild, mooney, melancholy vapoury
A sort of Chaucer *minus* Horace.

Spun out like those of William Loris,
   Who wrote of amorous red-tapery,
Behold the works of William Morris,
   Epics, and here and there wall-papery!

Long ladies, knights, and earls and choris-
   ters in the most appropriate drapery,
   Samite and silk and spotless napery,
Sunflowers and apple blossoms and orris,
Behold the works of William Morris!

ANON

Alfred Austin (1835–1913)

A Birthday Ode to Mr Alfred Austin

The early bird got up and whet his beak;
  The early worm arose, an easy prey;
This happened any morning in the week,
    Much as to-day.

The moke uplift for joy his hinder hoof;
  Shivered the fancy poodle freshly shorn;
The prodigal upon the attic roof
    Mewed to the morn.

His virile note the cock profusely blew;
  The beetle trotted down the kitchen tong;
The early bird above alluded to
    Was going strong.

All this refers of course to England's isle,
  But things were going on across the deep;
In Egypt – take a case – the crocodile
    Was sound asleep.

Buzzed the Hymettian bee; sat up in bed
  The foreign oyster sipping local drains;
The impious cassowary lay like lead
    On Afric's plains.

A-nutting went the nimble chimpanzee; –
  And what, you ask me, am I driving at?
Wait on: in less than twenty minutes we
    Shall come to that.

The bulbous crowfoot drained his dewy cup;
   The saxifrage enjoyed a morning crawl;
The ampelopsis slowly sidled up
      The garden wall.

Her petals wide the periwinkle flung;
   Blue gentian winked upon unweanèd lambs;
And there was quite a pleasant stir among
      The cryptograms.

May was the month alike in croft and wild
   When – here in fact begins the actual tale –
When forth withal there came an infant child,
      A healthy male.

Marred was his ruby countenance as when
   A blushing peony is moist with rain;
At first he strenuously kicked and then
      He kicked again.

They put the bays upon his barren crest
   Laid on his lap a lexicon of rhyme
Saying: 'You shall with luck attain the quest
      In course of time.'

Stolid he gazed as one that may not know
   The meaning of a presage – or is bored;
But when he loosed his lips it was as though
      The sea had roared.

That dreadful summons to a higher place
   He would not, if he could, have spurned away;
But, being a babe, he had, in any case,
      Nothing to say.

So they continued: 'Yes, on you shall fall
   The laurels; you shall clamber by-and-by
Where Southey sits, where lately sat withal
      The Poet Pye.

'As yet you are not equal to the task;
    A sense of euphony you still must lack;
Nor could you do your duty by the cask
        Of yearly sack.

'Just now, withal (that's twice we've said 'withal')
    The place is filled by someone sitting there;
Yet poets pass; he, too, will leave his stall
        And go elsewhere.

'Meanwhile, to trust you with a pointed pen,
    Dear babe, would manifestly be absurd;
Besides all well-conducted little men
        Are seen, not heard.

'First, how to tutor your prehensile mind
    Shall be the object of our deep concern;
We'll teach you grammar; *grammar, you will find,*
        Takes years to learn.

''Twixt – mark the pretty word – 'twixt boy and man
    You shall collate from every source that's known
A blended style; which may be better than
        One of your own.

'Your classic mould shall be completely mixed
    Of Rome's robustness and the grace of Greece;
And you shall be a Tory, planted 'twixt
        Plenty and peace.

'And lo! we call you Alfred! Kinglihood
    Lies in the name of Him, the Good and Great!
You may not rise to greatness; O, be good
        At any rate!'

Eight happy summers passed and Southey, too,
    And one that had the pull in point of age
Walked in; for Alfred still was struggling through
        The grammar-stage.

When William flowed out in Robert's wake,
  An alien Alfred filled the vacant spot,
Possibly by some clerical mistake,
      Possibly not.

Our friend had then achieved but fifteen years,
  Nor yet against him was there aught to quote;
For he had uttered in the nation's ears
      Not half a note.

Adult, no more he dreamed the laurel-wreath,
  But wandered, being credentialled to the Bar,
There where the Northern Circuit wheels beneath
      The polar star.

One day, asleep in Court, Apollo's crown
  All in a briefless moment his he saw;
Then cast his interloping wig adown
      And dropped the Law.

Henceforth with loyal pen he laboured for
  His England (situated on the main);
Wrote in the tragic, or satiric, or
      Some other vein.

At forty-one he let his feelings go: –
  'If he, that other Alfred, ever die,
And I am not appointed, I will know
      The reason why!'

Some sixteen further autumns bound their sheaves;
  With hope deferred wild battle he had waged,
And written books. At last the laurel leaves
      Were disengaged.

Felicitations, bursting through his bowers,
    Came on him hoeing roots. With mild surprise,
'Leave me alone,' he said, 'among my flowers
        To botanize.'

The Prime Elector, Man of Many Days,
    Though Allan's Muse adorned the Liberal side,
Seizing the swift occasion, left the bays
        Unoccupied.

The Peer that followed, having some regard
    For humour hitherto accounted sin,
Produced a knighthood for the blameless bard
        Of proud Penbryn.

At length a callous Tory Chief arose
    Master of caustic jest and cynic gibe,
Looked around the Carlton Club and lightly chose
        Its leading scribe.

And so with heaving heart and happy tears
    Our patient Alfred took the tardy spoil
Though spent with sixty venerable years
        Of virtuous toil.

And ever, when marsh-marigolds are cheap,
    And new potatoes crown the death of May,
If memory serve us, we propose to keep
        His natal day.

SIR OWEN SEAMAN

Sir William S. Gilbert (1836–1911)

A Policeman's Lot

'The progress of any writer is marked by those moments when he manages to outwit his own inner police system' – Ted Hughes

Oh, once I was a policeman young and merry (young and merry)
Controlling crowds and fighting petty crime (petty crime)
But now I work on matters literary (litererry)
And I am growing old before my time ('fore my time).
No, the imagination of a writer (of a writer)
Is not the sort of beat a chap would choose (chap would choose)
And they've assigned me a prolific blighter ('lific blighter) –
I'm patrolling the unconscious of Ted Hughes.

It's not the sort of beat a chap would choose (chap would choose)
Patrolling the unconscious of Ted Hughes.

All our leave was cancelled in the lambing season (lambing season)
When bitter winter froze the drinking trough (drinking trough)
For our commander stated, with good reason (with good reason)
That that's the kind of thing which starts him off (starts him off)
But anything with four legs causes trouble (causes trouble)
It's worse than organizing several zoos (several zoos)
Not to mention mythic creatures in the rubble (in the rubble),
Patrolling the unconscious of Ted Hughes.

It's worse than organizing several zoos (several zoos)
Patrolling the unconscious of Ted Hughes.

Although it's disagreeable and stressful (bull and stressful)
Attempting to avert poetic thought ('etic thought)
I could boast of times when I have been successful (been successful)
And conspiring compound epithets were caught ('thets were caught).
But the poetry statistics in this sector (in this sector)
Are enough to make a copper turn to booze (turn to booze)
And I do not think I'll make it to inspector (to inspector)

Patrolling the unconscious of Ted Hughes.

It's enough to make a copper turn to booze (turn to booze) –
Patrolling the unconscious of Ted Hughes.

WENDY COPE

I Am a Racist

I am a racist of the National Front
And a right good racist too!
I was never very smart
And I couldn't give a fart,
For the blacks – or the reds like you!
Bad language or abuse I never never use –
Unless it's on the BBC:
'Hey nigger!' I may shout –
If there's only one about,
But I never send him turds or pee.
'What never?'
'No never!'
'What never?'
'Well, *hardly* ever . . .'

I am a racist of the National Front
And a right good John Bull too!
For I want this country white
And I couldn't give a shite,
For the likes of your nignog crew!
I might overlook a Kraut but the darkies will be out –
How else to make this country free?
If a man is shaded brown –
It's my right to knock him down,
But I never send him turds or pee.
'What never?'
'No never!'
'What never?'
'Well, *hardly* ever . . .'

TIM HOPKINS

Algernon Charles Swinburne
(1837–1909)

Nephelidia

From the depth of the dreamy decline of the dawn through a notable
nimbus of nebulous noonshine,
    Pallid and pink as the palm of the flag-flower that flickers with
fear of the flies as they float,
Are the looks of our lovers that lustrously lean from a marvel of
mystic miraculous moonshine,
    These that we feel in the blood of our blushes that thicken and
threaten with throbs through the throat?
Thicken and thrill as a theatre thronged at appeal of an actor's
appalled agitation.
    Fainter with fear of the fires of the future than pale with the
promise of pride in the past;
Flushed with the famishing fullness of fever that reddens with
radiance of rathe recreation,
    Gaunt as the ghastliest of glimpses that gleam through the gloom
of the gloaming when ghosts go aghast?
Nay, for the nick of the tick of the time is a tremulous touch on the
temples of terror,
    Strained as the sinews yet strenuous with strife of the dead who is
dumb as the dust-heaps of death:
Surely no soul is it, sweet as the spasm of erotic emotional exquisite
error,
    Bathed in the balms of beatified bliss, beatific itself by beatitude's
breath.
Surely no spirit or sense of a soul that was soft to the spirit and soul
of our senses
    Sweetens the stress of suspiring suspicion that sobs in the sem-
blance and sound of a sigh;
Only this oracle opens Olympian, in mystical moods and triangular
tenses –
    'Life is the lust of a lamp for the light that is dark till the dawn of
the day when we die.'

Mild is the mirk and monotonous music of memory, melodiously
 mute as it may be,
  While the hope in the heart of a hero is bruised by the breach of
  men's rapiers, resigned to the rod;
Made meek as a mother whose bosom-beats bound with the bliss-
 bringing bulk of a balm-breathing baby,
  As they grope through the graveyard of creeds, under skies
  growing green at a groan for the grimness of God.
Blank is the book of his bounty beholden of old, and its binding is
 blacker than bluer:
  Out of blue into black is the scheme of the skies, and their dews
  are the wine of the bloodshed of things;
Till the darkling desire of delight shall be free as a fawn that is freed
 from the fangs that pursue her,
  Till the heart-beats of hell shall be hushed by a hymn from the
  hunt that has harried the kennel of kings.

ALGERNON CHARLES SWINBURNE

Octopus

Strange beauty, eight-limbed and eight-handed,
 Whence camest to dazzle our eyes?
With thy bosom bespangled and banded
 With the hues of the seas and the skies;
Is thy home European or Asian,
 O mystical monster marine?
Part molluscous and partly crustacean,
 Betwixt and between.

Wast thou born to the sound of sea-trumpets?
 Hast thou eaten and drunk to excess
Of the sponges – thy muffins and crumpets,
 Of the seaweed – thy mustard and cress?
Wast thou nurtured in caverns of coral,
 Remote from reproof or restraint?
Art thou innocent, or art thou immoral,
 Sinburnian or Saint?

Lithe limbs, curling free, as a creeper
  That creeps in a desolate place,
To enrol and envelop the sleeper
  In silent and stealthy embrace,
Cruel beak craning forward to bite us,
  Our juices to drain and to drink,
Or to whelm us in waves of Cocytus,
    Indelible ink!

O breast, that 'twere rapture to writhe on!
  O arms 'twere delicious to feel
Clinging close with the crush of the Python
  When she maketh her murderous meal!
In thy eight-fold embraces enfolden,
  Let our empty existence escape,
Give us death that is glorious and golden
  Crushed all out of shape!

Ah! thy red lips, lascivious and luscious,
  With death in their amorous kiss!
Cling round us, and clasp us, and crush us,
  With bitings of amorous bliss;
We are sick with the poison of pleasure,
  Dispense us the potion of pain;
Ope thy mouth to its uttermost measure
  And bite us again!

A. C. HILTON

A Melton Mowbray Pork Pie

Strange pie that is almost a passion,
  O passion immoral for pie!
Unknown are the ways that they fashion,
  Unknown and unseen of the eye.
The pie that is marbled and mottled,
  The pie that digests with a sigh:

For all is not Bass that is bottled,
  And all is not pork that is pie.

RICHARD LE GALLIENNE

Thomas Hardy (1840–1928)

A Luncheon (Thomas Hardy Entertains the Prince of Wales)

Lift latch, step in, be welcome, Sir,
Albeit to see you I'm unglad
And your face is fraught with a deathly shyness
Bleaching what pink it may have had,
Come in, come in, Your Royal Highness.

Beautiful weather? – Sir, that's true,
Though the farmers are casting rueful looks
At tilth's and pasture's dearth of spryness. –
Yes, Sir, I've written several books. –
A little more chicken, Your Royal Highness?

Lift latch, step out, your car is there,
To bear you hence from this antient vale.
We are both of us aged by our strange brief nighness,
But each of us lives to tell the tale.
Farewell, farewell, Your Royal Highness.

SIR MAX BEERBOHM

Transistors

On a rock-scattered shore, steeped in deep tristfulness,
Companioned by Ocean's unwearying wistfulness,
Pensive I sat, my sad thoughts pursuing,
Consoled by the seabirds' importunate mewing.
Two soul-struck young lovers came sauntering, clinging,
And each, in the hand unencumbered, held swinging
A 'tranny' emitting a music most mordant –
Instruments stridulant, voices discordant.
And so they trailed onwards, in bliss all unheeding,
The blare and their figures both slowly receding,
Until of their passing no vestige remained there –
No cries now but those of the gulls who still plained there.
An interlude harsh: in the Final Accounting,
Will Man be thus valued, his brief span amounting
To just such an eposide – dissonant, fleeting,
The transient whim of a Will quite Unweeting?

MARTIN FAGG

My Mouse

My Mouse nibbles swift at his cheeses,
His flavour-fraught whiskers astir.
'But no such small offering pleases',
    I cogitate, 'her.'

He all needless of tether and troth is:
Unperforcely our futures are twined:
'But she who might mistress us both is',
    I sigh, 'disinclined.'

EDWARD BLISHEN

146

The Morning's Journal

The morning's journal conning, I
'Flat-racing recommences' note;
Intelligence that, read awry –
A sadder quirk lent to the quote –
   Might well be deemed to fit the case
   Of a more rueful kind of race.

For – racehorse-wise, I ween, we thud
Along life's courses to the post:
Of Arab or of feebler blood,
Most end among the hindermost.
   While gods – old guileful manflesh-gaugers –
   Sit interchanging lackcare wagers.

EDWARD BLISHEN

Foes Beyond

As the fretful pulse of dayspring slows to slumbrous eventide,
While the fevered ghosts of bat-light swartly round the gables glide –
I, in trance forgetful musing, brooding by my hearth, behold
Firelight flickers flecking volumes, valiant in lettered gold.
Faintly now, I seem to catch, from sallowed pages, plaintive cries –
Creatures tremulously calling, creatures of my own devise.
'Us you shape from out the shadows, us', they groan, 'you limn and name;
Fashion all our happenstances, all our form and feature frame.
Dire the whim whereby you wrought us, ruin brought us late or soon –
Sunlit chances quickly clouding, portioning more bale than boon.
Wherefore do you wring and rack us, all our springtide strivings thwart;
Blasting youth and wasting prime, sweet summer's schemings all abort?

147

Soon our dreams you blear and blister, long our days with fardels
   freight;
Ne'er to win the love we're wanting, e'er in bedlock to mismate.
Sure, our lives could never breed such unrelenting unsuccess,
If you'd grafted Grace to Angel, Clym to Sue and Giles to Tess.'
'Man-trap Sex hath maimed and lamed us!' moans a spectre-pallid
   Jude.
'Hadst thou cast them celibate, my years had not been ghastly-
   hued!'
How to quieten their reproaches, how their peevish chidings quell?
Answer that, in lists of loving, I, alas, unlanced as well,
Ne'er did learn the chivalry to spell their hopeful heart-plans'
   thrive –
Since such long and wan disaster dogged the hour *I* went to wive?
Luckless wights of my contriving – pardon grant! The days are few
Till, quite incorporeal, I substanceless shall be as you!

MARTIN FAGG

Henry James (1843–1916)

The Guerdon

Written upon hearing that the Order of Merit was about to be conferred on Henry James.

That it hardly was, that it all bleakly and unbeguilingly *wasn't* for 'the likes' of *him* – poor decent Stamfordham – to rap out queries about the owner of the to him unknown and unsuggestive name that had, in these days, been thrust on him with such a wealth of commendatory gesture, was precisely what now, as he took, with his prepared list of New Year *colifichets* and whatever, his way to the great gaudy palace, fairly flicked his cheek with the sense of his having never before so let himself in, as he ruefully phrased it, without letting anything, by the same token, out.

'Anything' was, after all, only another name for *the* thing. But he was to ask himself what earthly good it was, anyhow, to have kept in its confinement the furred and clawed, the bristling and now all but audibly scratching domestic pet, if he himself, defenceless Lord Chamberlain that he was, had to be figured as bearing it company inside the bag. There wasn't, he felt himself blindly protesting, room in there for the two of them; and the imminent addition of a Personage fairly caused our friend to bristle in the manner of the imagined captive that had till now symbolized well enough for him his whole dim bland ignorance of the matter in hand. Hadn't he all the time been reckoning precisely *without* that Personage – *without* the greater dimness that was to be expected of *him* – without, above all, that dreadful lesser blandness in virtue of which such Personages tend to come down on you, as it were, straight, with demands for side-lights? There wasn't a 'bally' glimmer of a side-light, heaven help him, that he could throw. He hadn't the beginning of a notion – since it had been a point of pride with him, as well as of urbanity, not to ask – who the fellow, the so presumably illustrious and deserving chap in question *was*. This omission so loomed for him that he was to be conscious, as he came to the end of the great moist avenue, of a felt doubt as to whether he could, in his bemusement, now 'place' anybody at all; to which condition of his may have been due the impulse that, at the reached gates of the palace, caused him to pause and all vaguely, all peeringly inquire of one of the sentries: 'To whom do you beautifully belong?'

The question, however, was to answer itself, then and there, to the effect that this functionary belonged to whom *he* belonged to; and the converse of this reminder, presenting itself simultaneously to his consciousness, was to make him feel, when he was a few minutes later ushered into the Presence, that he had never so intensely, for general abjectness and sheer situational funk, belonged as now. He caught himself wondering whether, on this basis, he were even animate, so strong was his sense of being a 'bit' of the furniture of the great glossy 'study' – of being some oiled and ever so handy object moving smoothly on castors, or revolving, at the touch of a small red royal finger, on a pivot. It would be placed questioningly, that finger – and his prevision held him as with the long-drawn pang of nightmare – on the cryptic name. That it occurred, this name, almost at the very end of the interminable list, figured to him not as a respite but as a prolongment of the perspirational agony. So that when, at long last, that finger *was* placed, with a roll towards him of the blue, the prominent family eye of the seated reader, it was with a groan of something like relief that he faintly uttered an:

'Oh well, Sir, he *is*, you know – and with all submission, hang it, just *isn't* he though? – of an eminence!'

It was in the silence following this fling that there budded for him the wild, the all but unlooked-for hope that 'What *sort*, my dear man, of eminence?' was a question not, possibly, going to be asked at all. It fairly burst for him and blossomed, this bud, as the royal eye rolled away from his into space. It never, till beautifully now, had struck our poor harassed friend that his master might, in some sort, be prey to those very those inhibitive delicacies that had played, from first to last, so eminently the deuce with *him*. He was to see, a moment later, that the royal eye had poised – had, from its slow flight around the mouldings of the florid Hanoverian ceiling, positively swooped – on the fat scarlet book of reference which, fraught with a title that was a very beam of the catchy and the chatty, lay beside the blotting-pad. The royal eye rested, the royal eye even dilated, to such an extent that Stamfordham had anticipatively the sense of being commanded to turn for a few minutes his back, and of overhearing in that interval the rustle of the turned leaves.

That no such command came, that there *was* no recourse to the dreadful volume, somewhat confirmed for him his made guess that on the great grey beach of the hesitational and renunciational he was not – or wasn't all deniably not – the only pebble. For an instant, nevertheless, during which the prominent blue eye rested on a prominent blue pencil, it seemed that this guess might be, by an immense *coup de roi*, terrifically shattered. Our friend held, as for an eternity, his breath. He was to form, in later years, a theory that the name really *had* stood in peril of deletion, and that what saved it was that the good little man, as doing, under the glare shed by his predecessors, the great dynastic 'job' in a land that had been under two Jameses and no less than eight Henrys, had all humbly and meltingly resolved to 'let it go at that'.

SIR MAX BEERBOHM

A Blurb for the Dustjacket of The Turn of the Screw

In this, as one may not too precisely term it, *conte* (though, from its not being tied to, from its ever so slightly disdaining a too absolute contact with, events for which the word is, perhaps, 'normal', *conte surnaturel* might be the fuller term), the publishers allow themselves, but with no, as it were, 'cockiness', to come ever so cautiously close to feeling that, having regard to his, in the past, other and, indeed, 'tougher' work, Mr James has, not, since it so misleadingly hints at a search, *found*, but if it is not saying too much, *stumbled upon* a vein, and driven into that vein so very much the mere tip of his 'pickaxe', that may – to be made to shudder being, for so many, a better end to reading than, as one may put it, to be called upon for no 'creeping' of the flesh – bring him forth from his obscurity, as one of those more, indeed, 'talked of' than read, and lead him, if there is not too much hope in the word, *near* to being an, as it were, not best, but 'second-best-seller' . . .

EDWARD BLISHEN

Gerard Manley Hopkins (1844–1889)

Initial Poem

Grief gripes my midnight mood with clasping claws
Exquisite sharp, which clutch, clamp and cling
Ratch to my brooding breast; must I then sing
Anthems, Lord, to Your most lawful, most aweful lores or laws?
Rather writhe I 'neath Your chaste and cheerless chivvying,
Dumb, damn myself must and dam my work-jammed jaws.

Merciful Mother Mary, May's maiden, laden and cold
Allweary I cry theewards for comfort counsel: 'Is there naught,
None, none, nowhere, never, nothing of the sort?
Live must I wretched? Cannot my sins be cudgelled or cajoled
Else of me? Elsewhere, elsetaken like contraband to freeport,
Yoiked and yachted yonder a yard or so? Must ever I scold?'

Hold! there moves in mankindheart a chord so tender,
Orchestrate how you may, it will sound there,
Pulse and pound the ear with a pummel of Heaven's air,
Kiss the listening soul, *not* lost (list!), and render
Into bliss (list!) all sweat, all suffering unsweet care.
Nestle beneath the spirit's rustling wing; wrest there, repair
Share! Since God's love over globe casts morning splendour.

GERARD BENSON

Breakfast with Gerard Manley Hopkins

'*Delicious heart-of-the-corn, fresh-from-the-oven flakes are sparkled and spangled with sugar for a can't-be-resisted flavour*' – Legend on a packet of breakfast cereal

Serious over my cereals I broke one breakfast my fast
    With something-to-read-searching retinas retained by print on a
      packet;
Sprung rhythm sprang, and I found (the mind fact-mining at last)
    An influence Father-Hopkins-fathered on the copy-writing racket.

Parenthesis-proud, bracket-bold, happiest with hyphens,
    The writers stagger intoxicated by terms, adjective-unsteadied –
Describing in graceless phrases fizzling like soda siphons
    All things, crisp, crunchy, malted, tangy, sugared and shredded.

Far too, yes, too early we are urged to be purged, to savour
    Salt, malt and phosphates in English twisted and torn,
As, sparkled and spangled with sugar for a can't-be-resisted flavour,
    Come fresh-from-the-oven flakes direct from the heart of the corn.

ANTHONY BRODE

February Filldyke

Praiséd be God for February rain,
Fill dyke, flushmeadow, floatark, when from lower
Of skies stippled, dun-dappled, black-grey-hatched, shower
Cleanly descends on our oh in need of cleansing plain.
Restitution here repénts. Lént's the fit, fasting fit, tear-washed
   reason of
Racing these level with, rival with its rim stream.
Root-minded tree's tumble, eddy-gashed clay's fall, is water's seisin of
Earth, earth's of water, in foam's yellow cream.
But *this*, my Moses, bank *these* rushes rain-spent dawn to dark,
Wind-worried, flood-tugged into turbulent water,
No footing offer for a Pharaoh's fair daughter,
No haven, hid harbour, mooring for your pitched wattle ark.

R. J. P. HEWISON

Baked Beauty

My flour fetched, salt-sprinkled, sift in self-
Raised, self-unselving with raisins wrinkle-round:
Soon scones will, kitchen-cosseted, be sudden-found,
The crumble cake-scapes clustered, shaped for shelf.
O fingers linger, tender-tippéd, thus to mix
Thy marge in moist: most need must, mingling, knead.
And ah! in flour sour cream streams! So my creed
Is dough, deft dough, light-hefted, fair to fix.
Now punch-pleased, pat in pattern, pitter-pat,
Cut careful, all board-ordered. Best to bake
Brushed beaten-egg-neat, meet to eat. Lay flat,
Fresh-fashioned passion, gas-mark-eight to take
Ten tongue-tight, frightful minutes, while set platt-
ers placed: such grace my scone-skilled God will make.

BILL GREENWELL

Oscar Wilde (1854–1900)

A Play of No Importance

Scene: Lord Sidewinder's gun-room. Enter LORD SIDEWINDER *and* HARGREAVES *the gamekeeper.*

LORD SIDEWINDER: Game's pretty thin this year, Hargreaves.

HARGREAVES: Her Ladyship insists that Lent is strictly observed in the coverts, my Lord.

LORD SIDEWINDER: Eh?

(*Enter* RONALD, *Lord Sidewinder's son.*)

Ah, Ronald, I hear you've been sent down. Disgraceful!

RONALD: Oxford is like the train to Didcot. One is never certain where one will alight, due to the state of the track.

(*Enter* CELIA.)

(*Wearily*) Kissing one's sister is rather like looking at Duchamp's *Mona Lisa* – one wonders whether the moustache might not be dispensed with.

(CELIA *weeps.*)

HARGREAVES: Bear up, Miss, remember sisterly affection is like a butler watering the port, best kept within reasonable limits.

(*Gong sounds.*)

LORD SIDEWINDER: Good-oh, grub up.

(*They go in.*)

HARGREAVES: When the Last Trump sounds for the Upper Class it will be sounded on a dinner gong, as like as not.

J. DEAN

The Importance of Being Ernestine

JACK WORTHING: And now, Lady Bracknell, there is a question I must put to you.

LADY BRACKNELL: To me, sir?

JACK WORTHING: To speak plainly, I have noticed that you are somewhat reticent about your origins.

LADY BRACKNELL: (*Confused*) My origins! Pray, how can they concern you? I am married to a peer of the realm. Surely that is sufficient?

JACK WORTHING: Do not misunderstand me. I am prepared to overlook a trifling social indiscretion of that kind. But I have searched for your parentage in the *ABC of the Aristocracy*, and other works of sensational fiction – quite without success. (*Sternly*) Lady Bracknell – to whom were you born?

LADY BRACKNELL: (*Agitated*) Mr Worthing – I have a confession to make. I was not so much born as – 'located'.

JACK WORTHING: Located?

LADY BRACKNELL: In a warming-pan.

JACK WORTHING: A warming-pan?

LADY BRACKNELL: It was a brass warming-pan.

JACK WORTHING: The metal is immaterial.

LADY BRACKNELL: It was at a garden fête to provide woolly comforts for equatorial missions.

JACK WORTHING: The engagement is at an end. How can I possibly marry into a charity bazaar and wed the daughter of a white elephant? Good afternoon, Lady Bracknell. (*He leaves in dudgeon.*)

MARTIN FAGG

H. Rider Haggard (1856–1925)

from The Deathless Queen

We were all sitting together round our camp-fire somewhere about the middle of Africa, Sir Henry – a grand figure of a man for all the clumsy darns in his tattered shooting-jacket – Captain Wood, R.N., and myself. At a little distance squatted Wunpotobaas, that grim old warrior, crooning a Zulu *impi* to himself, as he ran his finger lovingly along the keen blade of his *kaross*.

'Well, I'm going on, anyhow,' Sir Henry was saying. 'Good Lord! We have stumbled on a tremendous thing by the merest fluke, and you fellows want to turn back.'

'I am thinking of the danger,' I said nervously. 'I am not a brave man by nature, and I have always had a certain curious desire to die quietly in my bed.'

Sir Henry burst into one of his tremendous laughs. 'My dear old Quarterslain,' he said, 'it's a bit late in the day to try and persuade us you're afraid, we know all about that.'

Old Wunpotobaas had caught the last few words, and looked up with a quiet smile.

'Ah, Mataigarleeli,' (this was a name given to me by the natives years ago, and means, 'the great chief, who always sleeps with one eye round the corner'), 'I also know that fear of thine, and love it. Wast thou afraid when we stood together before the picked warriors to T'Chaka, and slew each our thousand men? or when thou and I crept softly through the King's *biltong*, and rescued the little maid with the hair of gold? Ai, but our hands were wet and red that night, Mataigarleeli, mine and thine! Or rememberest thou –'

'Silence, Wunpotobaas,' I said sharply, for the old butcher's eyes were flaming with blood fever, and, besides, I did not care to be reminded of the occasions on which the excitement of adventure had proved too much for the natural prudence, not to say timidity, which is inherent in me. But I have never found it easy to convince others of my inherent cowardice – possibly because I insist upon it so frequently.

Well, we talked the matter up and down for a long time. Weeks ago we had heard vague rumours of a white-skinned people dwelling in the hollow of a great ring of inaccessible mountains far beyond that vast subterranean river, which sweeps for close on three hundred miles through the bowels of the world. This river we had already negotiated successfully in spite of the manifold perils of the swirling water and of a race of gigantic shrimps, from which we had barely escaped with our lives, and now we had come to the foot of these mysterious mountains. Through the leaves of the towering *sjamboks*, under which we had pitched our camp, we could see plainly the beetling crags and jagged precipices, which formed, as it were, a natural barrier to the inquisitive instinct of mankind. And Sir Henry was anxious to press on and see what was to be seen. I gave in at last with a sigh.

'Very well, we'll start first thing tomorrow morning.'

But, as it happened, the decision was taken out of our hands, for next morning, as I was lying in the half-doze of daybreak, I heard sounds of moving feet about our camp, and sprang up with a quick cry that roused the others. And then we saw that we were surrounded by a number of splendid, long-limbed warriors, who stood and looked at us in silence like statues, and – marvel of marvels – like statues of polished ivory.

'My Aunt!' said Wood, screwing his glass into his eye with a tremendous effort. 'So it's true, after all.'

Their leader, a dignified old gentleman with a flowing white beard, stepped forward, and began to speak. Truly Africa is a land of wonder, of unending surprises, for to our amazement he talked the purest Kokni. He told us briefly that the Queen, whom he described simply as 'She-Who-Must-Be-Decayed', had heard of our arrival, and desired our immediate attendance at her capital.

G. F. FORREST

George Bernard Shaw (1856–1950)

Opening Paragraph of his Memoirs

If anyone expects that the book about to be inflicted on her is the usual farrago of anecdote and inanity, faulty recollection and stale wit, which goes by the name of Memoirs, she is, I am afraid, wholly justified. In me the exuberance of youth has given place to the garrulity of age: what message I had to deliver I have repeated to the point of nausea: nothing remains for me now but the saltless hack-writing of the book maker. But I protest that I am not to blame. What man in my position, or in any position, could have the heart to reject an offer of a million pounds sterling (free of tax) for a single book? This is the breath-bereaving offer of the Amalgamated British and American Publishers, Inc., for the thin dregs of my genius's nectar. The offer, coming on top of the Greater War's disillusions, has been too much for me: I have succumbed.

But do not despair. I daresay I can vamp up enough literary virtuosity, even at a hundred, to persuade you that what you are reading is something dazzlingly new and important, though I must go on saying, whether you listen or not, that it is nothing of the kind . . .

ALLAN M. LAING

On Jane Austen

As for Miss Austen's novels, if the Government had the good sense to make me Cultural Dictator, I would unhesitatingly ban the lot as being immoral, subversive, and vulgar; immoral because they acquiesce joyously in the existence of idlers, Baronets, curates, Misses, and the whole tribe of unproductive parasites; subversive, because they tend to perpetuate the mischievous illusion, which I have decisively exploded in my Plays and Prefaces, that the initiative in sex transactions remains with Man; and vulgar, because Miss Austen is an Englishwoman. For there are two kinds of vulgarity, into one or other of which all English people fall: that of being no lady (or gentleman) and that of being ladylike (or gentlemanly). But I am a person of taste as well as a moralist, and since I am personally immune to these pernicious tendencies, being too intelligent to be demoralized, too well-instructed to be subverted, and, as an Irishman, congenitally incapable of vulgarity, I shall continue to solace my own leisure with the delectable Elizabeth Bennet while the public, under my Dictator's lash, are resentfully mis-understanding *Back to Methuselah*.

L. E. JONES

Joseph Conrad (1857–1924)

from Mystery

I hadn't seen Burleigh for some five years or more when I found him waiting for me that fine light evening in the long low-roofed room with the red curtains – all sailormen know it – at the back of the Ebb Tide. The front rooms of the tavern of course look out on the square grey shipping offices of the Ultramarine Company, just where the tramway forks – I never could make out, by the way, where that tramway goes to – but Robinson keeps his upstairs room with the bay windows, the one that looks out over the docks, for a few favoured customers, amongst whom I am privileged to count myself.

Robinson didn't seem to have altered much, I thought. The same white puffed-out cheeks like an elderly cherub in need of fresh air, and the thick black eyebrows that seemed to wave and rustle as if in some invisible wind. Mrs Robinson was much the same too – angular, moving obscurely in the background, with those thin lips and that faint everlasting smile.

The first part of Burleigh that I noticed when I went upstairs and opened the door was his broad back, encased as usual in a frockcoat of No. 1 sailcloth, the tails of which fell slightly apart as he bent downwards to light his pipe at the fire with a long twist of old newspaper. When he stood up and turned round I was relieved to see that he had not altered either. The ring of fine curly hair that ran round the crown of his otherwise bald head was thinner than it had been, but there was the same lugubrious drollery in his grey eyes and the same gentle murmuring voice that came so incongruously from his deep stalwart chest as though through a sort of syrup. He had that old trick, too, of his, of smiling so that one end of his mouth ran up suddenly against the barrier of his heavy moustache, like the curl of a wave on a spit of reef. The large white-cotton umbrella, badly rolled up, that he always carried when ashore, was still hanging by its crook from his huge right arm.

'Have a –' he said quizzically, and I signified assent in the usual manner. As we sat down at the gleaming mahogany table and looked at each other smiling across it, he knew, of course – how could he help knowing? – that I wanted to hear all about that remarkable cruise of the *Albatross* away in the Southern ice floes about which the whole waterside was talking and about which nobody surely was likely to know more than he did. But equally of course he wasn't going to tell me all at once, for that wasn't Burleigh's way. Instead he tugged dreamily at one of his big moustaches and smiled up into the end of the other as we looked out at the lighted tideway beneath. Lamps shone high, shone low there, shone with single eyes, shone in rows, were reflected in glittering ladders broken by the shadows of hawsers along the oily inquietude of the stream. Congregated and at rest, the ships seemed to cast gentle inquiring glances at one another, to ask how each had fared in the vast incalculable tangle of wet mysteriousness which passes under the name of the sea.

Burleigh gave a final tug at last and spoke.

'I've asked another man in here tonight to meet you in a kind of way,' he said with a sort of deprecatory wave of his big hand as though it was a species of liberty to ask one man to meet another. And then, clearing his throat and twisting his smile again – 'Man called Allotson, Jim Allotson'; and, as if with a sudden effort of memory and dragging the words up from some deep recess of his vast interior – 'second mate.'

'Not on the –' I began, but he stopped me at once with the heavy emphatic nod characteristic of him.

'First man up the berg-side,' he cooed in that surprisingly gentle voice. 'Girl on it. Sicilian dancer. I believe. Derelict. Polar bears too. Good man, Jim Allotson. I'll tell you about him before he comes.'

And bit by bit I came to piece out, between the nods of Burleigh's head and the tuggings of that moustache of his and his quick sideways smile, the history of Allotson's youth up to the day when, by one of those extraordinary coincidences that sailors call chance, he became second officer of the *Albatross* – became second officer and so had his share of the tragi-comedy that was to happen to the crew of about the most adventurous tramp that was ever beaten out of the trade routes into the frozen seas.

He had been the son of a rather superior ship's chandler, I gathered, of a pious disposition, who settled down in East Croydon of all places after retiring from the sight and smell of salt water as they came to him on the quayside at Singapore. Neither a gravel subsoil nor excessive church-going was able to ward off malaria for long. He soon went under – his wife had died some years before – and left the child to the care of his only surviving relative, a sister named Ann. I can see her now as Burleigh described her to me, with her tight lips, expressionless eyes, grey coils of hair and the black alpaca dress she always inhabited, checking, reproving, forbidding and instilling endless moral axioms into this tousle-headed waif who had the rover's blood so inalienably in his veins.

He ran away, of course. He was bound to run away, had always dreamed and thought of nothing but ropes and rigging and tar, had seen the alleyways of his snug suburban home as tidal inlets hung with tropical vegetation; ran away and got a berth as ship's boy, and at fifteen had seen as much of the strange places of the world as many of us achieve in a lifetime. He had frizzled in pestilential mudflats, been driven under stormsails by the stark spite of typhoons, opened up hidden creeks, the passionless offshoots of unknown estuaries, at a time when other lads were grinding away at their Rule of Three.

Somehow or other, Burleigh did not exactly know how, he had managed to get his second-mate's certificate. But what he did know was that all through those wanderings the young man had preserved a sort of simple charming piety that came perhaps from the early lessons of that vigorous uncompromising old lady in Croydon, intolerable though her maxims had seemed.

'Good man, Jim Allotson,' cooed Burleigh once more at the end of all this, as though it was a kind of refrain. And just then the door opened and a man came in. He was dressed in a blue reefer suit, stooped slightly and walked a little lame. So much I saw as I gradually drew my eyes upward from the bright spot of light at the bottom of Burleigh's grog glass, where they had been fixed with sort of fascination while he spoke. Raised now to the level of the stranger's own, they blinked a little, and I held my breath for a moment at the contrast between that fresh ruddy face with slight black whiskers and the crop of hair that surmounted it, white as a bank of snow. He had the grey eyes that seem to be searching out the eternal riddle of heaven and sea, even when they have no further to look than the end of a room. Down the left cheek ran a broad whitey-brown scar that shocked almost as though it were unnatural and had been painted on. I did not need Burleigh's purred introduction to the second mate of the *Albatross* to have my curiosity, already pretty lively, as you know, whipped up to fever-point; and my friend's 'This young man is very anxious to hear –' could have been read without trouble in my eyes.

'But how much have you told him already?' he asked, speaking with a slight stammer, as he raised his glass and held it out a little stiffly in front of him, as though this was a necessary preliminary before putting it to his lips. I found out later that this was an invariable trick of his. 'Have you told him how I got my second-mate's certificate?'

Burleigh shook his head. He didn't, of course, as I was aware, know. 'About fourteen years ago,' began Allotson, and I sighed a little; but before he had said another word the door opened again. There was something horribly uncanny about that opening of the door, not followed by the appearance of a body but only of a face, as if it had been cut off at the neck –

'Time, gentlemen, please,' said the voice of Robinson.

E. V. KNOX

A. E. Housman (1859–1936)

What, Still Alive at Twenty-two?

What, still alive at twenty-two,
A clean upstanding chap like you?
Sure, if your throat 'tis hard to slit,
Slit your girl's, and swing for it.

Like enough, you won't be glad,
When they come to hang you, lad:
But bacon's not the only thing
That's cured by hanging from a string.

So, when the spilt ink of the night
Spreads o'er the blotting pad of light,
Lads whose job is still to do
Shall whet their knives, and think of you.

HUGH KINGSMILL

Summer Time on Bredon

'Tis Summer Time on Bredon,
   And now the farmers swear;
The cattle rise and listen
   In valleys far and near,
   And blush at what they hear.

But when the mists in autumn
   On Bredon tops are thick,
The happy hymns of farmers
   Go up from fold and rick,
   The cattle then are sick.

HUGH KINGSMILL

The Man Who Hangs Head Downwards

The man who hangs head downwards
Against the shaking sky
Reflects me in the water;
And who he is or why;
He knows no more than I.

I stir, he shifts beneath me;
I halt, he stands stock still;
He knows not what constrains him
To move against his will;
He only knows it ill.

And both will drown together
The mirrored man and I;
One falls, one rises upwards
To break the painted sky;
But both of us will die.

KATHARINE WHITEHORN

Last Poem

On Wenlock Edge a lad's in trouble,
   His stomach at the Wrekin heaves;
'Tis not a spot of decent grub'll
   Remove the sickness he relieves.

In summertime on Bredon summit
   He sees the girl he used to know
Conveniently placed to plummet
   Into the churchyard just below.

His team is ploughing at the gallop
   The fields of Clunbury and Clun,
And all the ghostly clods of Salop
   Rise up to curse its famous son.

He didn't like the pubs he sat in;
   The rose-lipt girls he never laid;
A likely lad should stick to Latin –
   Less damaging and better paid.

MARY HOLTBY

Off Wenlock Edge

On Wenlock Edge the wood's in trouble,
   For no one's left to feel its breath;
The lightfoot lads beneath the stubble
   Have found the Roman road of death;

The roselipt girls I once ran after
   As frozen churchyard mounds survive;
And Wrekin-like, I heave with laughter
   That though I'm wheezing, I'm alive.

On Wenlock Edge a thousand curses;
   It's led my lungs a fearful dance.
Though Shropshire's featured in my verses,
   I much prefer the South of France.

That wind, it blew my backbone double;
   It blows me down the road of man;
And Housman's pulmonary trouble
   Rates theses in the Bod-lei-an.

PAUL GRIFFIN

The Sun It Shines

The sun it shines on boughs of may.
   It shines on Bredon hill.
It shines upon the light-foot lad
   That goes to kiss and kill.

It shines upon the rose-lipt girl
   He strook so good and hard.
It shines upon the blasted cop
   That comes from Scotland Yard.

So many friends on hangman's drops
  Have choked for what they done,
'Twill take a sight of malt – and hops –
  To justify that sun.

THOMAS DERRICK

Sir Arthur Conan Doyle (1859–1930)

The Adventure of the Diamond Necklace

As I pushed open the door, I was greeted by the strains of a ravishing melody. Warlock Bones was playing dreamily on the accordion, and his keen, clear-cut face was almost hidden from view by the dense smoke-wreaths, which curled upwards from an exceedingly filthy briar-wood pipe. As soon as he saw me, he drew a final choking sob from the instrument, and rose to his feet with a smile of welcome.

'Ah, good morning, Goswell,' he said cheerily. 'But why do you press your trousers under the bed?'

It was true – quite true. This extraordinary observer, the terror of every cowering criminal, the greatest thinker that the world has ever known, had ruthlessly laid bare the secret of my life. Ah, it was true.

'But how did you know?' I asked in a stupor of amazement.

He smiled at my discomfiture.

'I have made a special study of trousers,' he answered, 'and of beds. I am rarely deceived. But, setting that knowledge, for the moment, on one side, have you forgotten the few days I spent with you three months ago? I saw you do it then.'

He could never cease to astound me, this lynx-eyed sleuth of crime. I could never master the marvellous simplicity of his methods. I could only wonder and admire – a privilege, for which I can never be sufficiently grateful. I seated myself on the floor, and, embracing his left knee with both my arms in an ecstasy of passionate adoration, gazed up inquiringly into his intellectual countenance.

He rolled up his sleeve, and, exposing his thin nervous arm, injected half a pint of prussic acid with incredible rapidity. This operation finished, he glanced at the clock.

'In twenty-three or twenty-four minutes,' he observed, 'a man will probably call to see me. He has a wife, two children, and three false teeth, one of which will very shortly have to be renewed. He is a successful stockbroker of about forty-seven, wears Jaegers, and is an enthusiastic patron of Missing Word Competitions.'

'How do you know all this?' I interrupted breathlessly, tapping his tibia with fond impatience.

Bones smiled his inscrutable smile.

'He will come', he continued, 'to ask my advice about some jewels which were stolen from his house at Richmond last Thursday week. Among them was a diamond necklace of quite exceptional value.'

'Explain,' I cried in rapturous admiration. 'Please explain.'

'My dear Goswell,' he laughed, 'you are really very dense. Will you never learn my methods? The man is a personal friend of mine. I met him yesterday in the City, and he asked to come and talk over his loss with me this morning. *Voilà tout.* Deduction, my good Goswell, mere deduction.'

'But the jewels? Are the police on the track?'

'Very much off it. Really our police are the veriest bunglers. They have already arrested twenty-seven perfectly harmless and un-offending persons, including a dowager duchess, who is still prostrate with the shock; and, unless I am very much mistaken, they will arrest my friend's wife this afternoon. She was in Moscow at the time of the robbery, but that, of course, is of little consequence to these amiable dolts.'

'And have you any clue as to the whereabouts of the jewels?'

'A fairly good one,' he answered. 'So good, in fact, that I can at this present moment lay my hands upon them. It is a very simple case, one of the simplest I have ever had to deal with, and yet in its way a strange one, presenting several difficulties to the average observer. The motive of the robbery is a little puzzling. The thief appears to have been actuated not by the ordinary greed of gain so much as by an intense love of self-advertisement.'

'I can hardly imagine', I said with some surprise, 'a burglar, *qua* burglar, wishing to advertise his exploits to the world.'

'True, Goswell. You show your usual common sense. But you have not the imagination, without which a detective can do nothing. Your position is that of those energetic, if somewhat beef-witted enthusiasts, the police. They are frankly puzzled by the whole affair. To me, personally, the case is as clear as daylight.'

'That I can understand,' I murmured with a reverent pat of his shin.

'The actual thief', he continued, 'for various reasons I am unwilling to produce. But upon the jewels, as I said just now, I can lay my hand at any moment. Look here!'

He disentangled himself from my embrace, and walked to a patent safe in a corner of the room. From this he extracted a large jewel case, and, opening it, disclosed a set of the most superb diamonds. In the midst a magnificent necklace winked and flashed in the wintry sunlight. The sight took my breath away, and for a time I grovelled in speechless admiration before him.

'But – but how' – I stammered at last, and stopped, for he was regarding my confusion with evident amusement.

'*I* stole them,' said Warlock Bones.

G. F. FORREST

The Adventure of the Two Collaborators

Conan Doyle once collaborated with Sir James Barrie on a libretto for a light opera. After the disastrous first night, Barrie presented his friend and collaborator with the following:

In bringing to a close the adventures of my friend Sherlock Holmes I am perforce reminded that he never, save on the occasion which, as you will now hear, brought his singular career to an end, consented to act in any mystery which was concerned with persons who made a livelihood by their pen. 'I am not particular about the people I mix among for business purposes,' he would say, 'but at literary characters I drew the line.'

We were in our rooms in Baker Street one evening. I was (I remember) by the centre table writing out 'The Adventure of the Man without a Cork Leg' (which had so puzzled the Royal Society and all the other scientific bodies of Europe), and Holmes was amusing himself with a little revolver practice. It was his custom of a summer evening to fire round my head, just shaving my face, until he had made a photograph of me on the opposite wall, and it is a slight proof of his skill that many of these portraits in pistol shots are considered admirable likenesses.

I happened to look out of the window, and perceiving two gentlemen advancing rapidly along Baker Street asked him who they were. He immediately lit his pipe, and, twisting himself on a chair into the figure eight, replied:

'They are two collaborators in comic opera, and their play has not been a triumph.'

I sprang from my chair to the ceiling in amazement, and he then explained:

'My dear Watson, they are obviously men who follow some low calling. That much even you should be able to read in their faces. Those little pieces of blue paper which they fling angrily from them are Durrant's Press Notices. Of these they have obviously hundreds about their person (see how their pockets bulge). They would not dance on them if they were pleasant reading.'

Up I went to the ceiling, and when I returned the strangers were in the room.

'I perceive, gentlemen,' said Mr Sherlock Holmes, 'that you are at present afflicted by an extraordinary novelty.'

The handsomer of our visitors asked in amazement how he knew this, but the big one only scowled.

'You forget that you wear a ring on your fourth finger,' replied Mr Holmes calmly.

I was about to jump to the ceiling when the big brute interposed.

'That Tommy-rot is all very well for the public, Holmes,' said he, 'but you can drop it before me. And, Watson, if you go up to the ceiling again I shall make you stay there.'

Here I observed a curious phenomenon. My friend Sherlock Holmes *shrank*. He became small before my eyes. I looked longingly at the ceiling, but dared not.

'Let us cut the first four pages,' said the big man, 'and proceed to business. I want to know why –'

'Allow me,' said Mr Holmes, with some of his old courage. 'You want to know why the public does not go to your opera.'

'Exactly,' said the other ironically, 'as you perceive by my shirt stud.' He added more gravely, 'And as you can only find out in one way I must insist on your witnessing an entire performance of the piece.'

It was an anxious moment for me. I shuddered, for I knew that if

Holmes went I should have to go with him. But my friend had a heart of gold. 'Never,' he cried fiercely, 'I will do anything for you save that.'

'Your continued existence depends on it,' said the big man menacingly.

'I would rather melt into air,' replied Holmes, proudly taking another chair. 'But I can tell you why the public don't go to your piece without sitting the thing out myself.'

'Why?'

'Because,' replied Holmes calmly, 'they prefer to stay away.'

SIR JAMES BARRIE

Rabindranath Tagore (1861–1941)

A Spot of Verse

What is life, my brother, but a temple offering?
I walk through showers of dreams in the evening
Like a fly in the dust.
Weep not, my daughter,
In the morning a fire will be lit,
O thou blood-red trumpet, whose feet are weary.
Empty my heart, O brother, on the road,
As the gardener empties his *gumani*
When Ganges flows upwards,
In palsied pain, O jemadar.
There is no cure for death but life,
No life for death but life,
No death for life but death,
Go, then, and ask thy sister for a blue-bag.

J. B. MORTON ('BEACHCOMBER')

Sir Henry Newbolt (1862–1938)

The Little Commodore

It was eight bells in the forenoon and hammocks running sleek
   (*It's a fair sea flowing from the West*),
When the little Commodore came a-sailing up the Creek
   (*Heave Ho! I think you'll know the rest*).
Thunder in the halyards and horses leaping high,
Blake and Drake and Nelson are listenin' where they lie,
Four and twenty blackbirds a-bakin' in a pie,
   And the *Pegasus* came waltzing from the West.

Now the little Commodore sat steady on his keel
   (*It's a fair sea flowing from the West*),
A heart as stout as concrete reinforced with steel
   (*Heave Ho! I think you'll know the rest*).
Swinging are the scuppers, hark, the rudder snores,
Plugging at the Frenchmen, downing 'em by scores.
Porto Rico, Vera Cruz, and also the Azores,
   And the *Pegasus* came waltzing from the West.

So three cheers more for the little Commodore
   (*It's a fair sea flowing from the West*).
I tell you so again as I've told you so before
   (*Heigh Ho! I think you know the rest*).
Aged is the Motherland, old but she is young
(Easy with the tackle there – don't release the bung),
And I sang a song like all the songs that I have ever sung
   When the *Pegasus* came sailing from the West.

SIR JOHN SQUIRE

There's a Breathless Hush

There's a breathless hush in the Close tonight –
　Ten to make and the match to win
As our number eleven squared up for the fight.
　The first ball reared and grazed his chin,
And the second one jumped and split his thumb,
　But little he cared for life's hard knocks
Till the third ball beat him and struck him plumb
　In a place where wiser men wear a box.

He thought of his honour and thought of the School
　And thought of the threat to his manly twitch,
And a voice inside said to him, 'Don't be a fool',
　So 'Sod this!' he muttered, and limped from the pitch.
There's a breathless hush in the Close tonight –
　Harrow won't play us again, they say.
'What bounder was that?' hissed the Head, death-white.
　Matron blushed: 'It was Bond, sir, J.'

NOEL PETTY

William Butler Yeats (1865–1939)

I Will Arise

I will arise and go now, and seek a Ministry,
And a deep shelter find there of ferro-concrete made,
The Departmental personnel will all make room for me,
And I shall sleep through the b——— loud raid.

Yes, I shall wait for peace there, for peace keeps stopping short,
Stopping for the wail of warning that noon and darkness brings;
Here midnight's all a-jitter with the A.A. guns' report
And evening full of the Luftwaffe's wings.

I will arise and go now, for wandering astray
I hear from Whitehall's refuges that long untroubled snore;
As I duck in surface shelters the Blitz can blast away,
I hear it in the deep earth's core.

SAGITTARIUS

Rudyard Kipling (1865–1936)

To R.K. (1891)

As long as I dwell on some stupendous
And tremendous (Heaven defend us!)
Monstr'-inform'-ingens-horrendous
Demoniaco-seraphic
Penman's latest piece of graphic.

ROBERT BROWNING

Will there never come a season
Which shall rid us from the curse
Of a prose that knows no reason
And an unmelodious verse:
When the world shall cease to wonder
At the genius of an Ass,
And a boy's eccentric blunder
Shall not bring success to pass;

When mankind shall be delivered
From the clash of magazines,
And the inkstands shall be shivered
Into countless smithereens:
When there stands a muzzled stripling,
Mute, beside a muzzled bore:
When the Rudyards cease from Kipling
And the Haggards Ride no more?

J. K. STEPHEN

A Ballad

As I was walkin' the jungle round, a-killin' of tigers an' time;
I seed a kind of an author man a writin' a rousin' rhyme;
'E was writin' a mile a minute an' more, an' I sez to 'im, ' 'Oo are
    you?'
Sez 'e, 'I'm a poet – 'er majesty's poet – soldier an' sailor, too!'
An 'is poem began in Ispahan an' ended in Kalamazoo,
It 'ad army in it, an' navy in it, an' jungle sprinkled through,
For 'e was a poet – 'er majesty's poet – soldier an' sailor, too!

An' after, I met 'im all over the world, a doin' of things a host;
'E 'ad one foot planted in Burmah – an' one on the Gloucester coast;
'E's 'alf a sailor an' 'alf a whaler, 'e's captain, cook, and crew,
But most a poet – 'er majesty's poet – soldier an' sailor too!
'E's often Scot an' 'e's often not, but 'is work is never through,
For 'e laughs at blame, an' 'e writes for fame, an' a bit for revenoo, –
Bein' a poet – 'er majesty's poet – soldier an' sailor too!

'E'll take you up to the Ar'tic zone, 'e'll take you down to the Nile,
'E'll give you a barrack ballad in the Tommy Atkins style,
Or 'e'll sing you a Dipsy Chantey, as the bloomin' bo'suns do,
For 'e is a poet – 'er majesty's poet – soldier an' sailor too!
An' there isn't no room for others, an' there's nothin' left to do;
'E 'as sailed the main from the 'Arn to Spain, 'e 'as tramped the
    jungle through,
An' written up all there is to write – soldier an' sailor, too!

174

There are manners an' manners of writin', but 'is is the *proper* way,
An' it ain't so hard to be a bard if you'll imitate Rudyard K.;
But sea an' shore an' peace an' war, an' everything else in view –
'E 'as gobbled the lot! – 'er majesty's poet – soldier an' sailor, too!
'E's not content with 'is Indian 'ome, 'e's looking for regions new,
In another year 'e'll 'ave swept 'em clear, an' what'll the rest of us
    do?
'E's crowdin' us out! – 'er majesty's poet – soldier an' sailor too!

GUY WETMORE CARRYL

Spring Is Here

We was moochin' around near the barracks one evening after tea,
Browned orf and fed to the teeth we was, Bill Bugginton and me,
When suddenly that son of a gun stopped dead in his tracks in the
    lane;
'Blimey,' 'e said, 'if the bloody leaves ain't on the trees again.'

And there we stood a marvellin' 'ow spring 'ad done 'er stuff,
The bloomin' annual miracle of callin' winter's bluff;
The little buds was burstin' and the 'edgerows turnin' green
And the air was sort o' balmy, and the sky was rain-washed clean.

You can talk of yer TV programmes and yer cracked-up disco shows,
But give me a lane and a land-girl, and a spot where nobody goes,
A man's man's gotta swig 'is pint and enjoy 'is bit o' smut,
But if 'e don't thrill to an English spring 'e's the dopiest kind of a
    mutt.

For it's in the new sap risin' and the sweet birds twitterin' round
That you touch the 'eart of England. And the 'eart of England's
    sound
So long as one British bastard, 'mid April sun and rain,
Gets a kick out o' seein' the bloody leaves upon the trees again.

STANLEY J. SHARPLESS

Mummy

I went into the kitchen to get a cup o' tea
The boys they stopped their talking and their eyes all said to me
'Look, can't you see we've friends in?' and they 'eaved a pointed
sigh.
I climbed the staircase back to bed and to myself sez I:
    Oh, it's Mummy this and Mummy that and 'Mummy, do you
    mind!'
    But it's 'Mummy, can you help me?' when your boots are hard to
    find.
    'I've left my football kit at home, so could you bring it round?'
    'Oh thanks, that's grand – and by the way – you haven't got a
    pound?'

When kids start on their schooling, those darn teachers know it all,
'Could try harder ... must write neater ... keep your eye upon
the ball.'
If *you* should try and teach your kids – 'that's not the way it's done';
But you bet they'll blame 'is background if the boy goes on the run.
    Oh it's 'Mums keep out' and 'Mums don't fuss' from teachers that
    we've paid;
    But it's 'Thank you Mrs Atkins' when they want the lemonade,
    The biscuits and the costumes for the fourth-form pantomime;
    They're dead keen on us mothers when they want *our* overtime.

We're Mums, so we're the cleaners too, the washers and the cooks;
An' they think that's all we're good for, once we've lost our dolly
looks.
My 'usband doesn't mind to say I'm just a silly moo,
But 'e sees it all quite different when 'e wants my wages too.
    Oh it's 'Mum's too slow' and 'Mum's too fat' and 'Mum's a
    bleeding fool'
    But it's 'Mum could make some money' once the kids are off to
    school.
    They want us scrubbing saucepans and they think that's all we
    do –
    But they call us 'Superwoman' when they want our wages too.

We ain't no superwomen nor we ain't no numbskulls too,
But common thinking people, most remarkable like you.
And sometimes if our tempers isn't all your fancy paints,
Well, women stuck with 'ousework don't grow into plaster saints.
    The 'Mum, come 'ere' and 'Mum, get lost' would make you go
        berserk;
    But it's 'motherhood is precious' when it's men that want the
        work.
    It's washing and it's ironing and it's food to feed their gobs,
    But it's 'sacred task of motherhood' when men want all the jobs.

You talk o' better terms for us, playgroups an' nursery schools,
And think such things will settle it; you must think we're all fools.
It's a job without a let-up, and just when we think we're through
We find that we're expected to 'mother' Uncle too.
    Oh it's Mummy this and Mummy that and Mummy up and
        down;
    – But sailors all call 'Mother!' when they know they're goin' to
        drown.
    We love our kids and lump it; but all we get for pay
    Is the thin red bunch o' roses that you bring on Mother's Day.

                                    KATHARINE WHITEHORN

Christie's Minstrels

In their Rollses and their Jags, in their very gladdest rags,
They're a-pourin' down the lanes from far and wide,
For there's music in the air and they want their annual share
Of Op'ra with some champers on the side.
Yes, the kids are safe with nanny so it's off to *Don Giovanni*
For a classy bloomin' operatic fling.
Oh, there's nothing rag-and-taggy or the least bit Cav-and-Paggy
Down at Glyndebourne where the Christie minstrels sing.

Come the end of ev'ry May there's a call the toffs obey
To mix a bit of culture with their class,

And so you find them there in the balmy Sussex air
A-listenin' and a-strollin' on the grass.
They leave *La Traviata* to the lower social strata
And a Glyndebourne *Butterfly* just isn't done,
But if your cup of tea is stuff like *Dido and Aeneas*
Better put your black tie on and join the fun.

PETER VEALE

The Reunion Dinner

There was eighty-seven in our mob, when we sailed in '93,
And now, dear Bill, to sit and dine, there's only you and me.
Grog and pox put paid to twelve, the cholera nabbed four,
Beri-beri collared five, the *kraits* got seven more.
'Johnny Pathan' drilled thirty-eight, 'is Missus cut up nine,
The Sergeant-Major shot 'isself (too good for the rotten swine!).
The QMS was next to go (went '*must*' in Cooch Behar)
The rest was either poisoned, 'anged – or knifed in the bazaar.
So only you and me, old friend, are 'ome to tell the tale,
To sniff the sweet old London fog, and sit and sup our ale.
So 'ere's to our Reunion! For you and me what's roughed it,
It's nice to think we're in the pink, while all the rest 'as snuffed it.

MARTIN FAGG

Recruiting Song

If you can keep your head when all about you
Are losing theirs and aiming things at you;
If you can leave a class to work without you
And guarantee they'll keep hard at it, too;
If you can mark and not grow tired of marking,
Of counting money, writing your Reports;
If you can stand the end-of-term sky-larking,

And still have spirit left to watch the Sports;
If you can talk, nor lose your voice with talking,
Give punishments without a biased mind;
If you can stop an idle mob from squawking
At every doubtful meaning they can find;
If you can dream – and not make dreams your master;
Or talk with Heads – nor lose the common touch;
If you can save your subject from disaster
By tactfully not plugging it too much;
If you can bear to hear the truth you've spoken
Twisted and laughed at by moronic fools;
If you're prepared to watch equipment broken
By 'scholars' who have scant regard for rules;
If you can fill the unforgiving minute
With ninety seconds' worth of distance run,
Teaching's for you, and everything that's in it,
And – which is more – you're welcome to it, son!

MICHAEL FOSTER

H. G. Wells (1866–1946)

from The Peculiar Bird

''Eng!' said Mr Bottleby, addressing the eighteenth milestone with intense bitterness: ''Eng!'

The bright windy sunshine on that open downland road, the sense of healthy effort, of rhythmic trundling speed, the consciousness of the nearly new ready-to-wear gent's cycling costume which draped his limbs – it had been ticketed 'Enormous Reduction', and, underneath that again, 'Startling Sacrifice, 25/6', in Parkinson's great front window on the South Parade – none of these things had availed to dissipate the gradual gloom which had been settling like a miasma on Mr Bottleby's mind through the whole of that morning of May. Various causes, historical, social as well as physiological, had contributed their share towards that tenebrous exhalation which already seemed to hang about him like a tangible and visible cloud. But undoubtedly its immediate origin and the cause of his hasty flight was the state of the Breakfast Bacon. Greasy. Uneatable. Tck! How many times had he told Ann, a hundred times if he had told her once, that he liked it in little crisp hard pieces and the eggs poached separately on toast? He was Fed Up. That was it. Absobloominglutely Fed. Tck!

If some well-meaning social philosopher had attempted to explain to Mr Bottleby the exact processes whereby a wasteful and ill-organized civilization had condemned him to struggle Laocoön-like in the coils of the retail ironmongery and the embraces of an uncongenial spouse, it is doubtful whether Mr Bottleby would have clearly understood. But his resentment against fate was none the less profound because it was largely inarticulate and because he would probably have summed up all this mismanagement and stupidity and carelessness and insensate cruelty in some simple epigram like 'A bit too thick'. Vaguely, in the recesses of his being, Mr Bottleby knew that in some way or other there ought to have been for him a more beautiful and gracious existence, a life somehow different from the drudgery and pettiness that he endured . . . .

The shop . . . How he hated it! How he did hate it! Ironmongery! Fast bound – what was it they had said in the church he had strayed into one evening? Misery and iron? Yes, that was it. Fast bound in misery and iron. That was him. And Ann. Sometimes when he thought of Ann . . . Skinny. Complaining. And why the doose did she cook like that? . . . There were other things too. In fact, there was One Thing after Another.

' 'Eng!' repeated Mr Bottleby to the nineteenth milestone; ' 'Eng!'

And having come now to the rather precipitous winding lane which leads down into Fittlehurst village he placed his feet on the rests – it was long before the luxurious days of the free-wheel – folded his arms and began to coast. Perilously, but with a certain sense of satisfaction in his extreme recklessness, to coast . . .

One figures him, a slightly rotund shape of about three-and-thirty years of age, attired in the check knickerbocker suit which had meant such an earth-shaking sacrifice to Mr Parkinson; one figures him, I say, with his freckled face, pleasant brown eyes and that large tuft of hair which continually escaped the control of his cap peak, rushing rapidly, worried, tormented by destiny, between those tall hedges on which the hawthorn had already made patches of scented, almost delirious, bloom, rushing downwards – on . . .

Whuck!

I come now upon a difficulty. I find it exceedingly hard to describe to you the nature of that surprising existence to which Mr Bottleby awoke when, having caught the fallen telegraph wire – fallen in yesterday's gale so that it blocked the Fittlehurst road like a piece of paddock fencing – having caught this wire exactly under his chin, he was projected out and away into the Ultimate Beyond.

His first impression was agreeable enough. It was one of amazing lightness. And, looking down with those pleasant brown eyes of his, he found that there was indeed good reason for this. For all that lower corporeal part of Mr Bottleby, that envelope of complicated tubes and piping which had been the source of so much of his trouble, that foundation for the altruistic sartorial efforts of Mr Parkinson, had completely disappeared. The bicycling suit, and all that therein was, had ceased to be. It had been even more Greatly Reduced. It had been Sacrificed Entirely. And simultaneously Mr Bottleby was conscious of a kind of soft and feathery growth to right and left of him, a faint iridescent fluffiness a little way behind each of his ears. At the same moment he also became conscious of the fact that he was not alone. All about him, floating, if I may so put it, though the phrase is a singularly inapt one, were thousands of similarly bodiless beings with bright and tiny wings attached to their necks. There was a sound, too, as of a mighty chattering. All these beings were talking, talking hard, talking with a shrill pleasant chirrup like that of song-birds at dawn.

E. V. KNOX

Arnold Bennett (1867–1931)

from Scruts

Albert Grapp, ladies' man though he was, was humble of heart. Nobody knew this but himself. Not one of his fellow clerks in Clither's Bank knew it. The general theory in Hanbridge was 'Him's got a stiff opinion o' hisself.' But this arose from what was really a sign of humility in him. He made the most of himself. He had, for instance, a way of his own in the matter of dressing. He always wore a voluminous frockcoat, with a pair of neatly striped vicuna trousers, which he placed every night under his mattress, thus preserving in perfection the crease down the centre of each. His collar was of the highest, secured in front with an aluminium stud, to which was attached by a patent loop a natty bow of dove-coloured sateen. He had two caps, one of blue serge, the other of shepherd's plaid. These he wore on alternate days. He wore them in a way of his own – well back from his forehead, so as not to hide his hair, and with the peak behind. The peak made a sort of half-moon over the back of his collar. Through a fault of his tailor, there was a yawning gap between the back of his collar and the collar of his coat. Whenever he shook his head, the peak of his cap had the look of a live thing trying to investigate this abyss. Dimly aware of the effect, Albert Grapp shook his head as seldom as possible.

On wet days he wore a mackintosh. This, as he did not yet possess a greatcoat, he wore also, but with less glory, on cold days. He had hoped there might be rain on Christmas morning. But there was no rain. 'Like my luck,' he said as he came out of his lodgings and turned his steps to that corner of Jubilee Avenue from which the Hanbridge–Bursley trams start every half-hour.

Since Jos Wrackgarth had introduced him to his sister at the Hanbridge Oddfellows' Biennial Hop, when he danced two quadrilles with her, he had seen her but once. He had nodded to her, Five Towns fashion, and she had nodded back at him, but with a look that seemed to say 'You needn't nod next time you see me. I can get along well enough without your nods.' A frightening girl! And yet her brother had since told him she seemed 'a bit gone, like' on him. Impossible! He, Albert Grapp, make an impression on the brilliant Miss Wrackgarth! Yet she had sent him a verbal invite to spend Christmas in her own home. And the time had come. He was on his way. Incredible that he should arrive! The tram must surely overturn, or be struck by lightning. And yet no! He arrived safely.

The small servant who opened the door gave him another verbal message from Miss Wrackgarth. It was that he must wipe his feet 'well' on the mat. In obeying this order he experienced a thrill of satisfaction he could not account for. He must have stood shuffling his boots vigorously for a full minute. This, he told himself, was life. He, Albert Grapp, was alive. And the world was full of other men, all alive; and yet, because they were not doing Miss Wrackgarth's bidding, none of them really lived. He was filled with a vague melancholy. But his melancholy pleased him.

In the parlour he found Jos awaiting him. The table was laid for three.

'So you're here, are you?' said the host, using the Five Towns formula. 'Emily's in the kitchen,' he added. 'Happen she'll be here directly.'

'I hope she's tol-lol-ish?' asked Albert.

'She is,' said Jos. 'But don't you go saying that to her. She doesn't care about society airs and graces. You'll make no headway if you aren't blunt.'

'Oh, right you are,' said Albert, with the air of a man who knew his way about.

A moment later Emily joined them, still wearing her kitchen apron. 'So you're here, are you?' she said, but did not shake hands. The servant had followed her in with the tray, and the next few seconds were occupied in the disposal of the beef and trimmings.

The meal began, Emily carving. The main thought of a man less infatuated than Albert Grapp would have been 'This girl can't cook. And she'll never learn to.' The beef, instead of being red and brown, was pink and white. Uneatable beef! And yet he relished it more than anything he had ever tasted. This beef was her own handiwork. Thus it was because she had made it so . . . He warily refrained from complimenting her, but the idea of a second helping obsessed him.

'Happen I could do with a bit more, like,' he said.

Emily hacked off the bit more and jerked it on to the plate he had held out to her.

'Thanks,' he said; and then, as Emily's lip curled, and Jos gave him a warning kick under the table, he tried to look as if he had said nothing.

Only when the second course came on did he suspect that the meal was a calculated protest against his presence. This a Christmas pudding? The litter of fractured earthenware was hardly held together by the suet and raisins. All his pride of manhood – and there was plenty of pride mixed up with Albert Grapp's humility – dictated a refusal to touch that pudding. Yet he soon found himself touching it, though gingerly, with his spoon and fork.

In the matter of dealing with scruts there are two schools – the old and the new. The old school pushes its head well over its plate and drops the scrut straight from its mouth. The new school emits the scrut into the fingers of its left hand and therewith deposits it on the rim of the plate. Albert noticed that Emily was of the new school. But might she not despise as affectation in him what came natural to herself! On the other hand, if he showed himself as a prop of the old school, might she not set her face the more stringently against him? The chances were that whichever course he took would be the wrong one.

It was then that he had an inspiration – an idea of the sort that comes to a man once in his life and finds him, likely as not, unable to put it into practice. Albert was not sure he could consummate this idea of his. He had indisputably fine teeth – 'a proper mouthful of grinders' in local phrase. But would they stand the strain he was going to impose on them? He could but try them. Without a sign of nervousness he raised his spoon, with one scrut in it, to his mouth. This scrut he put between two of his left-side molars, bit hard on it, and – eternity of that moment! – felt it and heard it snap in two. Emily also heard it. He was conscious that at sound of the percussion she started forward and stared at him. But he did not look at her. Calmly, systematically, with gradually diminishing crackles, he reduced that scrut to powder, and washed the powder down with a sip of beer. While he dealt with the second scrut he talked to Jos about the Borough Council's proposals to erect an electric power station on the site of the old gas works down Hillport way. He was aware of a slight abrasion inside his left cheek. No matter. He must be more careful. There were six scruts still to be negotiated. He knew that what he was doing was a thing grandiose, unique, epical; a history-making thing; a thing that would outlive marble and the gilded monuments of princes. Yet he kept his head. He did not hurry, nor did he dawdle. Scrut by scrut, he ground slowly but he ground exceeding small. And while he did so he talked wisely and well. He passed from the power station to a first edition of Leconte de Lisle's *Parnasse contemporain* that he had picked up for sixpence in Liverpool, and thence to the Midland's proposal to drive a tunnel under the Knype Canal so as to link up the main line with the Critchworth and Suddleford loop line. Jos was too amazed to put in a word. Jos sat merely gaping – a gape that merged by imperceptible degrees into a grin. Presently he ceased to watch his guest. He sat watching his sister.

Not once did Albert himself glance in her direction. She was just a dim silhouette on the outskirts of his vision. But there she was, unmoving, and he could feel the fixture of her unseen eyes. The time was at hand when he would have to meet those eyes. Would he flinch? Was he master of himself?

The last scrut was powder. No temporizing! He jerked his glass to his mouth. A moment later, holding out his plate to her, he looked Emily full in the eyes. They were Emily's eyes, but not hers alone. They were collective eyes – that was it! They were the eyes of stark, staring womanhood. Her face had been dead white, but now suddenly up from her throat, over her cheeks, through the down between her eyebrows, went a rush of colour, up over her temples, through the very parting of her hair.

'Happen,' he said without a quaver in his voice, 'I'll have a bit more, like.'

She flung her arms forward on the table and buried her face in them. It was a gesture wild and meek. It was the gesture foreseen and yet incredible. It was recondite, inexplicable, and yet obvious. It was the only thing to be done – and yet, by gum, she had done it.

Her brother had risen from his seat and was now at the door. 'Think I'll step round to the Works,' he said, 'and see if they banked up that furnace aright.'

SIR MAX BEERBOHM

Hilaire Belloc (1870–1953)

At Martinmas

At Martinmas, when I was born,
Hey diddle, Ho diddle, Do,
There came a cow with a crumpled horn,
Hey diddle, Ho diddle, Do.
She stood agape and said, 'My dear,
You're a very fine child for this time of year,
And I think you'll have a taste in beer,'
Hey diddle, Ho diddle, Ho, do, do, do,
Hey diddle, Ho diddle, Do.

A taste in beer I've certainly got,
Hey diddle, Ho diddle, Do,
A very fine taste that the Jews have not,
Hey diddle, Ho diddle, Do.
And though I travel on the hills of Spain,
And Val-Pont-Côte and Belle Fontaine,
With lusty lungs I shall still maintain
Hey diddle, Ho diddle, Ho, do, do, do,
Hey diddle, Ho diddle, Do.

So Sussex men, wherever you be,
Hey diddle, Ho diddle, Do,
I pray you sing this song with me;
Hey diddle, Ho diddle, Do;
That of all the shires she is the queen,
And they sell at the 'Chequers' at Chanctonbury Green
The very best beer that ever was seen.
Hey Dominus, Domine, Dominum, Domini,
Domino, Domino.

SIR JOHN SQUIRE

New Tarantella

Do you remember an Inn, Matilda?
Do you remember an Inn?
And the clangs and the bangs of the gangs from the builder,
Do you remember an Inn, Matilda?
Do you remember an Inn?
And the porter mixing mortar with a bucketful of water,
And the floorless, doorless room?
And the stamp, stamp, stamp of the tramp in the damp
Of the workmen marching, putting up the arching,
Knocking off the copper from the roof;
And the woof! and the grrr!
And the stir
Of the long-tailed cur
Snapping at the chappies in the gloom?

Nevermore, Matilda, nevermore;
No Inn without a window or a door;
Only a neat, complete Hotel,
Not a cell with a smell on the Costa del Sol,
Not a hol
Like Hell.

PAUL GRIFFIN

New Cautionary Tale

Marmaduke Rupert Vere de Vere,
Anticipating Christmas cheer,
In wheedling tones said, 'Please, dear Mummy,
For fear I might constrict my tummy,
Let out the waistband of my shorts.'
To whom Mama, displeased, retorts,
'I haven't time. There is no need
For larger waists. Restrain your greed.'

The great day comes. The lad is right;
His nether garments are too tight,
And at the seventeenth mince-pie,
North, east, south, west his buttons fly,
Confusion reigns throughout the parlour,
The butler drops the old Marsala,
Papa is peppered, mother swoons.

MORAL
Don't shirk enlarging pantaloons.

VEN. H. F. KIRKPATRICK

On Mrs Beeton

O plump but ineffectual Book
That failed to teach me how to cook:
Lay banquets – use pistachio –
But fry two herrings? Oh dear no!
Book overdone, Book indigestible,
Book stodged with every rich comestible,
Book for a palace, Book majestic,
Book far too large to call domestic,
Book managerial, Book didactic,
Book with bicarb, as prophylactic,
Book which – oh crikey! – I must shut,
To cough and open windows, but
Believe me I shall soon return –
The frying pan! My herrings burn!
To say some more about this Book
That failed to teach *me* how to cook.

STEVIE EWART

W. H. Davies (1871–1940)

The Tales I Hear

I'm sure that you would never guess
  The tales I hear from birds and flowers,
Without them sure 'twould be a mess
  I'd make of all the summer hours;
But these fair things they make for me
A lovely life of joy and glee.

I saw some sheep upon some grass,
  The sheep were fat, the grass was green,
The sheep were white as clouds that pass,
  And greener grass was never seen;
I thought, 'Oh, how my bliss is deep,
With such green grass and such fat sheep!'

And as I watch bees in a hive,
  Or gentle cows that rub 'gainst trees,
I do not envy men who live,
  No fields, no books upon their knees.
I'd rather lie beneath small stars
Than with rough men who drink in bars.

SIR JOHN SQUIRE

J. M. Synge (1871–1909)

A Memory

When I was as high as that,
I saw a poet in his hat.
I think the poet must have smiled
At such a solemn gazing child.

Now wasn't it a funny thing
To get a sight of J. M. Synge,
And notice nothing but his hat?
Yet life is often queer like that.

L. A. G. STRONG

Walter de la Mare (1873–1956)

The Last Bus

Nid-nod through shuttered streets at dead of night
   Soundless the last grey motor-bus went home;
Hailed it no watcher in its phantasm flight;
   Up the steep belfry stair no passenger clomb.

Mute as a mammet, bowed above the wheel
   The driver. His moustache was green with moss.
Cobwebs about him had begun to steal;
   Deafer than dammit the conductor was.

Red rust was on the gear chain. Hung long trails
  Of bugloss and bindweed from the bonnet's crown;
Charlock and darnel cluttered up the rails;
  The destination boards were upside down.

Yet still the bus moved, billowy with grass,
  Tottered and laboured, spurted, swayed and slowed;
Stock still the constable beheld it pass;
  Bunched sat the cat and feared to whisk the road.

Doom-loud the vegetable transport train
  Thundered their hallos, ground the earth to grit;
Scavengers turned to wave and wave again,
  Night revellers screamed 'Toot-a-loot' to it.

And still no sound. Only a murmur, a sigh
  Showed it not all a thing of shadow and gleam;
Fled the tall soap-works, fled the brewery by,
  Fled the municipal baths as though in a dream.

None knew whence this shadowy motor-bus,
  What it was doing, why, and whither away
It sped on into the night adventurous,
  Covered with lichens and all a-shake with hay.

Aye, but the forms within! What face was that
  Glassily seen – and that one, mild yet mum?
There – with the pink petunia in her hat!
  There – with the purple pelargonium!

And some have parcels of meat and fish and tea,
  And some eat aniseed from paper bags,
And some with sightless eyes scan momently
  Novels – yet turn no page – and fictional mags.

Fares are not asked. Time here is all withdrawn;
  A tenderness is here most tranquil and sweet;
As the still bus incessantly sails on
  Nobody stamps on anybody's feet.

Till see! They are out beyond the shuttered streets,
  Beyond the edge of the pavement and the trams.

A wonderful change! The ghosts stir in their seats.
　　Dawn glints. The first grey light shows fields of lambs.

Lollops a coney; peeps from tangled hedge
　　Bright eye of weasel (so unvexed the route):
Sits tit and sways on perilous blossom's edge;
　　Squabbles a squirrel; ululates a coot.

Bluebells start up, fantastically long,
　　Cowslip and cuckoo pint; all around the wheels
Dactyls wave arms and extra syllables throng
　　Looping the felloes. Topples the bus and heels.

And now an amazing sense of freedom from care
　　Deliciously moves their hearts as out they get.
This is the terminus. Rose-sweet the air,
　　Although underfoot the ground is still quite wet.

Leaves his sad perch the driver. Laughing and gay,
　　Lands the conductor a friendly slap on the snout;
They bind the engine anew with a twist of hay;
　　All breathe, dance, skip, take breakfast, scamper about.

E. V. KNOX

The Bug-eyed Listeners

'Is there anybody there?' signalled Voyager,
　　Travelling through outer space;
And it focused its television cameras
　　On Jupiter, just in case:
And it switched on all its computers,
　　And its telescopes infra-red,
And waggled its antennae again a second time:
　　'Come in, if you're there,' it said.
But no one responded to Voyager;
　　No extra-terrestrial things
Replied as the peering spacecraft

Took a butcher's at Saturn's rings.
But only a group of green-eyed creatures
   Looked upwards in dumb dismay,
And whispered behind their spatulate feelers,
   'Perhaps it will go away.'
And Voyager released its cargo
   Through the dark galactic sky,
A record of one hand clapping,
   And Bach and a baby's cry.
And they listened to President Carter,
   And the sound of a Rolling Stone,
And they knew the world Voyager came from
   Was less civilized than their own.

ROGER WODDIS

G. K. Chesterton (1874–1936)

In Praise of Non-central Heating

Before the Roman came to Kent, acquisitive and dire,
The Ancient British housewife made the Ancient British fire,
A smoky fire, a poky fire, a fire of coal and wood,
And one that didn't always burn as hotly as it should.

The Ancient British fire within the Ancient British grate
For years has warmed one half of every body in the State.
But Britons are a curious lot; we really do not mind
If we are nicely cooked in front and frozen hard behind.

You came, our last invaders, from your brash America,
With jeers and dirty cracks about our *frigidaria*;
You tried to educate us in your funny foreign ways,
With talk of central heating, like the Roman of old days.

But Britons are conservative and independent folk.
We love an independent fire, a fire that we can poke;
And, as the Roman failed, so all must fail who would aspire
To rob the Modern Briton of his Ancient British fire.

H. A. C. EVANS

When I Leapt over Tower Bridge

When I leapt over Tower Bridge
   There were three that watched below,
A bald man and a hairy man,
   And a man like Ikey Mo.

When I leapt over London Bridge
   They quailed to see my tears,
As terrible as a shaken sword
   And many shining spears.

But when I leapt over Blackfriars
   The pigeons on St Paul's
Grew ghastly white as they saw the sight
   Like an awful sun that falls;

And all along from Ludgate
   To the wonder of Charing Cross,
The devil flew through a host of hearts –
   A messenger of loss;

With a rumour of ghostly things that pass
   With a thunderous pennon of pain,
To a land where the sky is as red as the grass
   And the sun as green as the rain.

SIR JOHN SQUIRE

A Song Against Supermarkets

When God created Eden,
And all was going well,
The Devil upset everything
By tempting Eve. She fell.
Now he runs supermarkets,
With miles of gleaming shelves,
And whispers to Eve's daughters,
'Come in and help yourselves.'

They cram the yawning trolleys
With oven-ready stuff,
And Frozen This and Instant That,
And none cries, 'Hold, enough!'
The posters in the window
For fish-fingers and beer
Should warn instead, 'Abandon hope
All ye who enter here.'

STANLEY J. SHARPLESS

W. Somerset Maugham (1874–1965)

from First Person Circular

I do not often care for company on getting back to England from abroad. A slow process of adjustment is both necessary and pleasant, and I find one savours the pleasure a little more sharply if one is alone. On this occasion, however, after attending to arrears of correspondence and putting into order the two or three volumes of notes I had accumulated on my travels, I was finding London, for some reason or other, a trifle flat.

In a longer stay at Kuala than I had foreseen I had contracted the habit of an early Pilsener. How my man Ransom knew this I do not pretend to understand, even though I am, as you might say, a professional observer. It may have been through one of those indefatigable news agencies that collect bits about writers. Certain it was that Pilsener was always waiting for me. I sipped it now wondering whether, after all, London had anything that I could not have got in Tanga Orabiv, or for that matter Claustrophobia, where I had spent an unexpectedly tolerable week as the guest of the local FMG. It may have been due to this slight distaste of mine for London that, when Ransom entered to say that Mrs Waterson was on the telephone, I said at once, 'Put her through.' Yet if since my return Ransom had answered one call with a polite prevarication he must have answered a dozen.

Mary Waterson, on the telephone at least, has a voice which would move the angels, and I soon discovered that she had an appeal to make.

'Oh!' she said, 'so you *are* back! I had so hoped it was true, and that you weren't after all still out in one of those extraordinary places of yours at the ends of the earth – Now, did you get my invitation?'

'I may have,' I said. 'I haven't opened any.'

'That's positively wicked of you. But you will come, won't you?'

'Come? Where? And when?'

'Here, to Felstock. For the weekend.'

I thought one moment. Mary Waterson was after all a very friendly person. And they were using a pneumatic drill outside the flat. By comparison her house would be restful. So I said, 'Yes, I'll come.'

'That's delightful of you! Jack and Gloria will look forward to seeing you as much as myself – If you don't come by road your best train is the two forty-six.'

'Good,' I said, 'I'll do my best to catch it. Tomorrow. Goodbye.'

I was roused to look through the two dozen or so invitations I had idly put aside. Among them, though none was very exciting, was one from the Duchess of Glynning. Had I opened it earlier, and Mary had not telephoned, and had I felt more inclined to see the Duchess than to drink two or three afternoon bottles of Pilsener at home I might have accepted it, and this story would not have been written. Though no doubt another one would have been . . .

L. A. PAVEY

Short Story – Opening Paragraph

I am not altogether sure that I like my Aunt Maud. There is much, it is true, to be said in her favour. She provides an excellent tea; her conversation, though gushing and loud, is not wholly demeaning; and I never leave her house in Bayswater without a gift of some kind. But in return for her hospitality she makes demands that strike me as a trifle excessive. It was not always so. Once, there was the merest ruffling of my hair to set against hot crumpets succulent with butter, meringues as light and fragile as bubbles, thick wedges of cake, and afterwards five shillings (ten, when I wore my sailor suit) pressed into my politely reluctant palm. But as time passed, her pudgy fingers took to tweaking my cheeks. Her powdered face, drooping with fat under its loose, lined skin, was presented more frequently for kissing. I bore up, thinking of crumpets, but worse was to come.

W. J. WEBSTER

Cats!

It was just before the war. I was working in the garden at Cap Ferrat on the stories in *The Mixture As Before*. Beverley, who was understandably a little nervous about the effect of sunlight on his peaches-and-cream complexion, had chosen to work indoors. He too was engaged upon a task that stretched his creative powers to their uttermost – the compilation of his Annual Cat Calendar. I finished the first draft of 'The Three Fat Women of Antibes' – a deliciously adroit tale, although I say it myself – and wandered contentedly indoors.

'Martini time, Beverley,' I said, poking my head into his room.

The poor dear was enisled by literally hundreds of full-plate pussy-pictures. He had to choose twelve, garlanding each with a paragraph of his inimitably breathless prose. Most of them were calculatedly endearing, but there was also one of an alley-cat – scarred, predatory, malignant.

Beverley held it up. 'I think I shall call this one Gerald,' he said, with a feline smirk.

I mixed him a really *filthy* cocktail.

MARTIN FAGG

Robert Frost (1874–1963)

Mr Frost Goes South to Boston

When I see buildings in a town together,
Stretching all around to touch the sky,
I like to know that they come down again
And so I go around the block to see,
And, sure enough, there is the downward side.
I say to myself these buildings never quite
Arrived at heaven although they went that way.
That's the way with buildings and with people.
The same applies to colts and cats and chickens
And cattle of all breeds and dogs and horses.
I think the buildings Boston has are high
Enough. I like to ride the elevator
Up to the top and then back I come again.
Now, don't get me wrong. I wouldn't want
A ticket to New York to ride up higher.
These buildings come as close to heaven now
As I myself would ever want to go.

FIRMAN HOUGHTON

John Buchan (1875–1940)

Nunsmantle

Permissive London oppressed me mightily. The long parade of ringleted youth, as unwashed as it was epicene; the sleaziness of Soho oozing out to infect the whole capital; the unmistakable stench of moral *fetor* – all this set me yearning for the cool starlit intoxication of a night on the *veldt*. My unease was compounded by what I read in the *Telegraph* of the latest nun-running mystery. Fifty pure English girls abducted – and still not a trace! I am a peacable man but I dearly craved five minutes alone with a *sjambok* with the swine responsible.

A nun came and sat at the other end of my park bench. I have always sat lightly to religion – the Church of Rhodesia is an undemanding institution – but there are times when one envies the sweet certainties of Rome.

'Congratulations, Dick, on your peerage.'

I gaped. '*Sandy!*'

'Keep your voice down, Dick,' she murmured. 'This is the tightest spot that even you and I have ever shared.'

MARTIN FAGG

from The Queen of Minikoi

We were talking of coincidences. It had been a hard day. For eleven hours we had stalked a shootable sixteen-pointer over the Runnoch screes and up and down the corries of Sgurr Beoch, until Old Mac, who had been with me in the Bourlon Wood show, groaned: 'Yon beastie's a deil.' Finally Lord Trasker had flung himself down and fired upwind into the eddies of mist; a chance shot, the outcome of overwrought nerves. But as he fired, the stag came loping from behind a knoll, and took the shot full in the mazzard.

'Deid,' cried old Mac, 'a straucht shot for a braw cantlin. I wull no' ha' seen mony better shots at all.'

'It was a fluke, you know,' said Trasker, 'I just had an instinct . . .'

We dragged our quarry down Glenlivet and across Ruiseach Side to the Tollig, and arrived back at Sir Robert Manningham's shooting lodge, weary but well pleased with ourselves. And then, after an admirable dinner, prepared by Marston, who had been with Sir Robert in the Festubert show, somebody had remarked that Lord Trasker's shot had been a coincidence. And General the Hon. Derrick McQuantock had said, in that voice which always brought Eton back to me:

'Yes, but what is coincidence? There are forces outside the world of which we know next to nothing. Why did I meet Eric' – he pointed his pipe stem at Sir Eric Chalmers Troope – 'Why did I meet Eric in Zerka when we were both supposed to be in Bigadich? Or what made Philip' (indicating Admiral Sir Philip Delmode) 'suspect our Dutch friend Joos Vuyterswaelt?'

We all laughed at the memory of the neat way in which the Admiral had outwitted the Romanian Secret Service. And while we were still laughing, the squat little figure of Sandy Argyll, that astounding baker from Forfar, who had become a merchant adventurer and had helped to save the Queen of Holland from the Red Hand Society – that squat figure moved in a chair by the fire. 'Coincidence,' he said. 'Hm! Ask Graham to tell you about the hat that didn't fit.'

We all turned to the Earl of Moorswater, and in a silence deeper than that of the night-shrouded Whang Scaur outside the windows, he told this story.

'Any of you fellows ever hear of Minikoi? No, it's not the name of a girl. It's an island in the Arabian Sea, and I myself had only heard of it vaguely, when, on a certain spring day after the war, I came out of the Premier, and turned down Pall Mall. I had dined well, and old Fossett, who was with me in the St Quentin show, had brought up a bottle of the club port – '58. I was feeling pretty pleased with life. As I passed through the door into the street I noticed that Carson, the head hall porter –'

'Sorry to butt in,' said the General, 'but wasn't he given the DCM after the Cambrai stunt? I thought so. A white man.'

'– Old Carson,' continued the Earl, 'stared at me curiously. At the same time I felt a pressure on my head. Now as you all know, I get my hats from Challoner, and no man in town makes a better hat. And yet my hat was too tight. I took it off, and to my amazement found a thick piece of paper stuffed inside the lining. There was writing on it, and I stood under a lamp-post to read it. Now, I'm considered pretty good at languages, as you all know, but I must confess this screed puzzled me. It was written in faded red ink, and it seemed to be no modern tongue. Well – it wasn't any modern tongue. After puzzling over it for some minutes, I noticed a certain syllable which recurred very frequently, and at once I knew what the writing was. It was the language of the old Icelandic sagas of Snorre Sturlason – the Heimskringla – stories of the Norsemen just before they were Christianized by the Anglo-Saxons. I recognized it thanks to a job of work I had done for the Foreign Office towards the end of the war. I took the paper home with me, intending to get to work on it, but my man Truslove – you remember him, Derrick, at Le Cateau' – the General nodded – 'Truslove informed me that there was a gentleman waiting for me in the library. It turned out to be Sir Ronald Waukinshaw, my old chief at the FO. You should have seen his face when I said: "Ronnie, ever heard of Minikoi?" The old boy glanced round nervously. Then he said: "In heaven's name, Graham, what on earth do you know about it?" I produced the bit of paper, and he whistled softly.

' "This is a pretty big thing," he said. "It's old Icelandic, of course. But how did you come by it?" I told him that I had found it in my hat. "Then somebody," said he, "must have mistaken your hat for someone else's."

' "But what does it mean?" I asked.

' "Read it yourself," he replied dryly.

'I read slowly: "The sword of the giant-queen of the rock and snow, the ring-bearer, shall be dyed in the gore of Geysa's sons on May 4th at Minikoi."

' "Isn't it clear?" asked Ronnie.

' "Not particularly," I said.

' "We must go back to your club at once," he rejoined. And in the taxi he told me the most incredible story I have ever listened to.

'It appeared that for some time past the Foreign Office had been worried by signs of unrest in the Laccadive and Maldive Islands. There was talk of an ancient Arabian Queen who had returned to earth to lead the islanders against the English in India, and to re-establish a vast heathen Empire from the Malabar coast to the Himalayas. As the sign that she was the expected monarch she was to show a heavy ring of beaten gold to her followers, chief among whom was a certain Afghan, at present in England to raise money for the rising, which, it was hoped, would quickly spread to the islands in the Bay of Bengal and the South China Sea. "This message," he said, "must have been intended for that Afghan's hat, for it gives the date of the rising."

' "But what has the Icelandic business to do with it?"

' "They thought they'd be safe if they used that language. As it is, you and I are probably about the only people who understand it."

' "And why are we going back to the club?"

' "To hunt for that Afghan – unless –"

'We met each other's eyes, as men do at such moments, and I read his purpose. "You want me to be that Afghan, and put a stopper on the whole affair."

' "It's almost certain death," he said.

' "That's one's job," I answered.

' "Good man," he said. "Today's May 1st. Not much time."

'Ronnie came back to my flat and watched while my man made me up as an Afghan. Then we rang up Donald Ritchie, who had been with my mob in the first Somme push. To my delight he was just starting off on one of his mad flights round the world, for though he had left an ear at Loos and a thumb at Suvla, he was the same old Donald who had trekked across Greenland to cure his insomnia. He said he could have his plane ready in an hour.'

J. B. MORTON ('BEACHCOMBER')

John Masefield (1878–1967)

Sea-chill

When Mrs John Masefield and her husband, the author of 'I Must Go Down to the Seas Again', arrived here on a liner, she said to a reporter, 'It was too uppy-downy and Mr Masefield was ill' – News item.

I must go down to the seas again, where the billows romp and reel.
So all I ask is a large ship that rides on an even keel,
And a mild breeze and a broad deck with a slight list to leeward,
And a clean chair in a snug nook and a nice, kind steward.

I must go down to the seas again, the sport of wind and tide,
As the gray wave and the green wave play leapfrog over the side.
And all I want is a glassy calm with a bone-dry scupper,
A good book and a warm rug and a light, plain supper.

I must go down to the seas again, though there I'm a total loss,
And can't say which is worst, the pitch, the plunge, the roll, the toss.
But all I ask is a safe retreat in a bar well tended,
And a soft berth and a smooth course till the long trip's ended.

ARTHUR GUITERMAN

Bank-holiday Fever

I must go down to the seas again, for the old bank 'oliday bash,
An' all I ask is a good boot an' a bird oo's got some cash,
An' the sea-front an' the small shop with the goods worth nickin',
An' the fat slob with the flash car an' shins worth kickin'.

I must go down to the seas again, to remember pints I sank,
When all I asked was a full gut an' some two-star in the tank;
But the cold wind an' the flung spray an' the black clouds hov'rin'
Are a bad scene an' I do feel it's not worth bovv'rin'.

RICHARD QUICK

The Everlasting Percy, or,
Mr John Masefield on the Railway Centenary

I used to be a fearful lad,
The things I did were downright bad;
And worst of all were what I done
From seventeen to twenty-one
On all the railways far and wide
From sinfulness and shameful pride.

For several years I was so wicked
I used to go without a ticket,
And travelled underneath the seat
Down in the dust of people's feet,
Or else I sat as bold as brass
And told them 'Season', in first-class.
In 1921, at Harwich,
I smoked in a non-smoking carriage;
I never knew what Life nor Art meant,
I wrote 'Reserved' on my compartment,
And once (I was a guilty man)
I swopped the labels in guard's van.

From 1922 to 4
I leant against the carriage door
Without a-looking at the latch;
And once, a-leaving Colney Hatch,
I put a huge and heavy parcel
Which I were taking to Newcastle,
Entirely filled with lumps of lead,
Up on the rack above my head;
And when it tumbled down, oh Lord!
I pulled communication cord.
The guard came round and said, 'You mule!
What have you done, you dirty fool?'
I simply sat and smiled, and said
'Is this train right for Holyhead?'
He said, 'You blinking blasted swine,
You'll have to pay the five-pound fine.'

I gave a false name and address,
Puffed up with my vaingloriousness.
At Bickershaw and Strood and Staines
I've often got on moving trains,
And once alit at Norwood West
Before my coach had come to rest.
A window and a lamp I broke
At Chipping Sodbury and Stoke
And worse I did at Wissendine:
I threw out bottles on the line
And other articles as be
Likely to cause grave injury
To persons working on the line –
That's what I did at Wissendine.
I grew so careless what I'd do
Throwing things out, and dangerous too,
That, last and worst of all I'd done,
I threw a great sultana bun
Out of the train at Pontypridd –
It hit a platelayer, it did.
I thought that I should have to swing
And never hear the sweet birds sing.
The jury recommended mercy,
And that's how grace was given to Percy.

And now I have a motor-bike
And up and down the road I hike,
Seeing the pretty birds and flowers,
And windmills with their sails and towers,
And all the wide sweep of the downs,
And villages and country towns,
And hear the mowers mowing hay,
And smell the great sea far away!
And always keeping – cars be blowed! –
Well on the wrong side of the road,
And never heeding hoots nor warners,
Especially around the corners,
For even down the steepest hill
Redemption saves me from a spill.

I have a flapper on the carrier
And some day I am going to marry her.

E. V. KNOX

E. M. Forster (1879–1970)

What Really Happened in the Malabar Caves

'What is that?'

'It is I. It is only Aziz. Do not be afraid.'

'I meant the noise.'

'It is only an echo, Miss Quested. Nothing to worry about I assure you! Ah! Excuse me. I hope I have caused you no embarrassment?'

'What a funny way of putting it! I think the strap's broken, that's all.'

'The stone is so slippery. It is treacherous. May I assist you?'

'Oh, Aziz!'

'Merciful Heavens! What would the City Magistrate think?'

'Who's going to tell him? Don't worry. This must be the first really private spot I've found in India. Why are you giggling?'

'I am thinking of dear Mr Fielding's face if he knew.'

'I like dark hairy men. You can call me Adela if you like.'

'Oh, Miss Quested – Adela . . . This is beyond the dreams of a humble Indian doctor like myself . . . To be in the arms of a beautiful English lady. I am dreaming.'

'Kiss me and see. Aren't I real? What's the matter?'

'Ah, what is real? I have a confession. I lied to you at the entrance. My wife is dead.'

'Silly! Ronny told me that days ago. You must be feeling very frustrated.'

T. GRIFFITHS

Lytton Strachey (1880–1932)

The Death of King Edward VII

He was not afraid to die; had he not been punctual in attendance at Divine Service? Besides, God was known to be merciful. But in another, less placable, quarter a report would certainly be demanded. Would it be possible, there whither he was bound, to meet Papa without Mama? He must ask the Archbishop. Of some things Papa must surely approve: there had been the Entente Cordiale; there had been the Hospital Fund; there had even been the Royal College of Music. No mention need be made of Minoru. And that reminded him. 'Tell Marky,' he whispered, 'I'm glad his horse won.' A few more mutterings followed, too faint to catch. Might those words have been, if caught, 'Don't let poor Cassel starve'? The words were not caught. The friendly hearted King was dead, and the Edwardian Age, exuberant, brittle, and amusing, saw no point in surviving him.

L. E. JONES

Mary Webb (1881–1927)

from Cold Comfort Farm

A strange film passed over Adam's eyes, giving him the lifeless primeval look that a lizard has, basking in the swooning southern heat. But he said nothing.

'And another thing,' continued Judith, 'you will probably have to drive down into Beershorn tonight to meet a train. Robert Poste's child is coming to stay with us for a while. I expect to hear some time this morning what time she is arriving. I will tell you later about it.'

Adam shrank back against the gangrened flank of Pointless.

'Mun I?' he said piteously. 'Mun I, Miss Judith? Oh, dunna send me. How can I look into her liddle flower-face, and me knowin' what I know? Oh, Miss Judith, I beg of 'ee not to send me. Besides,' he added, more practically, ' 'tes close on sixty-five years since I put hands to a pair of reins, and I might upset the maidy.'

Judith, who had slowly turned from him while he was speaking, was now halfway across the yard. She turned her head to reply to him with a slow, graceful movement. Her deep voice clanged like a bell in the frosty air:

'No, you must go, Adam. You must forget what you know – as we all must, while she is here. As for the driving, you had best harness Viper to the trap, and drive down into Howling and back six times this afternoon, to get your hand in again.'

'Could not Master Seth go instead o' me?'

Emotion shook the frozen grief of her face. She said low and sharp:

'You remember what happened when he went to meet the new kitchenmaid . . . No. You must go.'

Adam's eyes, like blind pools of water in his primitive face, suddenly grew cunning. He turned back to Aimless and resumed his mechanical stroking of the teat, saying in a sing-song rhythm:

'Ay, then I'll go, Miss Judith. I dunnamany times I've thought as how this day might come . . . And now I mun go to bring Robert Poste's child back to Cold Comfort. Ay, 'tes strange. The seed to the flower, the flower to the fruit, the fruit to the belly. Ay, so 'twill go.'

Judith had crossed the muck and rubble of the yard, and now entered the house by the back door.

In the large kitchen, which occupied most of the middle of the house, a sullen fire burned, the smoke of which wavered up the blackened walls and over the deal table, darkened by age and dirt, which was roughly set for a meal. A snood full of coarse porridge hung over the fire, and, standing with one arm resting upon the high mantel, looking moodily down into the heaving contents of the snood, was a tall young man whose riding boots were splashed with mud to the thigh, and whose coarse linen shirt was open to his waist.

The firelight lit up his diaphragm muscles as they heaved slowly in rough rhythm with the porridge.

He looked up as Judith entered, and gave a short, defiant laugh, but said nothing. Judith slowly crossed over until she stood by his side. She was as tall as he. They stood in silence, she staring at him, and he down into the secret crevasses of the porridge.

'Well, mother mine,' he said at last, 'here I am, you see. I said I would be in time for breakfast, and I have kept my word.'

His voice had a low, throaty, animal quality, a sneering warmth that wound a velvet ribbon of sexuality over the outward coarseness of the man.

Judith's breath came in long shudders. She thrust her arms deeper into her shawl. The porridge gave an ominous, leering heave; it might almost have been endowed with life, so uncannily did its movement keep pace with the human passions that throbbed above it.

'Cur,' said Judith, levelly, at last. 'Coward! Liar! Libertine! Who were you with last night? Moll at the mill or Violet at the Vicarage? Or Ivy, perhaps, at the ironmongery? Seth – my son . . .' Her deep, dry voice quivered, but she whipped it back, and her next words flew out at him like a lash.

'Do you want to break my heart?'

'Yes,' said Seth, with an elemental simplicity.

The porridge boiled over.

STELLA GIBBONS

P. G. Wodehouse (1881–1975)

Bertie and Emma

'I'm so unhappy,' Emma Bovary sighed, as she rested her head on Bertie's shoulder.

'I say, cheer up old thing,' he exhorted, patting her back with imprudent familiarity. He quivered as her warm flesh seared his trembling body. She raised her mouth towards his and Bertie snorted with undisguised passion. 'I'm not terribly good at this sort of rot,' he confided, before clamping his lips against her.

'Take me dearest,' she moaned helplessly.

His knees buckled with excitement and he slithered to the carpet with Emma. Bertie closed his eyes discreetly as he glimpsed her bared shoulders, yet held on with the resolution of an unmitigated bounder.

'Now,' she insisted urgently.

Bertie was engulfed by panic. 'Would you mind dreadfully if I phoned Jeeves?' he bleated.

RUSSELL LUCAS

Bertie Gulliver in Brobdingnag

'What ho! What ho! What ho!' I yodelled, as the governess female prepared to plank me down on the pleasure boat. 'A life on the jolly old ocean wave, what?'

It wasn't, you understand, that I felt so frightfully chirpy at being in the clutches of a girl beside whom Honoria Glossop would have seemed twin sister to the midget in Barnum and Bailey's: but one likes to say the polite thing on these occasions. *Nobless oblige*, and all that.

Well, I don't know whether or not the cheery Wooster salutation startled her, but at that precise moment the young idiot dropped me into thin air, and, believe me, I've never known it feel thinner.

For about a century and a half I plummeted like one of those dud rockets these military johnnies are continually firing: and then, wham! there was Bertram, dangling from the head of a pin the wretched female had stuck into her apron. It was at this frightful moment that a discreet 'Allow me, Sir!' sounded in my ears; and there was Jeeves, the gallant fellow, leaning from the ship's topmast to transfer the young master to the rigging.

G. J. BLUNDELL

I Say, Give Over, Jeeves!

'Jeeves,' I called, 'rally round the young master with a stiff B and S and get the old brain cells whizzing. Gussie's in trouble again.' He entered with a lurching walk and the sort of face that would have dragged an admiring gasp from a passing gorilla. 'Jeeves,' I cried, 'this is no time for amateur theatricals. You look like that rummy bloke in the play with the low thingummy.'

'I fancy, sir, you mean the monster Caliban, whose forehead, the Bard assures us, was villainous low. However, my appearance is not due to any Thespian activity, but to indulgence in a tonic beverage called Buck-U-Uppo left by a Mr Mulliner. Mr Fink-Nottle also called, wearing a tie whose design caused me considerable pain.'

'Live and let live Jeeves, I trust you were not churlish with him?'

'No, sir, I fear I strangled him with it.'

CLIVE JACQUES

Daisy Ashford (1881–1972)

The Wages of Sin Is Deth

Dam and blarst said Mr Salteena flinging aside his wifes prayer book I shall go and see Ethel today. He cheered up and put on his suit of velvit cote and green knickerbockers. He carefully rubbd the seat part with oderclone witch had gone shiny from horse galloping. He poked the doorbell of Ethels manshon with his riding crop. If this is sin I like it thought Mr Salteena. A maid showed him into a costly room with gay sofas. He helped himself to a large wiskey and took a fat sigar. A lovely vishon came it was Ethel. Mr Salteena sprang to his feet and said egerly I cannot stand sour grapes and ashes any longer come away with me. You filty beast gasped Ethel the wages of Sin is Deth. She took a little gun from a fringy evenig bag and shot him. Mr Salteena died.

P. M. ROBERTSON

Virginia Woolf (1882–1941)

A Cricket Commentary

Mr Botham rubs the ball on his trousers with a swift circular motion – some ritual propitiation of the gods. Now he runs like the wind towards what I think is called the crease, while the man with the bat at the other end awaits the onslaught with what seems like resignation born of despair. The score stands at 137 for 3, or it may be 8; my eyes have misted over with the sudden realization of the sheer poetry of the scene; the worn stretches of grey-green sod, the lowering sky, the line of diseased elms, the handful of pale-faced spectators with their secret joys and sorrows. I am transfixed by the consideration of inability to understand (let alone communicate) the transcendental inwardness of it all. And now bad light has stopped play. Gloom and sorrow have descended upon us. I weep for England.

STANLEY J. SHARPLESS

Advertisement Copy

'Oh, thank you, dear.'

(*Thinks*) And now I must be kissed, must smile, his scowl, his grumpiness – how strange men are! – utterly vanished. And still one gropes, like a blind man with a stick, for the reason; the late-night malted drink – was that it? – the crispy breakfast cereal – was that it? How could they spirit away that monster, those hooves trampling the pale leaves of my content, that near hatred? This, then: the teeming suds; white sheets flapping (like great swans fighting to be free); Monday, and his dinner not scamped; his wife gracious with leisure. It is to Rinsil, then, my thanks should go!

ELAINE MORGAN

A. A. Milne (1882–1956)

from When We Were Very Silly

SOMEONE ASKED THE PUBLISHER

Some one asked
The publisher,

Who went and asked
The agent:
'Could we have some writing for
The woolly folk to read?'
The agent asked
His partner,
His partner
Said: 'Certainly.
I'll go and tell
The author
Now
The kind of stuff we need.'

The partner
He curtsied,
And went and told
The author:
'Don't forget the writing that
The woolly folk need.'
The author
Said wearily:
'You'd better tell
The publisher
That many people nowadays
Like hugaboo
To read.'

NOW WE ARE SICK

Hush, Hush,
Nobody cares,
Christopher Robin
Has fallen downstairs.

JOHN PERCY

John Percy
Said to his nursy:
  'Nursy,' he said, said he,

'Tell father
I'd much rather
    He didn't write books about me.'
'Lawkamercy!'
Shouted nursy,
    'John Percy,' said she,
'If dad stopped it,
If dad dropped it,
    We shouldn't have honey for tea!'

J. B. MORTON ('BEACHCOMBER')

God Bless Nanny

God bless Nanny, she's my Delight –
Wasn't she Fun in the bath tonight!
The soft so soft and the firm so firm –
God – don't send me to school next term!
If I open my diary a little bit more
I can see her undressing me by the shore;
It's a beautiful view, and she hasn't a stitch –
Oh, bless us both, and make us rich!
Next, a Wedding, with Wedding Cake –
(I call her Nanny for old times' sake) –
And a Honeymoon, and Bed for Two –
So get stuffed, Tigger, and Winnie the Pooh!

W. F. N. WATSON

No Daddy

One of the latchkey children although only twice times three,
A blazered Christopher Robin pockets his friend, ET,
And says to his one-parent mother, 'Come on, Mother,' says he,
    'You can lecture all day at the V & A
    But leave me the front-door key.'

Christopher Robin's mother, dressed in her sweater and jeans,
Leaves on the kitchen table a teatime tin of baked beans.
Christopher Robin's mother says to herself, says she,
　'I can earn my pay at the V & A
　And get home soon after tea.'

Christopher Robin's mother didn't get home after tea,
So Christopher's playing truant, won't learn his ABC.
'S'pose she's off with the milkman,' he says to his friend, ET.
　'But *I* don't care 'cos I have the key
　And she jolly now can't lecture *me*.'

MONICA G. RIBON

James Joyce (1882–1941)

from The Tents of Wickedness

He awoke in a strange bed. Not awoke exactly, but felt it penetrate his consciousness that it was a strange bed in a strange place, before sinking into even deeper slumber . . .

. . . Then for some reason he could not explain, except within the logic of dreams where no explanations are required but oddity itself imposes its kind of clarity, he was in one of those places where people take their laundry to wash it in automatic machines. The public Laundromat. It would be a mistake to say he was there in person: he was rather there in spirit, to witness the two old women who were the only customers as they drew the soiled family clothes from their bags and chucked them into the washers. The machines were side by side, the centre pair in a glistening white row of perhaps ten. The women sat side by side on a bench to gossip, and as the machines simultaneously commenced the first of the cycles, the drone of their words mingled with the hum of the motors and the wash and splash of the water and the clothes, while all of it seemed to be going on in Swallow's head itself, where it merged in an endlessly flowing river of dialogue.

FIRST WOMAN

It was a literary friendship. (*Laughter from the toothless crones.*) Can't you see them in their trysting shanty, talking about books. Well, it's the sterne realities they'll be facing now.

SECOND WOMAN

What he minds most they say is the being a laughing stock. It's his *rire* end to be seen sticking through the britches he was too big for.

FIRST WOMAN

And hers out front. They must have known it would illicit comment.

SECOND WOMAN

That sort's not practical, the artistic – and when it comes to the poets! I understand he could be treacly in his tastes for all that. Not even above a little Tennyson.

FIRST WOMAN

Chacun à son goo. And that's not all. Think o' them fancy composers they must have cuddled up listening to. Everything was fine and d'indy then, but I de falla now to see a bright side to the situation. Now don't fly off the handel about the modern stuff, Molly, that's not what the subject is about. Let's stick to it for once, for a luscious one it is, my duck.

SECOND WOMAN

I'm not shootin' me mouth off about that aspect of it either. There ought to be a law against all these illicit relations. What's needed is some good plain penal reform.

FIRST WOMAN

Beginning with his. Cut it off without a pity – and don't stop there either. Let him die intestate, him on his Castro convertible.

SECOND WOMAN

So he'll never go whole hog again? (*Laughter.*) But he won't soon again anyway, I'll be bound. Still, it'd be a stop in the right direction.

(*There is a pause and they suddenly turn silent and thoughtful, even sad. There is a transition in the machine and a change of tempo in the wash.*)

FIRST WOMAN

(*Half humming*) Ha hee ha ho a low ... It's keening the sound of these machines makes me feel like doing. A mournful ancient seadark sound it is, this in the Laundromat, as of all the waters washing all the shores in the weary world. The splash and swish of the suds reminds me of all the rivers running into the sea, yet the sea not full. There, the pre-rinse is over, and now it's the water frothing and swirling in the seacove, lonely beyond knowing, my Molly, the last outlet of Time ... the wash everything comes out in as they do be sayin'.

SECOND WOMAN

Stop your lip, woman, and leave the poetry to them as can moan it proper. Poets are born, not made.

FIRST WOMAN

Aye, but we know one was made, don't we now? And proper too she was. She priapubly had them lined up waiting their turn. Had I the queue for passion she has I wouldn't be doin' me own washin', let alone others'. There's food for thought there – intravenus injection. Still 'twas she, not I, met with a foetal accident.

SECOND WOMAN

Ah, you're a foul-mouthed sweet old soul. Yes, made she was I must admit – and made once, maid no more.

FIRST WOMAN

Stop grinning with them two remaining teeth. They remind me of cloves, which reminds me I've got to get home and fix a ham for the poor old clod I've remaining to me. An incurable rheumatic. Ah well I love him just the same, the same. He's persona non Groton, but he's mine, and he wouldn't go cheatin' on me even if he had the opportunity, like that other blatherskite.

SECOND WOMAN

Oh, let's not blacken the lad to the point of using him as a sinonim for all ruttin' off the reservation. I've heard rumours *he* was the one prevailed upon. The soft sell and then the hard sell, and him so young and rubicund. It's the company he kept.

FIRST WOMAN

Kept is it now? *He* keeps anyone, that cheapskate, at least to hear tell? He'd never get in that deep – he'd never get fiscally involved if he could help. Furs and flowers, and then Christmas coming round and she up there in the flat waiting over the eggnog, in hopes that St Necklace soon would be there. And him with his Santa Claustrophobia. No, not him. Just once he slipped and now he's slapped and that's the long and the short of it. Slapped around just like that clothes behind the glass there. Did you ever hear the one about the woman who looked at one of these and said, 'Well, if that's television . . .'?

SECOND WOMAN

Oh, woman, if you can't tell jokes at least no older than yourself, button up. Here comes the Spin-dry. Then you can spread your washin' proper and get home to cook that ham. How do you cook a ham?

FIRST WOMAN

(*Growing absent*) So little thyme. Sanctuary much, he'll say ironiclike. He was good for the jests he was, once and many a spare quid for a case of bottles. Remembrance of Things Pabst, that's the story of our life, and ah, how we lay dreaming on the grass. Him reading to me books with plots. How Greene Was My Valley of Decision then. Yes right off, and him with the wherewithal to hitch us up straight off. Legal Tender Is the Night. Him laying in bed drunk singing as I dropped my shift on the cold hotel room floor, Sister Carrie Me Back to old Virginibus Puerisque. It's all a welter mitty in my head, thinkin' back so fondly. For the lad it's Beth In the Afternoon. As I went walking down the street I metamorphosis. It's like that Spin-dry in my head as it must be in his too. I hear he's mental now, aw, let's have a kind thought for the chap. This is the end for him: delirium: tear-a-lira-lirium: stream of conscience: you pays your money and you takes your joyce.

PETER DE VRIES

Franz Kafka (1883–1924)

A's Trial

A, presumably an acquaintance of Kafka's K, attempts to renew his British Museum Reading Room ticket.

Adam, or A as he would now more vaguely have identified himself, had been all through this before, but could not be sure whether he had dreamed it or actually experienced it. He was trapped. Behind him was a locked, guarded door; in front of him a long corridor terminating in a room. He could not go back. He could not stay where he was – the men in the room at the end of the corridor, warned by the bell, were expecting him. He went reluctantly forward, down the long corridor, between the smooth polished wooden cabinets, locked and inscrutable, which formed the walls, stretching high out of reach. Craning his neck to see if they reached the high ceiling, A felt suddenly dizzy, and leaned against the wall for support.

The room at the end of the corridor was an office, with a long, curving counter behind which sat two men, neat, self-possessed, expectant. A approached the nearer man, who immediately began writing on a piece of paper.

'Yes?' he said, after a few minutes had passed, and without looking up.

A, his mouth unaccountably dry, enunciated with difficulty the words, 'Reading Room Ticket.'

'Over there.'

A sidled along the counter to the second man, who immediately began writing in a ledger. A waited patiently.

'Yes?' said the second man, closing his ledger with a snap that made A jump.

'IwanttorenewmyReadingRoomTicket,' gabbled A.

'Over there.'

'But I've just been over there. He sent me to you.' Out of the corner of his eye, A saw the first man watching them intently.

The second man scrutinized him for what seemed a very long time, then spoke. 'One moment.' He went over to the first man, and they held a whispered conference, at the conclusion of which the first man came over to A and sat down in the second man's seat.

'What is it you want, exactly?' he asked.

'I want to renew my Reading Room Ticket,' said A patiently.

'You want to *renew* it? You mean you have a ticket already?'

'Yes.'

'May I see it?'

A presented his ticket.

'It's out of date,' observed the man.

'That's why I want to renew it!' A exclaimed.

'When did you last use the Reading Room?'

'Two months ago,' lied A, cunningly.

'You haven't used it since your ticket expired?'

'No.'

'It wouldn't matter if you had,' said the man. 'As long as you're not lying.' He tore A's ticket neatly into four sections, and deposited them in a waste-paper basket. It distressed A to see his ticket torn up. He experienced a queasy, empty feeling in his stomach.

'So now you want to renew your annual ticket?'

'Please.'

'You see, you didn't make that clear to me just now.'

'I'm sorry.'

'I assumed you were a casual reader wanting a short-term ticket. That's why I sent you to my colleague.' He nodded in the direction of the second man. 'But when he realized you wanted an annual ticket, he directed you back to me. That is the reason for our apparently contradictory behaviour.'

He flashed a sudden smile, displaying a row of gold-filled teeth.

'I see. I'm afraid it was my fault,' A apologized.

'Don't mention it,' said the first man, opening the ledger and beginning to write.

'Could I have my new ticket now?' said A, after some minutes had passed.

'Over there.'

'But you just said you were responsible for renewing annual tickets!' protested A.

'Ah, but that was when I was sitting over there,' said the first man. 'We've changed places now. We do that from time to time. So that if one of us should fall ill,' he continued, 'the other can cover his work.'

A made his way wearily to the second man.

'Good morning. Can I help you?' said the second man, as if greeting him for the first time.

'I want to renew my annual Reading Room Ticket,' said A.

'Certainly. May I see your old ticket?'

'No, the other man – gentleman – has torn it up.'

'It *was* an annual ticket you had?'

'Yes. He just tore it up. Didn't you see him?'

The second man shook his head gravely. 'This is very irregular. You shouldn't have given him the ticket. He's on short-term tickets now.'

'Look, all I want is to have my ticket renewed. What does it matter which of you does it?'

'I'm afraid I can't renew a ticket which, as far as I'm concerned, doesn't exist.'

A gripped the counter tightly and closed his eyes. 'What do you suggest I do then?' he whispered hoarsely.

'I could give you a short-term ticket . . .'

'No that won't do. I'm working here every day. My livelihood depends upon my being here every day.'

'Then I can only suggest that you come back when my colleague and I have changed places again,' said the second man.

'When will that be?'

'Oh there's no telling. You can wait if you like . . .'

DAVID LODGE

Damon Runyon (1884–1946)

On Henry James

If Henry James ever keeps a speak, I am not one of his customers. I am a guy that reads more than somewhat, but Henry's merchandise is harder to take in than Good Time Charley's. And that is more than talking. Indeed, if I see one of Henry's tales coming, I haul off and walk away, because he is a guy from whom I get no literary scratch. I never give the large hello to the guys and dolls in his pieces. They have too much tongue, and however long they snow, I am not getting their drift, so what is the use of going around with them? I will only wish to poke them in the smush. There is a writing guy that says Henry is like a hippopotamus picking up a pea. That seems right to me. Let him get on with it. But me, I am no piker. I like to run around with simple, tough guys that have a guy's slant on dolls and guys. I do not care to see a guy all tangled up in his mind over a thin dime. I get sored up. So that is how Henry strikes me. I do not mind playing the chill on him like this, because he never packs a Betsy, and even if I try to cool him off he will just argue with me till I am daffy. Also he dies quite a while back. But I still wish he is never born.

ALLAN M. LAING

The Fable of the Hare and the Tortoise

It happens I am around Joe's place and how I come to be around Joe's place is this way. There is a guy called Harry the Hare known to all and sundry as the fastest runner on Broadway on account of how he has done nothing but run from the cops since he was a kid in short pants. Now Harry the Hare is to race three times round the block against a guy called Tommy the Tortoise. So Joe's place is filled with guys and dolls anxious to place money on Harry, and maybe it is good business for Joe, and maybe it isn't as nobody who is wise to Joe's whisky will have any part of it, and most of Broadway is wise to Joe's whisky these days. Harry the Hare is drinking lime juice for training, but I get straight to the bar and slip a century on Tommy at twenty to one. Well, Harry gets away to a flying start, but in the second lap he gives a little moan and drops to the ground, and before the guys with money at stake can help him up Tommy has won. Upon which there is much argument, many citizens announcing their intention of laying into Harry the Hare more than somewhat for having sold them the old phonus bolonus. Personally I collect the two thousand smackers owing to me and disappear, saying nothing of how I have doped Harry's lime juice with Joe's whisky before the race.

L. W. BAILEY

Ivy Compton-Burnett (1884–1969)

Little Brothers and Sisters

'So we were heard and not seen,' said Hector, reaching the school-room.

'It is not what children are supposed to be.'

'It is the opposite,' said Lesbia. 'We must be heard occasionally, though. It is expected of us.'

The Caistor children had been given the Christian names of rich God-parents, the richest of whom, Lesbia Chaveling, had had parents whose respect for the classics was matched by their ignorance of them. Lady Caistor regarded objections to the name as frivolous. The Chaveling fortune was large.

'Miss Wates will not let us know she heard,' said Hector. 'It is a good thing we saw her.'

'Yes. Forewarned is forearmed. Servants always listen, and governesses tell parents.'

'This one will not do so,' said Hector, at the window. 'Miss Wates is floating face down in the lake.'

'She will be seen and not heard,' said Lesbia.

MARGARET ROGERS

D. H. Lawrence (1885–1930)

On a Football-pool Winner

In the blue October twilight, she watched from behind the lace curtains of the house in Scargill Street, as his black figure came shamblingly up the path from the Bottoms. Her hands tightened on

224

the little envelope, but she thrust it deep into her apron pocket. She would not tell him yet, before he had had his supper. The corrupt breath of the flaring chrysanthemums, that stood in their cheap vase on the dark piano, stifled her in the little parlour, and she hurried out into the gas-lit kitchen. She would tell him as she rubbed his back with the warm flannel in front of the fire. Soon she heard his heavy pit boots slurring along the entry, and he stood in the doorway. There was no greeting between them. He lowered himself on to his chair and waited for her to serve him. The old flame that had burned between them, a live thing licking into the secret places of their being, was low and ashy after ten years. But he saw that she was roused, quickened about something. With his dark husband knowledge he saw it, and before he took a mouthful he asked, 'What's biting thee tonight then, ma lass?'

PETER SHELDON

The Lost Girl Trespasser

'Was it tha supped oor Quaker oats?' he asked gently.

She was ermine-white with the empty shining sky-eyes of the Western female. 'I was right clemmed,' she admitted. 'We get only half an apple each for breakfast at the Remand Home.'

'I've a hunger too, lass,' he said even more gently, laying buttercups about her nose.

'I can see something. What is it? Tha doesn't need an umbrella with tha in bedroom on such a sunny day.'

He felt the tightening in his loins, the inscrutable dark wash of male bear power flooding and ascending his hind legs and prehensile hairs, the old, old ursine urge to stand upright in dominant need for honey, older, darker than that for 'O' levels, electricity, technology or hibernation.

'He's John Thomas, lass,' he said. 'Put a little chaplet of buttercups and bluebells round the maypole for him.'

'Nay, I couldn't.'

'Why canna tha?' he asked tenderly.

'Matron said we could play with teddy-bears, but to keep off jigging bears and maypoles.'

'She sounds a right old Puritan, your matron.'

'She swears that Persil washes sheets whiter. You're lucky being a bear and not needing sheets and bed-clothes.'

There was the crash of a door and the thud of paws downstairs.

'It's me mam and dad back, god damn,' he moaned. 'They'll have my pelt if they find a human female up here with me. Quick! Through the window on to the washhouse roof. Meet me in the scouts' hut in the wood tonight. I'm a cub, so I'll teach tha how to light a fire, and tha can be my girl guide.'

GEORGE MOOR

The British Museum Reading Room

He passed through the narrow vaginal passage, and entered the huge womb of the Reading Room. Across the floor, dispersed along the radiating desks, scholars curled, foetus-like, over their books, little buds of intellectual life thrown off by some gigantic act of generation performed upon that nest of knowledge, those inexhaustible ovaries of learning, the concentric inner rings of the catalogue shelves.

The circular wall of the Reading Room wrapped the scholars in a protective layer of books, while above them arched the vast, distended belly of the dome. Little daylight entered through the grimy glass at the top. No sounds of traffic or other human business penetrated to that warm, airless space. The dome looked down on the scholars, and the scholars looked down on their books; and the scholars loved their books, stroking the pages with soft pale fingers. The pages responded to the fingers' touch, and yielded their knowledge gladly to the scholars, who collected it in little boxes of file cards. When the scholars raised their eyes from their desks they saw nothing to distract them, nothing out of harmony with their books, only the smooth, curved lining of the womb. Wherever the eye travelled, it met no arrest, no angle, no parallel lines receding into infinity, no pointed arch striving towards the unattainable: all was curved, rounded, self-sufficient, complete. And the scholars dropped their eyes to their books again, fortified and consoled. They curled themselves more tightly over their books, for they did not want to leave the warm womb, where they fed upon electric light and inhaled the musty odour of yellowing pages . . .

DAVID LODGE

Slug

A slug came to my lettuce patch
on a wet, wet day, and I in my wellies
        to the netty alfresco.
In the deep, skin-soaking shadow of the
        thunder cloud
I came down the path with my bucket
And nearly slipped, nearly slipped and fell,
        for he had slimed on the path before me.

He had crawled from a crack in the path in the night
and trailed his bright-black plumpness soft-bellied
        over, down across the edge of the stone path
and reached his head (I think it was his head) into the
        lettuce patch
and where a leaf, a green, green leaf, had sprung from
        the crown over the path (see diagram)
he nibbled through his tiny mouth (I think it was his
        mouth) into his bright black round plump body
hungrily.

Someone was before me at the toilet
and I, the second comer, waiting.
So I watched him.

The voice of my horticulture said to me,
He must be killed (the slug, that is),
for in Bradford the black black slugs are ravenous
(and so are the pink).

And voices in me said If you were a man
you would take some salt and pour it on him
        now, and finish him off.
But how I admired him, and I was honoured
        that he had come to leave his trail of slime
Across my path.
But even as I admired him
and liked him for his phlegm and his black delicacy
I felt disgusted.

Where had he come from?
Out of what pile of dirt, what pile of rotten filth
had he crept to defile my path,
my clean, my clear, my clean hard,
my clear stone path with his filthy trail?

Those voices: If you were a man you'd not wait (for the salt)
          you'd squash him.

Yet how I admired him.

Then, Go, signor, I thought.
How dare you spoil my path?
My clean, etc., path.
I will not have it.
I hated him (although I admired him) for defiling my path.

And as he moved his end into the lettuces,
I thought about my lettuces, my crisp, green lettuces,
and how I should find his progeny
under my leaves in the autumn,
his little pink progeny, like amputated tonsils,
defiling my salads,
as he was defiling my path.

So I stepped out to squash him.
I stepped forward to put my boot on him,
my big, black boot.
I put my boot at his black blob of defilement.

No, I said,
Non, Nein, Niet.
I shall not let you defile my path,
my clean, clear, hard stone path.
And I brought my boot down on him.
I brought it down on his shiny darkness.
And he spread over the path,
my clean, clear, hard stone path.

He spread like a star,
spread like a dark, wet star,
or a meringue.

How I admired him.

And immediately I regretted it.
I thought how petty, how petty and paltry and sweaty
      and salty
was his little wet life,
dispersed under my welligog.
I felt as defiled as if I had eaten him.

So I missed my chance at the toilet
(for a third comer had passed me down the path –
how I hated him) by killing a slug.
And I have something to eradicate –
A sogginess.

ANDREW STIBBS

Ezra Pound (1885–1972)

Another Canto

Monsieur Ezra Pound croit que
By using foreign words
He will persuade the little freaks
Who call themselves intellectuals
To believe that he is saying
Quelque chose très deep, ma foi!

J. B. MORTON ('BEACHCOMBER')

Siegfried Sassoon (1886–1967)

Initial Poem

Some morning, far from shrieking guns,
Inspired to attack the Huns,
Egged on by staff they never saw,
Gallant lads went off to war.

'Fine chaps,' the Major-General said,
'Recruits who'll fight until they're dead.'
In England's shires, tending cattle,
Earnest uncles fought their battle.

Drowned and gassed, and doused by rain,
Some were never seen again;
A boy of eighteen, cold and wet,
Slithered from the parapet.

So, stand and cheer, you hypocrites,
Over bodies blown to bits,
Obedient to your marching hymns,
Newly home with missing limbs.

BILL GREENWELL

Dame Edith Sitwell (1887–1964)

Contours

Round – oblong – like jam –
Terse as virulent hermaphrodites;
Calling across the sodden twisted ends of Time.

Edifices of importunity
Sway like Parmesan before the half-tones
Of Episcopalian Michaelmas;
Bodies are so impossible to see in retrospect –
And yet I know the well of truth
Is gutted like pratchful Unicorn.
Sog, sog, sog – why is my mind amphibious?
That's what it is.

SIR NOËL COWARD

Sunday Morning at Wiesbaden

I sometimes think that shrimps and sprats
Should wear enormous Homburg hats,
And swim about with cricket bats
  Suspended from their ears.

Importunate the rolling downs,
Like very rude provincial clowns,
In knitted Jaeger dressing-gowns
  Upon the ends of piers.

SIR NOËL COWARD

The Three Calenders

I

Rhinoceros-glum
The tramcars come
With a quick bastinado
To shake the façado
Of the stout riverado,
And
Simpering simian viziers stare
Through the zebraed gloom in the thick furred air
Of the blue bandanaed,
Unzenanaed
Come-away-and-let's-get-a-ripe-bananaed
Strand.

Canned
Peaches are sold and peppermint drops,
But the West Ham motor-bus never stops.
Don Magnifico down in hell
Dances the shimmy-shake really well;
Te-he, tittering, sighs Mamzelle
To the bland
Titanesque, picaresque
Young clerk from the desk
Where the light creaks soft under rose-petalled trellises,
Bought it for ninepence at Simpson & Ellis's,
'Ain't the band
Sumfin' grand?'

II

The fluted plasters of the sky
Come off in long grey strips to try

And snare the clockwork birds like fish
(Fat carp with feathers). No winds swish

Our faces, peering under hats
As we walk home from Wanstead Flats;

Long lines of lamp-posts tulip-stark
Wave beards of light that flap the dark.

Mamzelle insists this is not so,
Yet were we two alone, I know,

On Wanstead Flats, unfurred by fear,
With no wood-carved policeman near,

Mamzelle would break away from me
And climb these tall posts gingerly,

And seize the tender gas-flame buds
And bite them off and chew their cuds,

As cows digest fruit-hairy Springs:
Mamzelle does most *peculiar* things.

When
  Dan Mephistopheles cursed at his coffee-lees
    Down in Gehenna –
    He swore they were senna
    (But the barmaid cried 'Go hon'),
  Alfred Lord Tennyson, eating cold venison
  Granting his benison, roared to each denizen,
    Rat-faced professor and don,
  That the inquisitorial Albert Memorial
  (Madam Queen Venus uplifted on horsehair
     but where was the corsair?
  Why ruling the waves of a pantomime sea)
    Was gone.
    Break, break, break;
    But free,
    And wholly audacious
    And quite contumacious
  And squirting some pomegranate juice in the eye
    Of Methuselah's ape as it fox-trots by
  On the rim of the hippopotamus sky
  Where the nightingale (stuffed) lets her singing die,
    Are we.

E. V. KNOX

T. S. Eliot (1888–1965)

Chard Whitlow

Mr Eliot's Sunday Evening Postscript

As we get older we do not get any younger.
Seasons return, and to-day I am fifty-five,
And this time last year I was fifty-four,
And this time next year I shall be sixty-two.
And I cannot say I should like (to speak for myself)
To see my time over again – if you can call it time:

Fidgeting uneasily under a draughty stair,
Or counting sleepless nights in the crowded tube.

There are certain precautions – though none of them very reliable –
Against the blast from bombs and the flying splinter,
But not against the blast from heaven, *vento dei venti*,
The wind within a wind unable to speak for wind;
And the frigid burnings of purgatory will not be touched –
By any emollient.
                I think you will find this put,
Better than I could ever hope to express it,
In the words of Kharma: 'It is, we believe,
Idle to hope that the simple stirrup-pump
Will extinguish hell.'
                Oh, listeners,
And you especially who have turned off the wireless,
And sit in Stoke or Basingstoke listening appreciatively to the
    silence,
(Which is also the silence of hell) pray, not for your skins, but your
    souls.
And pray for me also under the draughty stair.
As we get older we do not get any younger.

And pray for Kharma under the holy mountain.

HENRY REED

A Letter to Harriet Weaver, in the Style of *The Waste Land*

Rouen is the rainiest place getting
Inside all impermeables, wetting
Damp marrow in drenched bones.
Midwinter soused us coming over Le Mans
Our inn at Niort was the Grape of Burgundy
But the winepress of the Lord thundered over that
        grape of Burgundy
And we left it in a hurgundy.
  (Hurry up, Joyce, it's time!)

I heard mosquitoes swarm in old Bordeaux
So many!
I had not thought the earth contained so many
  (Hurry up, Joyce, it's time)

Mr Anthologos, the local gardener,
Greycapped, with politeness full of cunning
Has made wine these fifty years
And told me in his southern French
Le petit vin is the surest drink to buy
For if 'tis bad
Vous ne l'avez pas payé
  (Hurry up, hurry up, now, now, now!)

But we shall have great times,
When we return to Clinic, that waste land
O Esculapios!
  (Shan't we? Shan't we? Shan't we?)

JAMES JOYCE

The Picnic Land

Here I am, an old man with a dry mouth,
Bitten by flies among the cow-pats,
Eating dead winkles with a crooked pin.
And the end is the beginning, and tomorrow
It will be wasps at Runnymede. Last week
Lil had hysterics, throwing sandwiches
In the damp woods after a hard night's rain.
Here, on the waste ground behind the gasworks,
Gulls wheel and flock in the grey sky
Like the stones beneath an old man's bony buttocks.
I ache, much of the time, and long for winter.
O Vishnu, Vishnu, (atishoo! atishoo!) – Lord,
Grant me a little peace before I die!
    Mub! Eros! Llareggub!

J. A. LINDON

from The Eumenides at Home

It does not worry me that this verse has three stresses,
Why shouldn't it since the glass in my car is triplex?
One must move with the times,
As the old maid said in the musical comedy
On meeting a young gent Oxonianly debagged.
Nor does it worry me that this verse does not tinkle.
I do not expect modern art to sound nice,
Or even to look nice.
I am not alarmed because a horse by Chirico bears no resemblance
   to one by Solario.
Or perturbed when Hindemith sounds like somebody shooting
   coals.
Or distressed when a block of luxury flats looks like a ship or a
   warehouse.
That the pretty-pretty should give place to the ferro-concrete
Is just the age expressing itself.
What does worry me about this play is something altogether differ-
   ent –
The sneaking suspicion that I may not be intellectually up to it.
'*Il est si facile,*' said Balzac, '*de nier ce que l'on ne comprend pas.*'
Meaning that the fool sees not the same tree that the wise man sees.
Perhaps it might be easier if I had the Eumenides nearer my finger-
   tips,
In which case I should know whether moaning becomes Agatha as
   mourning became Electra.
Before it all opened the Dowager Lady Amy lost her husband,
A good easy man, who bred pigs and took
Prizes and even championships at the local shows,
But had a kink, which was to do his lady in.
(Pass the expression: *Pygmalion* uses it.)
And in his nefarious design would have succeeded
But that his sister-in-law, the aforesaid Agatha,
Rumbled him.
Quoth Aggie to herself:
'Amy's with child; otherwise 'twere quate all reaight!'
And used her power of veto.

The child was born, called Harry, grew up, married,
And every evening plotted wife-deletion. One day
On a cruise convenient for the purpose, the moon lanthorn,
And nobody on deck but just the two of them,
He did as he had planned, pleaded accident, and then
Repaired to the ancestral home,
To talk the matter over with Aunt Agatha, who –
Here out of bag comes cat –
Wished that her nephew had been her son,
And that, it seems, is exactly what was biting her,
Though what was biting him it was very hard to tell,
Except that whatever it was it wasn't murder.
Something, perhaps, about the truth of opposites,
How sleeping's waking, event not happening (or vice versa),
Nothing is changed except the status quo and a lot more
Of Mr Polly's Sesquippledan Verboojuice!

CHORUS
Twice two are four
But twice three are not five
Cows neigh in the byre
Herb-o'-grace looks for Sunday
Octaves wilt
Fifths grow consecutive
Moon and green cheese
Have come to terms
Fog horns summon
The household to supper
The bones of the majordomo
Rap out curses
Methylated spirits
Wait round the corner.

JAMES AGATE

Sweeney Aesthetic

In the room the women come and go/Talking of Michelangelo – 'The Love Song of J. Alfred Prufrock'

DORIS: Why, it's Lou.
MRS PORTER: Oh, it's Lou.
DORIS: We thought it was Pereira.
MAY: We were afraid it was Pereira.
MME SOSOSTRIS: We were just making tea.
MRS PORTER: And talking of Michelangelo.
LOU: You don't want Pereira?
DORIS: Nobody wants Pereira.
MME SOSOSTRIS: Except to pay the rent.
LOU: Pereira pays the rent?
DORIS: Well, yes, that's true.
LOU: But what's this about Michelangelo?
MAY: I must be going. I have to get
          My hair dyed and set.
MME SOSOSTRIS: Pereira can do hair. Did you know
                    He had a broken nose?
LOU: Pereira has a broken nose?
MRS PORTER: No, not Pereira, Michelangelo.
MAY: I must be going. Well, goo'bye all.
     (*Exit.*)
MME SOSOSTRIS: A boy broke it in a fight.
MRS PORTER: Pereira is fond of boys.
     (*Enter* LIL.)
LOU: Hullo, Lil. Did you know
          Pereira was fond of boys?
LIL: Pereira likes women too.
MME SOSOSTRIS: Pereira will always do
                    Any woman's hair
                    For a consideration. Can you spare
                    Just half a cup? Well, then,
                    I'll slip along.
MRS PORTER: I'm coming too. Goo'bye.
     (*Exeunt.*)

238

LOU: Goo'bye.
DORIS: Goo'bye.
LOU: I like to talk
        Of cultured things. Why, Lil, you look
        A picture in your teeth.

                    J. A. LINDON

McQuiddity

McQuiddity, McQuiddity, there's no one like McQuiddity,
His errors are so vulgar and so coarse in their solidity;
You may walk along the pavement, you may step upon the stair –
It's odorously evident McQuiddity's been there.

McQuiddity, McQuiddity, there's no one like McQuiddity,
He doesn't know the meaning of decorum or timidity;
He barks at friends and neighbours and will give the boss a scare,
But when burglars cart the silver off he doesn't turn a hair.

If you stagger through a doorway with an overloaded tray
You can bet that old McQuiddity is lying in the way;
If chocolates vanish overnight, or gloves vacate a chair,
Then it's absolutely certain that McQuiddity's been there . . .

McQuiddity, McQuiddity, there's no one like McQuiddity,
He's totally unrivalled in the depth of his stupidity;
His canine infelicities no cretin could surpass,
And he's undisputed champion of the Disobedience Class.

                    MARY HOLTBY

The Pooch

I have an old jet Podger Pooch, his name is Jellywobblechow
Around the garden he will mooch, as slow and placid as a cow.
Soon he will flop and fall asleep, then lumber up again, and mooch;
He's either sleeping or he's slow – and that's what makes a Podger
    Pooch.

But though he may amble so fatly, and snore
So long on his mat by the cool of the door,
His fuddled old brain runs the reel of his prime
Of bold derring-do and depraved doggy crime.
His bleary old eye sees as clear as it did
His puppyhood pranks and the slippers he hid,
And the nose in his head wrinkles moistly and black,
Bringing many cats' bottoms deliciously back.

I have an old jet Podger Pooch, his name is Jellywobblechow.
He likes a little drop of hooch – a saucer*ful* I don't allow.
For he will try to frisk, and fall, and snore, then up again and
    mooch:
He's either sleeping or he's slow – and that's what makes a Podger
    Pooch.

J. A. LINDON

Katherine Mansfield (1888–1923)

A Football-pool Winner

But I didn't even *choose* them! shrieked Clara silently. A few random
crosses on a piece of paper, and hey presto! a cheque for one hundred
thousand pounds was pressed into her hand. ('No really – I must

confess, I did it with my eyes shut!') Yet here it was, a real cheque, not to mention the fifty-three letters, the idiotic telegrams from people she hadn't spoken to for years, and heavens above! the newspapers – that awful, simpering photograph ripped out, of all things, from a *hockey* group! Surely the world had gone quite mad. She rushed into the window, fearing shattered houses and a people fled . . . A milk bottle squatted on every doorstep, and the black-and-white cat opposite was placidly laundering his chest. She felt it was all some terrible mistake. It's no use – her mouth opened – we must send it back! But before the words could escape, another thought winged out without so much as an excuse-me: Could we really, now, afford to buy a *whole* island? One hand, aghast, flew to her mouth, but she gazed enraptured across the breakfast table. Breathing a little heavily, totally absorbed, Bill had not heard her (perhaps she didn't really say it). He went on stroking the glossy pages of one of the seventeen television catalogues . . .

MARGARET TIMS

Raymond Chandler (1888–1959)

Mr Big

I was sitting in my office, cleaning the debris out of my thirty-eight and wondering where my next case was coming from. I like being a private eye, and even though once in a while I've had my gums massaged with an automobile jack, the sweet smell of greenbacks makes it all worth it. Not to mention the dames, which are a minor preoccupation of mine that I rank just ahead of breathing. That's why, when the door to my office swung open and a long-haired blonde named Heather Butkiss came striding in and told me she was a nudie model and needed my help, my salivary glands shifted into third. She wore a short skirt and a tight sweater and her figure described a set of parabolas that could cause cardiac arrest in a yak.

'What can I do for you, sugar?'

'I want you to find someone for me.'

'Missing person? Have you tried the police?'

'Not exactly, Mr Lupowitz.'

'Call me Kaiser, sugar. All right, so what's the scam?'

'God.'

'God?'

'That's right, God. The Creator, the Underlying Principle, the First Cause of Things, the All Encompassing. I want you to find Him for me.'

I've had some fruit cakes up in the office before, but when they're built like she was, you listened.

'Why?'

'That's my business, Kaiser, you just find Him.'

'I'm sorry, sugar. You got the wrong boy.'

'But why?'

'Unless I know all the facts,' I said, rising.

'OK, OK,' she said, biting her lower lip. She straightened the seam of her stocking, which was strictly for my benefit, but I wasn't buying any at the moment.

'Let's have it on the line, sugar.'

'Well, the truth is – I'm not really a nudie model.'

'No?'

'No. My name is not Heather Butkiss, either. It's Claire Rosensweig and I'm a student at Vassar. Philosophy major. History of Western Thought and all that. I have a paper due January. On Western religion. All the other kids in the course will hand in speculative papers. But I want to *know*. Professor Grebanier said if anyone finds out for sure, they're a cinch to pass the course. And my dad's promised me a Mercedes if I get straight As.'

I opened a deck of Luckies and a pack of gum and had one of each. Her story was beginning to interest me. Spoiled co-ed. High IQ and a body I wanted to know better.

'What does God look like?'

'I've never seen Him.'

'Well, how do you know He exists?'

'That's for you to find out.'

'Oh, great. Then you don't know what He looks like? Or where to begin looking?'

'No. Not really. Although I suspect He's everywhere. In the air, in every flower, in you and I – and in this chair.'

'Uh huh.' So she was a pantheist. I made a mental note of it and said I'd give her case a try – for a hundred bucks a day, expenses, and a dinner date. She smiled and okayed the deal. We rode down in the elevator together. Outside it was getting dark. Maybe God did exist and maybe He didn't, but somewhere in that city there were sure a lot of guys who were going to try and keep me from finding out.

My first lead was Rabbi Itzhak Wiseman, a local cleric who owed me a favour for finding out who was rubbing pork on his hat. I knew something was wrong when I spoke to him because he was scared. Real scared.

'Of course there's a you-know-what, but I'm not even allowed to say His name or He'll strike me dead, which I could never understand why someone is so touchy about having His name said.'

'You ever see Him?'

'Me? Are you kidding? I'm lucky I get to see my grandchildren.'

'Then how do you know He exists?'

'How do I know? What kind of question is that? Could I get a suit like this for fourteen dollars if there was no one up there? Here, feel a garbardine – how can you doubt?'

'You got nothing more to go on?'

'Hey – what's the Old Testament? Chopped liver? How do you think Moses got the Israelites out of Egypt? With a smile and a tap dance? Believe me, you don't part the Red Sea with some gismo from Korvette's. It takes power.'

'So He's tough, eh?'

'Yes, very tough. You'd think with all that success He'd be a lot sweeter.'

'How come you know so much?'

'Because we're the chosen people. He takes best care of us of all His children, which I'd also like to someday discuss with Him.'

'What do you pay Him for being chosen?'

'Don't ask.'

So that's how it was. The Jews were into God for a lot. It was the old protection racket. Take care of them in return for a price. And from the way Rabbi Wiseman was talking, He soaked them plenty. I got into a cab and made it over to Danny's Billiards on Tenth Avenue. The manager was a slimy little guy I didn't like.

'Chicago Phil here?'

'Who wants to know?'

I grabbed him by the lapels and took some skin at the same time.

'What, punk?'

'In the back,' he said, with a change of attitude.

Chicago Phil. Forger, bank robber, strong-arm man, and avowed atheist.

'The guy never existed, Kaiser. This is the straight dope. It's a big hype. There's no Mr Big. It's a syndicate. Mostly Sicilian. It's international. But there is no actual head. Except maybe the Pope.'

'I want to meet the Pope.'

'It can be arranged,' he said, winking.

'Does the name Claire Rosensweig mean anything to you?'

'No.'

'Heather Butkiss?'

'Oh, wait a minute. Sure. She's that peroxide job with the bazooms from Radcliffe.'

'Radcliffe? She told me Vassar.'

'Well, she's lying. She's a teacher at Radcliffe. She was mixed up with a philosopher for a while.'

'Pantheist?'

'No. Empiricist, as I remember. Bad guy. Completely rejected Hegel or any dialectical methodology.'

'One of those.'

'Yeah, he used to be a drummer with a jazz trio. Then he got hooked up on Logical Positivism. When that didn't work, he tried Pragmatism. Last I heard he stole a lot of money to take a course in Schopenhauer at Columbia. The mob would like to find him – or get their hands on his textbooks so they can resell them.'

'Thanks, Phil.'

'Take it from me, Kaiser. There's no one out there. It's a void. I couldn't pass all those bad checks or screw society the way I do if for one second I was able to recognize any authentic sense of Being. The universe is strictly phenomenological. Nothin's eternal. It's all meaningless.'

'Who won the fifth at Aqueduct?'

'Santa Baby.'

I had a beer at O'Rourke's and tried to add it all up, but it made no sense at all. Socrates was a suicide – or so they said. Christ was murdered. Nietzsche went nuts. If there was someone out there, He sure as hell didn't want anybody to know it. And why was Claire Rosensweig lying about Vassar? Could Descartes have been right? Was the universe dualistic? Or did Kant hit it on the head when he postulated the existence of God on moral grounds?

That night I had dinner with Claire. Ten minutes after the check came, we were in the sack and, brother, you can have your Western thought. She went through the kind of gymnastics that would have won first prize in the Tia Juana Olympics. After, she lay on the pillow next to me, her long blond hair sprawling. Our naked bodies still intertwined. I was smoking and staring at the ceiling.

'Claire, what if Kierkegaard's right?'

'You mean?'

'If you can never really *know*. Only have faith.'

'That's absurd.'

'Don't be so rational.'

'Nobody's being rational, Kaiser.' She lit a cigarette. 'Just don't get ontological. Not now. I couldn't bear it if you were ontological with me.'

She was upset. I leaned over and kissed her, and the phone rang. She got it.

'It's for you.'

The voice on the other end was Sergeant Reed of Homicide.

'You still looking for God?'

'Yeah.'

'An all-powerful Being? Great Oneness, Creator of the Universe? First Cause of All Things?'

'That's right.'

'Somebody with that description just showed up at the morgue. You better get down here right away.'

It was Him all right, and from the looks of Him it was a professional job.

'He was dead when they brought Him in.'

'Where'd you find Him?'

'A warehouse on Delancey Street.'

'Any clues?'

'It's the work of an existentialist. We're sure of that.'

'How can you tell?'

'Haphazard way how it was done. Doesn't seem to be any system followed. Impulse.'

'A crime of passion?'

'You got it. Which means you're a suspect, Kaiser.'

'Why me?'

'Everybody down at headquarters knows how you feel about Jaspers.'

'That doesn't make me a killer.'

'Not yet, but you're a suspect.'

Outside on the street I sucked air into my lungs and tried to clear my head. I took a cab over to Newark and got out and walked a block to Giordiano's Italian Restaurant. There, at a back table, was His Holiness. It was the Pope, all right. Sitting with two guys I had seen in half-a-dozen police line-ups.

'Sit down,' he said, looking up from his fettucine. He held out a ring. I gave him my toothiest smile, but didn't kiss it. It bothered him and I was glad. Point for me.

'Would you like some fettucine?'

'No thanks, Holiness. But you go ahead.'

'Nothing? Not even a salad?'

'I just ate.'

'Suit yourself, but they make a great Roquefort dressing here. Not like at the Vatican, where you can't get a decent meal.'

'I'll come right to the point, Pontiff. I'm looking for God.'

'You came to the right person.'

'Then He does exist?' They all found this very amusing and laughed. The hood next to me said, 'Oh, that's funny. Bright boy wants to know if He exists.'

I shifted my chair to get comfortable and brought the leg down on his little toe. 'Sorry.' But he was steaming.

'Sure He exists, Lupowitz, but I'm the only one that communicates with him. He speaks only through me.'

'Why you, pal?'

'Because I got the red suit.'

'This get-up?'

'Don't knock it. Every morning I rise, put on this red suit, and suddenly I'm a big cheese. It's all in the suit. I mean, face it, if I went around in slacks and a sports jacket, I couldn't get arrested religionwise.'

'Then it's a hype. There's no God.'

'I don't know. But what's the difference? The money's good.'

'You ever worry the laundry won't get your red suit back on time and you'll be like the rest of us?'

'I use the special one-day service. I figure it's worth the extra few cents to be safe.'

'Name Claire Rosensweig mean anything to you?'

'Sure. She's in the science department at Bryn Mawr.'

'Science, you say? Thanks.'

'For what?'

'The answer, Pontiff.' I grabbed a cab and shot over the George Washington Bridge. On the way I stopped at my office and did some fast checking. Driving to Claire's apartment, I put the pieces together, and for the first time they fit. When I got there she was in a diaphanous peignoir and something seemed to be troubling her.

'God is dead. The police were here. They're looking for you. They think an existentialist did it.'

'No, sugar. It was you.'

'What? Don't make jokes, Kaiser.'

'It was you that did it.'

'What are you saying?'

'You baby. Not Heather Butkiss or Claire Rosensweig, but Doctor Ellen Shepherd.'

'How did you know my name?'

'Professor of physics at Bryn Mawr. The youngest one ever to head a department there. At the mid-winter hop you get stuck on a jazz musician who's heavily into philosophy. He's married, but that doesn't stop you. A couple of nights in the hay and it feels like love. But it doesn't work out because something comes between you. God. Y'see, sugar, he believed, or wanted to, but you, with your pretty little scientific mind, had to have absolute certainty.'

'No, Kaiser, I swear.'

'So you pretend to study philosophy because that gives you a chance to eliminate certain obstacles. You get rid of Socrates easy enough, but Descartes takes over, so you use Spinoza to get rid of Descartes, but when Kant doesn't come through you have to get rid of him too.'

'You don't know what you're saying.'

'You made mince-meat out of Leibnitz, but that wasn't good enough for you because you knew if anybody believed Pascal you were dead, so he had to be gotten rid of too, but that's where you made your mistake because you trusted Martin Buber. Except, sugar, he was soft. He believed in God, so you had to get rid of God yourself.'

'Kaiser, you're mad!'

'No, baby. You posed as a pantheist and that gave you access to Him – *if* He existed, which He did. He went with you to Shelby's party and when Jason wasn't looking, you killed Him.'

'Who the hell are Shelby and Jason?'

'What's the difference? Life's absurd now anyway.'

'Kaiser,' she said, suddenly trembling. 'You wouldn't turn me in?'

'Oh yes, baby. When the Supreme Being gets knocked off, *somebody's* got to take the rap.'

'Oh, Kaiser, we could go away together. Just the two of us. We could forget about philosophy. Settle down and maybe get into semantics.'

'Sorry, sugar. It's no dice.'

She was all tears now as she started lowering the shoulder straps of her peignoir and I was standing there suddenly with a naked Venus whose whole body seemed to be saying, take me – I'm yours. A Venus whose right hand had picked up a forty-five and was holding it behind my back. I let go with a slug from my thirty-eight before she could pull the trigger, and she dropped her gun and doubled over in disbelief.

'How could you, Kaiser?'

She was fading fast, but I managed to get it in, in time.

'The manifestation of the universe as a complex idea unto itself as opposed to being in or outside the true Being of itself is inherently a conceptual nothingness or Nothingness in relation to any abstract form of existing or to exist or having existed in perpetuity to laws of physicality or motion or ideas relating to non-matter or the lack of objective Being or subjective otherness.'

It was a subtle concept but I think she understood before she died.

WOODY ALLEN

Wilfred Owen (1893–1918)

A Third World War Poem

What passing words for these stacked up as chattels?
    – Only the silence of ten searing suns.
    – Only the muttering wireless' chat of battles
Is stammering out some sum of megatons.
No saccharine speech – they have no hair, no balls,
    Nor had they word of warning, just the fires,
    The whirling, white-hot fires which melted walls;
Now shovels shift some bits for massive pyres.

What petrol may be found to burn them all?
    Not from the North Sea fields shall come the gas
To brighten up the last appalling Mass.
    The acid, crass old lies are now their gall;
Their only trace shall be some blackened rind;
Their last trump one charred fart from God's behind.

BILL GREENWELL

e. e. cummings (1894–1962)

poets

poets have their ear to the ground more than most people
if only because more than most they are beating their heads
against it
thus, Mad
        ame,
every true artist is a p
                 i
                 o
                 neer
eliot was streamlining in 1912
dali's limp watches ant
                     icipated cheeseburgers
  and I burr
        o
        k
        e the ground for S
                 c
                 r
                 a
                 b
                 b
                 l
                 e

PETER DE VRIES

Aldous Huxley (1894–1963)

from Told in Gath

Vulgarity is the garlic in the salad of charm – St Bumpus

It was to be a long weekend, thought Giles Pentateuch apprehensively, as the menial staggered up the turret stairs with his luggage – staggered all the more consciously for the knowledge that he was under observation, just as, back in Lexham Gardens, his own tyrannical Amy would snort and groan outside the door to show how steep the backstairs were, before entering with his simple vegetarian breakfast of stinkwort and boiled pond weed. A long weekend; but a weekend at Groyne! And he realized, with his instinct for merciless analysis that amounted almost to torture, that in spite, yes, above all, in spite of the apprehension, because of it even, he would enjoy all the more saying afterwards, to his friend Luke Snarthes perhaps, or to little Reggie Ringworm, 'Yes, I was at Groyne last weekend,' or 'Yes, I was there when the whole thing started, down at Groyne.'

The menial had paused and was regarding him. To tip or not to tip? How many times had he not been paralysed by that problem? To tip was to give in, yes, selfishly to give in to his hatred of human contacts, to contribute half a crown as hush money, to obtain 'protection', protection from other people, so that for a little he could go on with the luxury of being Giles Pentateuch, 'scatologist and eschatologist', as he dubbed himself. Whereas not to tip . . .

For a moment he hesitated. What would Luke Snarthes have done? Stayed at home, with that splayed ascetic face of his, or consulted his guru, Chandra Nandra? No – no tip! The menial slunk away. He looked round the room. It was comfortable, he had to admit; a few small Longhis round the walls, a Lupanar by Guido Guidi, and over the bed an outsize Stupruj Sabinarum, by Rubens – civilized people, his hosts, evidently.

He glanced at the books on the little table – the *Odes of Horace*, Rome, 23 BC, apparently a first edition, the *Elegancies of Meursius* (Rochester's copy), *The Piccadilly Ambulator, The Sufferings of Saint*

Rose of Lima, *Nostradamus* (the Lérins Press), *Swedenborg*, *The Old Man's Gita*. 'And cultivated,' he murmured, 'too.' The bathroom, with its sun lamp and Plombières apparatus, was such as might be found in any sensible therapeutic home. He went down to tea considerably refreshed by his lavage.

The butler announced that Lady Rhomboid was 'serving' on the small west lawn, and he made his way over the secular turf with genuine pleasure. For Minnie Rhomboid was a remarkable woman.

'How splendid of you to come,' she croaked, for she had lost her voice in the old suffragette days. 'You know my daughter, Ursula Groyne.'

'Only too well,' laughed Giles, for they had been what his set at Balliol used to call 'lovers'.

'And Mrs Amp, of course?'

'Of course!'

'And Mary Pippin?'

'Decidedly,' he grimaced.

'And the men,' she went on, 'Giles Pentateuch – this is Luke Snarthes and Reggie Ringworm and Mr Encolpius and Roland Narthex. Pentateuch writes – let me see? – like a boot, isn't it?' (Her voice was a husky roar.) 'Yes, a boot with a mission! Oh, but I forgot' – and she laughed delightedly – 'you're all writers!'

'*Encantado*, I'm sure!' responded Giles. 'But we've all met before. I see you have the whole Almanach de Golgotha in fact,' he added.

Mary Pippin, whose arm had been eaten away by termites in Tehuantepec, was pouring out with her free hand. 'Orange Pekoe or *Chandu*, Giles?' she burbled in her delicious little voice. 'Like a carrier pigeon's,' he thought.

'*Chandu*, please.' And she filled him a pipe of the consoling poppy, so that in a short while he was smoking away like all the others.

'Yes, yes,' continued Mr Encolpius, in his oily voice which rose and fell beneath the gently moving tip of his nose, 'Man axolotl here below but I ask very little. Some fragments of Pamphylides, a Choctaw blood-mask, the prose of Scaliger the Elder, a painting by Fuseli, an occasional visit to the all-in wrestling, or to my meretrix; a cook who can produce a passable '*poulet à la Khmer*', a Pong vase. Simple tastes, you will agree, and it is my simple habit to indulge them!'

Giles regarded him with fascination. That nose, it was, yes, it was definitely a proboscis . . .

'But how can you, how can you?' It was Ursula Groyne. 'How *can* you when there are two million unemployed, when Russia has reintroduced anti-abortionary legislation, when Iceland has banned *Time and Tide*, when the Sedition Bill hangs over us all like a rubber truncheon?'

Mary Pippin cooed delightedly; this was intellectual life with a vengeance – definately haybrow – only it was so difficult to know who was right. Giles, at that moment, found her infinitely desirable.

CYRIL CONNOLLY

William Faulkner (1897–1962)

Requiem for a Noun, *or* Intruder in the Dusk

The cold Brussels sprout rolled off the page of the book I was reading and lay inert and defunctive in my lap. Turning my head with a leisure at least three-fourths impotent rage, I saw him standing there holding the toy with which he had catapulted the vegetable, or rather the reverse, the toy first then the fat insolent fist clutching it and then above that the bland defiant face beneath the shock of black hair like tangible gas. It, the toy, was one of those cardboard funnels with a trigger near the point for firing a small celluloid ball. Letting the cold Brussels sprout lie there in my lap for him to absorb or anyhow apprehend rebuke from, I took a pull at a Scotch highball I had had in my hand and then set it down on the end table beside me.

'So instead of losing the shooter which would have been a mercy you had to lose the ball,' I said, fixing with a stern eye what I had fathered out of all sentient and biding dust; remembering with that retroactive memory by which we count chimes seconds and even minutes after they have struck (recapitulate, even, the very grinding of the bowels of the clock before and during and after) the cunning furtive click, clicks rather, which perception should have told me then already were not the trigger plied but the icebox opened. 'Even a boy of five going on six should have more respect for his father if not for food,' I said, now picking the cold Brussels sprout out of my lap and setting it – not dropping it, setting it – in an ashtray; thinking how across the wax bland treachery of the kitchen linoleum were now in all likelihood distributed the remnants of string beans and cold potatoes and maybe even tapioca. 'You're no son of mine.'

I took up the thread of the book again or tried to: the weft of legitimate kinship that was intricate enough without the obbligato of that dark other: the sixteenths and thirty-seconds and even sixty-fourths of dishonouring cousinships brewed out of the violable blood by the ineffaceable errant lusts. Then I heard another click; a faint metallic rejoinder that this time was neither the trigger nor the icebox but the front door opened and then shut. Through the window I saw him picking his way over the season's soiled and sun-frayed vestiges of snow like shreds of rotted lace, the cheap upended toy cone in one hand and a child's cardboard suitcase in the other, toward the road.

I dropped the book and went out after him who had forgotten not only that I was in shirtsleeves but that my braces hung down over my flanks in twin festoons. 'Where are you going?' I called, my voice expostulant and forlorn on the warm numb air. Then I caught it: caught it in the succinct outrage of the suitcase and the prim churning rear and marching heels as well: I had said he was no son of mine, and so he was leaving a house not only where he was not wanted but where he did not even belong.

'I see,' I said in that shocked clarity with which we perceive the truth instantaneous and entire out of the very astonishment that refuses to acknowledge it. 'Just as you now cannot be sure of any roof you belong more than half under, you figure there is no housetop from which you might not as well begin to shout it. Is that it?'

Something was trying to tell me something. Watching him turn off on the road – and that not only with the ostensible declaration of vagabondage but already its very assumption, attaining as though with a single footfall the very apotheosis of wandering just as with a single shutting of a door he had that of renunciation and farewell – watching him turn off on it, the road, in the direction of the Per-misangs', our nearest neighbours, I thought *Wait; no; what I said was not enough for him to leave the house on; it must have been the blurted inscrutable chance confirmation of something he already knew, and was half able to assess, either out of the blown facts of boyhood or pure male divination or both.*

'What is it you know?' I said springing forward over the delicate squalor of the snow and falling in beside the boy. 'Does any man come to the house to see your mother when I'm away, that you know of?' Thinking *We are mocked, first by the old mammalian snare, then, snared, by the final unilaterality of all flesh to which birth is given; not only not knowing when we may be cuckolded, but not even sure that in the veins of the very bantling we dandle does not flow the miscreant sniggering wayward blood.*

'I get it now,' I said, catching in the undeviating face just as I had in the prim back and marching heels the steady articulation of disdain. 'Cuckoldry is something of which the victim may be as guilty as the wrong-doers. That's what you're thinking? That by letting in this taint upon our heritage I am as accountable as she or they who have been its actual avatars. More. Though the foe may survive, the sleeping sentinel must be shot. Is that it?'

'You talk funny.'

Mother-and-daughter blood conspires in the old mammalian office. Father-and-son blood vies in the ancient phallic enmity. I caught him by the arm and we scuffled in the snow. 'I will be heard,' I said holding him now as though we might be dancing, my voice intimate and furious against the furious sibilance of our feet in the snow. Thinking how revelation had to be inherent in the very vegetable scraps to which venery was probably that instant contriving to abandon me, the cold boiled despair of whatever already featureless suburban Wednesday Thursday or Saturday supper the shot green was the remainder. 'I see another thing,' I panted, cursing my helplessness to curse whoever it was had given him blood and wind. Thinking *He's glad; glad to credit what is always secretly fostered and fermented out of the vats of childhood fantasy anyway (for all childhood must conceive a substitute for the father that has conceived it; finding that other unconceivable?)*; thinking *He is walking in a nursery fairy tale to find the king his sire.* 'Just as I said to you "You're no son of mine" so now you answer back "Neither are you any father to me."'

The scherzo of violence ended as abruptly as it had begun. He broke away and walked on, after retrieving the toy he had dropped and adjusting his grip on the suitcase which he had not, this time faster and more urgently.

The last light was seeping out of the shabby sky, after the haemorrhage of sunset. High in the west where the fierce constellations soon would wheel, the evening star in single bombast burned and burned. The boy passed the Permisangs' without going in, then passed the Kellers'. Maybe he's heading for the McCullums', I thought, but he passed their house too. Then he, we, neared the Jelliffs'. He's got to be going there, his search will end there, I thought. Because that was the last house this side of the tracks. And because *something was trying to tell me something*.

'Were you maybe thinking of what you heard said about Mrs Jelliff and me having relations in Spuyten Duyvil?' I said in rapid frantic speculation. 'But they were talking about mutual kin – nothing else.' The boy said nothing. But I had sensed it instant and complete: the boy felt that, whatever of offence his mother may or may not have given, his father had given provocation; and out of the old embattled malehood, it was the hairy ineluctable Him whose guilt and shame he was going to hold preponderant. *Because now I remembered.*

'So it's Mrs Jelliff – Sue Jelliff – and me you have got this all mixed up with,' I said, figuring he must, in that fat sly nocturnal stealth that took him creeping up and down the stairs to listen when he should have been in bed, certainly have heard his mother exclaiming to his father behind that bedroom door it had been vain to close since it was not soundproof: 'I saw you. I saw that with Sue. There may not be anything between you but you'd like there to be! Maybe there is at that!'

Now like a dentist forced to ruin sound enamel to reach decayed I had to risk telling him what he did not know to keep what he assuredly did in relative control.

'This is what happened on the night in question,' I said. 'It was under the mistletoe, during the holidays, at the Jelliffs'. Wait! I will be heard out! See your father as he is, but see him in no baser light. He had his arms around his neighbour's wife. It is evening, in the heat and huddled spiced felicity of the year's end, under the mistletoe (where as well as anywhere else the thirsting and exasperated flesh might be visited by the futile pangs and jets of later lust, the omnivorous aches of fifty and forty and even thirty-five to seize what may be the last of the allotted lips). Your father seems to prolong beyond its usual moment's span that custom's usufruct. Only for an instant, but in that instant letting trickle through the fissures of appearance what your mother and probably Rudy Jelliff too saw as an earnest of a flood that would have devoured that house and one four doors away.'

A moon hung over the eastern roofs like a phantasmal bladder. Somewhere an icicle crashed and splintered, fruits of the day's thaw.

'So now I've got it straight,' I said. 'Just as through some nameless father your mother has cuckolded me (you think), so through one of Rudy Jelliff's five sons I have probably cuckolded him. Which could give you at least a half-brother under that roof where under ours you have none at all. So you balance out one miscreance with another, and find your rightful kin in our poor weft of all the teeming random bonded sentient dust.'

Shifting the grip, the boy walked on past the Jelliffs'. Before him – the tracks; and beyond that – the other side of the tracks. And now out of whatever reserve capacity for astonished incredulity may yet have remained I prepared to face this last and ultimate outrage. But he didn't cross. Along our own side of the tracks ran a road which the boy turned left on. He paused before a lighted house near the corner, a white cottage with a shingle in the window which I knew from familiarity to read, 'Viola Pruett, Piano Lessons', and which, like a violently unscrambled pattern on a screen, now came to focus. Memory adumbrates just as expectation recalls. The name on the shingle made audible to listening recollection the last words of the boy's mother as she'd left, which had fallen short then of the threshold of hearing. '. . . Pruett,' I remembered now. 'He's going to have supper and stay with Buzzie Pruett overnight . . . Can take a few things with him in that little suitcase of his. If Mrs Pruett phones about it, just say I'll take him over when I get back.' I recalled now in that chime-counting recapitulation of retroactive memory – better than which I could not have been expected to do. Because the eternal Who-instructs might have got through to the whisky-drinking husband or might have got through to the reader immersed in that prose vertiginous intoxicant and unique, but not to both.

'So that's it,' I said. 'You couldn't wait till yóu were taken much less till it was time but had to sneak off by yourself, and that not cross-lots but up the road I've told you a hundred times to keep off even the shoulder of.'

The boy had stopped and now appeared to hesitate before the house. He turned around at last, switched the toy and the suitcase in his hands, and started back in the direction he had come.

'What are you going back for now?' I asked.

'More stuff to take in this suitcase,' he said. 'I was going to just sleep at the Pruetts' overnight, but now I'm going to ask them to let me stay there for good.'

PETER DE VRIES

257

Enid Blyton (1897–1968)

The Famous Five Take Tea with Gaius Caesar Augustus Germanicus and Family

'I say,' said Dick when the Emperor went out to fetch some more pop, 'I think he's beastly, don't you?'

'Rather,' said Anne. 'He's had twice as many buns as anyone else. And what a jolly rotten way to treat a sister in company! I'm glad you're not like that, Julian.'

'So am I,' said Julian with a puzzled look.

'Gosh,' laughed George. 'His uncle's jolly funny, though. Fancy talking like that all the t–t–t–time!' The children were all enjoying a good laugh when Caligula returned and ripped Timmy's leg off so he could stir his drink.

'That's almost as bad as the buns!' said Julian grimly.

N. J. WARBURTON

Thornton Wilder (1897–1975)

Just Plain Folks

The curtain has just fallen on William Faulkner's *Requiem for a Nun* (Royal Court). It has been performed with imposing devoutness by Ruth Ford, Bertice Reading, Zachary Scott and John Crawford. The production (by Tony Richardson) and the settings (by Motley) have been austerely hieratic. Let us now imagine that there steps from the wings the Stage Manager of Thornton Wilder's *Our Town*. Pulling on a corn-cob pipe, he speaks.

Well, folks, reckon that's about it. End of another day in the city of Jefferson, Yoknapatawpha County, Mississippi. Nothin' much happened. Couple of people got raped, couple more got their teeth kicked in, but way up there those faraway old stars are still doing their old cosmic criss-cross, and there ain't a thing we can do about it. It's pretty quiet now. Folk hereabouts get to bed early, those that can still walk. Down behind the morgue a few of the young people are roastin' a nigger over an open fire, but I guess every town has its night-owls, and afore long they'll be tucked up asleep like anybody else. Nothin' stirring down at the big old plantation house – you can't even hear the hummin' of that electrified barbed-wire fence, 'cause last night some drunk ran slap into it and fused the whole works. That's where Mr Faulkner lives, and he's the fellow that thought this whole place up, kind of like God. Mr Faulkner knows everybody round these parts like the back of his hand, 'n most everybody round these parts knows the back of Mr Faulkner's hand. But he's not home right now, he's off on a trip round the world as Uncle Sam's culture ambassador, tellin' foreigners about how we've got to love everybody, even niggers, and how integration's bound to happen in a few thousand years anyway, so we might just as well make haste slowly. Ain't a thing we can do about it.

(*He takes out his watch and consults it.*)

Along about now the good folk of Jefferson City usually get around to screamin' in their sleep. Just ordinary people havin' ordinary nightmares, the way most of us do most of the time.

(*An agonized shrieking is briefly heard.*)

Ayeah, there they go. Nothin' wrong there that an overdose of Seconal won't fix.

(*He pockets his watch.*)

Like I say, simple folk fussin' and botherin' over simple, eternal problems. Take this Temple Stevens, the one Mr Faulkner's been soundin' off about. Course, Mr Faulkner don't pretend to be a real play-writer, 'n maybe that's why he tells the whole story backwards, 'n why he takes up so much time gabbin' about people you never met – and what's more, ain't going to meet. By the time he's told you what happened before you got here, it's gettin' to be time to go home. But we were talkin' about Temple. Ain't nothin' special about her. Got herself mixed up in an auto accident – witnessed a killin' – got herself locked up in a sportin' house with one of these seck-sual perverts – witnessed another killin' – got herself married up 'n bore a couple of fine kids. Then, just's she's fixing to run off with a blackmailer, her maid Nancy – that's the nigger dope-fiend she met in the cathouse – takes a notion to murder her baby boy. That's all about Temple – just a run of bad luck that could happen to anyone.

And don't come askin' me why Nancy murders the kid. Accordin' to Mr Faulkner, she does it to keep him from bein' tainted by his mother's sins. Seems to me even an ignorant nigger would know a tainted child was better'n a dead one, but I guess I can't get under their skins the way Mr Faulkner can.

(*He glances up at the sky.*)

Movin' along towards dawn in our town. Pretty soon folks'll start up on that old diurnal round of sufferin' and expiatin' and spoutin' sentences two pages long. One way or another, an awful lot of sufferin' gets done around here. 'Specially by the black folk – 'n that's how it should be, 'cause they don't feel it like we do, 'n anyways, they've got that simple primitive faith to lean back on.

(*He consults his watch again.*)

Well, Temple's back with her husband, and in a couple of minutes they'll be hangin' Nancy. Maybe that's why darkies were born – to keep white marriages from bustin' up.

Anyways, a lot of things have happened since the curtain went up tonight. Six billion gallons of water have tumbled over Niagara Falls. Three thousand boys and girls took their first puff of marijuana, 'n a puppy-dog in a flyin' coffin was sighted over Alaska. Most of you out there've been admirin' Miss Ruth Ford's play-actin', 'n a few of you've been wonderin' whether she left her pay-thos in the dressing room or whether maybe she didn't have any to begin with. Out in Hollywood a big producer's been readin' Mr Faulkner's book and figurin' whether to buy the movie rights for Miss Joan Crawford. Right enough, all over the world, it's been quite an evening. 'N now Nancy's due for the drop.

(*A thud offstage. The* STAGE MANAGER *smiles philosophically.*)

Ayeah, that's it – right on time.

(*He repockets his watch.*)

That's the end of the play, friends. You can go out and push dope now, those of you that push dope. Down in our town there's a meetin' of the Deathwish Committee, 'n a fund-raisin' rally in aid of Holocaust Relief, 'n all over town the prettiest gals're primping themselves up for the big beauty prize – Miss Cegenation of 1957. There's always somethin' happenin'. Why – over at the schoolhouse an old-fashioned-type humanist just shot himself. *You* get a good rest, too. Goodnight.'

(*He exits. A sound of Bibles being thumped momentarily fills the air.*)

KENNETH TYNAN

Ernest Hemingway (1899–1961)

For Whom the Gong Sounds

The mouth of the cave was camouflaged by a curtain of saddle-blankets, matadores' capes and the soles of old espadrilles. Inside it smelt of man-sweat, acrid and brown ... horse-sweat sweet and magenta. There was the leathery smell of leather and the coppery smell of copper and borne in on the clear night air came the distant smell of skunk.

The wife of Pablo was stirring *frijoles* in a Catalonian wineskin. She wore rope-soled shoes and a belt of hand grenades. Over her magnificent buttocks swung a sixteenth-century cannon taken from the Escorial.

'I obscenity in the obscenity of thy unprintable obscenity,' said Pilar.

'This is the Ingles of the street car. He of the board walk to come soon.'

'I obscenity in the unprintable of the milk of all street cars.' The woman was stirring the steaming mess with the horns of a Mura bull. She stared at Robert Jordan then smiled. 'Obscenity, obscenity, obscenity,' she said, not unkindly.

'*Qué va*,' said Robert Jordan. '*Bueno*. Good.'

'*Menos mal*,' said El Sordo. 'Not so good.'

'Go unprint thyself,' said Pilar. The gypsy went outside and unprinted himself.

The girl with the shaved head filled a tin pail full of *petite marmite* and handed it to him and she gave him a great swig from the wineskin and he chewed the succulent bits of horsemeat and they said nothing.

And now Esteban stood beside him on the rim of the gorge. This is it, Robert Jordan said to himself. I believe this is it. I did not think it was this to be it but it seems to be it, all right. Robert Jordan spat down the gorge. Pablo watched the fast disappearing globule of man-saliva then slowly, softly spat down the gorge. Pilar said obscenity thy saliva then she too spat down the gorge. This time it was Pablo's gorge.

The girl was walking beside him.

'*Hola, Ingles*,' she said. 'Hello, English.'

'Equally, *guapa*,' said Robert Jordan.

'*Qué va*,' said the girl.

'Rabbit.'

Robert Jordan pulled the pistol lanyard up, cocked his *maquina* and tightened the ropes of his rope-soled shoes.

'*Vamos*,' he said, 'Let's go.'

'*Si*,' said Maria. 'Yes.'

They walked on in silence until they came to a rocky ledge. There were rough rocks and thistles and a wild growth of Spanish dagger. Robert Jordan spread his buffalo robe out for himself and allowed Maria to lie near him on a bed of nettles. The earth moved.

'Rabbit,' said Robert Jordan. 'Hast aught?'

'Nay, naught.'

'Maria,' he said. 'Mary. Little shaved head.'

'Let me go with thee and be thy rabbit.'

The earth moved again. This time it was a regular earthquake. Californians would have called it a temblor.

Robert Jordan had reached the boardwalk. He lay in the gorse and rubble. He had his infernal machine beside him, some hand grenades, a blunderbuss, an arquebus and a greyhound bus. His *maquina* was held securely in his teeth. Across the ravine Anselmo was sniping off sentries as they passed.

Listen, Robert Jordan said to himself, only the fascist bombs made so much noise he couldn't hear. You had to do what you did. If you don't do what you do now you'll never do what you do now. Not now you won't. Sure it does. He lashed the wire through the rings of the cotter pins of the release levers of the wires of the main spring of the coil, insulating it with a piece cut off the bottom of his rope-soled shoes.

What about the others . . . Eladio and Ignacio . . . Anselmo and St Elmo? And Rabbit? I wonder how Rabbit is. Stop that now. This is no time to think about Rabbit . . . Or rabbits. Better think about something else. Think about llamas. It's better to breathe, he thought. It's always much better to breathe. Sure it is. The time was gradually, inevitably drawing near. Someone in the valley was singing an old Catalonian song. A plane crashed quietly overhead. Robert Jordan lay still and listened for the gong to sound . . .

CORNELIA OTIS SKINNER

Sir Noël Coward (1899–1973)

The Archers

DAN: Where have you been lately?

DORIS: To feed the cows.

DAN: Very big, cows.

DORIS: I also fed the chickens.

DAN: Very small, chickens.

DORIS: And you?

DAN: Oh, here and there, you know Borchester.

DORIS: Did you see the Town Hall by moonlight? They say it's . . . very exciting by moonlight.

DAN: Rather disappointing, I found.

DORIS: I'm sorry.

DAN: It's hardly your fault. Or is it? All those fake beams.

DORIS: Horrid.

DAN: Very.

DORIS: I suppose you called in at the Bull?

DAN: Yes.

DORIS: Very beery, the Bull.

DAN: Yes. Very beery.

DORIS: Oh, Dan! Where did we go wrong?

E. O. PARROTT

from The Caretaker . . . *or* Private Life

A basement. Dingy perhaps, but not actually dirty. Old furniture, but tastefully arranged. ASTON *is alone in the room; he wears an old leather jacket but well-cut trousers off which he's elegantly flicking the cigarette ash. Enter* DAVIES, *a tramp, but picturesquely dressed and with rather distinguished greying hair.*

ASTON: Hello, matey, who are you?

DAVIES: I came, er, I come for my papers. Here, they said, or Sidcup.

ASTON: Very flat, Sidcup.

DAVIES: There's no need to be unpleasant.

ASTON: It was no reflection on the papers, unless of course they made it flatter. Do you come here often?

DAVIES: No, Budleigh Salterton, mostly. A better class of papers, there, and the moonlight on the bus-station roof is peculiarly attractive.

ASTON: Moonlight can be cruelly deceptive. How will you recognize it?

DAVIES: The moonlight?

ASTON: No, no, Sidcup.

DAVIES: There's bound to be a sign. If not, I shall ask. I'm told that people at bus stations, if asked, often reply.

ASTON: In what?

DAVIES: English, mostly, or so they tell me: nowadays one must never be too hopeful.

ASTON: I remember a station. Long ago, it was, and terribly far away. Up north, well past Watford. Maybe even Berkhamsted. Or Bletchley. It was in the war – everyone terribly busy with rationing and rock cakes and killing Germans and dressing up in those funny tin hats and there, quite suddenly, unexpectedly, almost surprisingly, there was this woman. An ordinary, middle-aged woman, terribly ordinary and terribly, terribly middle-aged and with a funny sort of look in her eye as if she was really supposed to be wearing glasses. We knew at once, of course.

DAVIES: Knew?

ASTON: That we were terribly, terribly in love.

(*He goes over to the piano, old but Bechstein, and starts to play softly.*) It was impossible, of course – too, too impossible for words and I suppose that was why we never actually spoke. Just stood there and stared and stared and wished the platform announcer could also have been to elocution classes. Then a train came – quite unexpectedly, really, out of a tunnel and with no sense of timing, and suddenly we knew it was all over. But sometimes, even now, I wake up in the night and wonder somehow if it could all have been different; if there hadn't been that awful fire at the Reichstag and then that common little man with the strange haircut shouting so much, would we have managed to speak? It all seems so terribly terribly sad and often, in the sudden chill of an autumn evening, or whenever spring breaks through again, I know . . .

DAVIES: A dark, secluded place, where no . . .
ASTON: Did you say something?
DAVIES: No, no, I was just wondering about the papers and Sidcup
and somehow everything seems so terribly complicated nowadays.

ALAN COREN

Ogden Nash (1902–1971)

Just a Few Friends

There are all kinds of parties, but the kind I don't like are
Those where the host is a piker –
The kind of guy who puts you on rations,
Like a handful of pecans, four canapés, and two Old Fashioneds –
And where, instead of dancing the rhumba
With a cute little number,
You end up heartbroken
On a sofa with some little old lady from Hoboken,
Usually a Seventh Day Adventist,
Who son is – guess what? – a dentist.
I don't know what's worse – hearing about the jerk's enviable
salary
Or surviving all evening on about half a calorie.

BASIL RANSOME-DAVIES

On Patience Strong

While I personally can't see that a simile or metaphor
Is any the better for
Being printed in a square and illuminated with bluebirds and
　Canterbury bells –
That's a thing that all creative writers must decide for themsells.
And I hasten right here at this verse's inception to
State that Miss Strong's philosophy is such as neither you nor I nor
　anyone else can take exception to;
There are probably happy couples this very minute murmuring, 'It
　was Patience
Whose timely counsel healed the rift in our domestic relatience.'
But to me her genius lay in this: in founding a coterie
Of poets who lay their lines end to end so that folks who are easily
　scared need never suspect it's poterie.

ELAINE MORGAN

Daddy's Not Taking You to the Zoo Tomorrow, Not If I Can Help It

If there is one thing that gets me in a sweat quicker than a sauna,
That is a visit with my precocious niece to the zoo to admire the
　exotic fauna;
Not that I have anything against animals, I haven't,
I admire them as much as any other revered uncle or savant,
But I have to hasten my niece past the coneys because they are
　mating,
And I say, 'Come and see the bears!' only nobody can see the bears,
　because the bears are hibernating;
And she says, 'Anyway, I want to see the coneys because it's funny
　the way they jump on each other',
And I wonder what I am going to tell her mother,
And distract her attention by taking her to the parrot house, which
　is excessively raucous

Because the inmates are all very good, if foul-mouthed and re-
    petitive talkers.
And when we get home and her mother says, 'How did you like the
    zoo? Was it nice?'
She replies, 'No, it was horrid. Uncle wouldn't let me watch the
    coneys playing, and he didn't buy me a chocolate ice.'

GERARD BENSON

Stevie Smith (1902–1971)

On Herself

Oh, I am full of love and joy,
I could dance and sing aloud.
My mother said I would make a handsome boy,
Although my head was often in a cloud.

Now my head is in this flowery hat,
To hide my hair that won't curl,
Thank goodness for that.
Mother thought I was rather a plain girl.

Can I tell how I look?
Perhaps Mother was right.
She was a good plain cook,
But never wanted me to look a fright.

JOHN STANLEY SWEETMAN

Hound Puss

I have a cat: I call him Pumpkin,
A great fat furry purry lumpkin.
Hi-dee-diddle hi-diddle dumpkin.

He sleeps within my bed at night,
His eyes are Mephistopheles-bright:
I dare not look upon their blight.

He stalks me like my angry God,
His gaze is like a fiery rod:
He dines exclusively on cod.

Avaunt, you creeping saviour-devil,
Away with thy angelic evil!

MARTIN FAGG

Graham Greene (1904–   )

Extract from a Biography of Sir Hugh Greene

Hugh lost his faith the day I hit him on the head with a croquet
mallet, and years later at his desk in Broadcasting House, arranging
some series of talks by atheists, he would feel his mind darkened by
the shadow of the falling mallet as by the wing of a great bird.

I was twelve that summer and already conscious of God moving
among the weeds between the raspberry canes. Hugh was six. The
nursery maid of the day (our mother changed them with the fre-
quency of young girls in a Gran Bassa brothel) crunched by on the
gravel, her thighs sleek as a cat's. But it was in one of her plump
calves that Hugh sank his teeth, through the acrid black stockings to
the succulent flesh.

I swung the mallet. Was it a foretaste of adult jealousy? I had known her for a week as an instrument of pleasure. Or was it that, as the blood spurted, I had some vague presentiment of my brother's future, the godless and orgiastic roads he was to follow, the too brilliant ascent, the sudden fall exactly fifty years later under the goads of the Puritans, the seedy and mysterious end.

SIR HUGH GREENE ('SEBASTIAN ELEIGH')

Verse Autobiography

A dead dog I remember in my pram,
It had a vulpine air even in death.
I cried out to the squint-eyed nurse, but words
Were still a miracle I had not learned.
Only I knew the hour had struck for me –
A businessman went grumbling into dark,
The District Officer I'd never be
Spared from my pram for darkest Africa.
I lay and watched that vulpine grin of death
Until the squint-eyed nurse to comfort me
Delved in her tomb-like bag and found interred,
Long, slim and pink, a stick of Brighton Rock.

GRAHAM GREENE ('H. A. BAXTER')

Extract from an Imaginary Novel

As usual the Euston train was twenty minutes late by the time it reached Berkhamsted. Through Watford, King's Langley and Boxmoor Sergeant had picked thoughtfully at the sore place on his lower lip until the blood was running down his chin. What did the General want, he wondered with impatient affection? What could he want so many years since the mugging in Belize?

At Berkhamsted station he walked rapidly along the tiled passage smelling of urine, like an elongated public lavatory, and came out into the misty Hertfordshire rain. Under the weeping willows on the canal bank a child was crying and a dog barked.

Driver was waiting for him on the canal bridge. How much time, he thought, the General must have spent all those years ago on acquiring a sergeant called Driver and a driver called Sergeant. 'Whom are we to kill this time?' he asked, almost cheerfully.

SIR HUGH GREENE ('SEBASTIAN ELEIGH')

Nothing Succeeds like Failure

Such chronic success was, thought Declan, a deep hereditary taint corrupting every cell of his otherwise morbidly healthy being. Not for him the rancid bliss of papering bedsitters with rejection slips, the sardine-and-apple dinners, the furtive applications for Supplementary Benefit. Constant bestsellerdom, international celebrity and obligatory tax exile: all these coated, like stale smegma, the doomed prosperity of his days.

He had flung wide the door even before the telegraph boy stopped ringing. A quick rip – then a rictus of sheer exultation. Once again he had failed to win the Nobel Prize for Literature! If, as Father Banjax had once muttered drunkenly in the confessional in Derry, all success was merely a kind of delayed failure, such failure was, surely, a sort of instantaneous success. But then, if all *success* was merely . . . ? He flapped his arms in a hopeless gesture, achieving thereby perfect crucifixion on the sun-dazed Cypriot wall.

MARTIN FAGG

Early Writing

The moment their eyes met, Gray knew the wisky priest wanted to steal his golden po. He stood there blinking in the pale autumn sunshine, for the interior of the shed had been dark, wondering what to do. A cigarete hung loosely from the man's lips, and his smile was not a holy one. Would the boy shout and struggle, he wondered, wincing a little as he felt in imagination the young fists pounding his fleshy stomack and the sturdy boots with blakeys hacking at his shins. It was a seedy world, he decided biterly, his eyes cuveting the lusterous utensil, which was just what he wanted to keep in his church for after Mass, because plain china seemed somehow disrespectful to the Lord. Gray wondered if he should dart back into the gloom of the shed, but it would be horrible to be caught in there by the priest. But it is for Doreen's birthday, he told himself again, I have painted it golden especially for her, and she will sit on it for hours thinking of me, he muttered fiercely, and he clutched the precious burden tightly to his thin chest. 'Good morning, father,' he said.

J. A. LINDON

Nun-running

Foskett locked the nuns in their cabin for the night. He fought down his longing for their young brown bodies by telling himself they belonged to God.

In the tiny saloon aft, the Mauritian steward squashed a fly in the glass before pouring him a Hong Kong whisky. Drinking down the hot sourness, Foskett mused on the whole squalid business.

He no longer asked himself why he got mixed up in it, but he did wonder how the ascetic Father Ramgoolam would spend the money he received for the air fares.

The Maltese with gold teeth approached. 'Mr Foxy, those very fine girls you have. I pay good for them.'

Foskett said, 'They are brides of the Church.'

'I understand,' the Maltese said. 'I am good Catholic too.'

Dear God, why were they all good Catholics? Downside had been so different.

PETER VEALE

C. P. Snow (1905–1980)

The Cloisters of Power

Paunceley was regaling us with the clarets of '56.

'This is very civil of you, Senior Tutor,' observed Mainwaring.

'Thank you, Professor of Palaeontology and Sometime Fellow of Jesus,' replied Paunceley. He seemed nervous, drawn, tense.

It was a languorous February night, heady with the rich evocative reek of sweet william. The chrysanthemums blazed in the court, a Scotch mist draped the plane trees and above, in the sky, shimmered the stars – countless, desolate, shining.

I felt increasingly uneasy about my tendency to fire off adjectives in threes. It was compulsive, embarrassing, ineluctable; but at least it fostered the illusion of a mind that was diamond-sharp, incisive, brilliant.

'I have asked you to come here before breakfast,' continued Paunceley, 'because I have a most unsavoury revelation to make to you about one of your colleagues.'

I glanced at Grimsby-Browne. He seemed suddenly immensely old, haggard, shrivelled. Had he committed the unforgivable and falsified a footnote? I studied Basingstoke, the Bursar. He too seemed suddenly bowed, broken, desiccated. Had he done the unspeakable and embezzled the battels? The scent of old man's beard saturated the combination room.

'It concerns Charles Snow,' said Paunceley.

The tension was now unbearably taut, torturing, tense. The plangent aroma of montbretia seemed to pervade every electron of my being.

The Senior Tutor's tone was dry, aloof, Olympian.

'I have discovered that his real name is Godfrey Winn.'

MARTIN FAGG

Lewis Eliot's Revolution Diary

Friday: Opening *The Times* to discover whether anybody who was anybody was dead, I noticed that Guttering, having deposited my breakfast tray, was hovering. He looked haggard, broken, slightly troubled.

'Excuse me, sir,' he stuttered with wholly excusable deference, 'but the College has risen.'

At first, a vision of the College as some kind of vast, academic soufflé filled my mind. Sternly suppressing such frivolous but witty fantasy, I was shocked, outraged, mildly surprised. With an icy calm matured by ruthless self-discipline, I seized the telephone and began dialling intrepidly.

'Is that you, Tutor of Admissions, Estates Bursar, Tufnell Gold Medallist for Latin Elegiacs and Sometime Chauntecleere Fellow of Comparative Philology?' I rapped out, grimly aware that there was not a moment to lose if we were to mount an effective counterstroke against the insurrectionists, who might even now be swilling vintage Dow's in the Combination Room . . .

MARTIN FAGG

Samuel Beckett (1906–   )

from Slamm's Last Knock

The den of Slamm, the critic. Very late yesterday. Large desk with throne behind it. Two waste-paper baskets, one black, one white, filled with crumpled pieces of paper, on either side of the stage. Shambling between them – i.e. from one to the other and back again – an old man, SLAMM. *Bent gait. Thin, barking voice. Motionless, watching* SLAMM, *is* SECK. *Bright grey face,*

273

holding pad and pencil. One crutch. SLAMM *goes to black basket, takes out piece of white paper, uncrumples it, reads. Short laugh.*

SLAMM: (*Reading*) '. . . the validity of an authentic tragic vision, at once personal and by implication cosmic . . .'
(*Short laugh. He recrumples the paper, replaces it in basket, and crosses to other – i.e. white – basket. He takes out piece of black paper, uncrumples it, reads. Short laugh.*)
(*Reading*) '. . . Just another dose of nightmare gibberish from the so-called author of Waiting for Godot . . .'
(*Short laugh. He recrumples the paper, replaces it in basket, and sits on throne. Pause. Anguished, he extends fingers of right hand and stares at them. Extends fingers of left hand. Same business. Then brings fingers of right hand towards fingers of left hand, and vice versa, so that fingertips of right hand touch fingertips of left hand. Same business. Breaks wind pensively.* SECK *writes feverishly on pad.*)
We're getting on. (*He sighs.*) Read that back.

SECK: (*Produces pince-nez with thick black lenses, places them on bridge of nose, reads:*) 'A tragic dose of authentic gibberish from the so-called implication of *Waiting for Godot*. Shall I go on?

SLAMM: (*Nodding head*) No. (*Pause.*) A bit of both, then.

SECK: (*Shaking head*) Or a little of neither.

SLAMM: There's the hell of it. (*Pause. Urgently*) Is it time for my Roget?

SECK: There are no more Rogets. Use your loaf.

SLAMM: Then wind me up, stink-louse! Stir your stump!
(SECK *hobbles to* SLAMM, *holding rusty key depending from piece of string round his [*SECK'S*] neck, and inserts it into back of* SLAMM'S *head. Loud noise of winding.*)
Easy now. Can't you see it's hell in there?

SECK: I haven't looked. (*Pause.*) It's hell out here, too. The ceiling is zero and there's grit in my crotch. Roget and over.
(*He stops winding and watches. Pause.*)

SLAMM: (*Glazed stare*) Nothing is always starting to happen.

SECK: It's better than something. You're well out of that.

SLAMM: I'm badly into this. (*He tries to yawn but fails.*) It would be better if I could yawn. Or if you could yawn.

SECK: I don't feel excited enough. (*Pause.*) Anything coming?

SLAMM: Nothing, in spades. (*Pause.*) Perhaps I haven't been kissed enough. Or perhaps they put the wrong ash in my gruel. One or the other.

SECK: Nothing will come of nothing. Come again.

SLAMM: (*With violence*) Purulent drudge! *You* try, if you've got so much grit in your crotch! Just one pitiless, pathetic creatively critical phrase!

SECK: I heard you the first time.

SLAMM: You can't have been listening.

SECK: Your word's good enough for me.

SLAMM: I haven't got a word. There's just the light, going. (*Pause.*) Are you trying?

SECK: Less and less.

SLAMM: Try blowing down it.

SECK: It's coming! (*Screws up his face. Tonelessly*) Sometimes I wonder why I spend the lonely night.

SLAMM: To many Fs. We're bitched.
(*Half a pause.*)

SECK: Hold your pauses. It's coming again. (*In a raconteur's voice, dictates to himself*) Tuesday night, seven-thirty by the paranoid barometer, curtain up at the Court, Sam Beckett unrivalled master of the unravelled revels. Item: *Krapp's Last Tape*, Krapp being a myopic not to say deaf not to say eremetical eater of one and one-half bananas listening and cackling as he listens to a tape-recording of twenty years' antiquity made on a day, the one far gone day, when he laid his hand on a girl in a boat and it worked, as it worked for Molly Bloom in Gibraltar in the long ago. Actor: Patrick Magee, bereaved and aghast-looking grunting into his Grundig, probably perfect performance, fine throughout and highly affecting at third curtain call though not formerly. Unique, oblique, bleak experience, in other words, and would have had same effect if half the words *were* other words. Or any words.
(*Pause.*)

SLAMM: Don't stop. You're boring me.

SECK: (*Normal voice*) Not enough. You're smiling.

KENNETH TYNAN

LGA-ORD

Then, Beckett decided to become a commercial pilot . . . 'I think the next little bit of excitement is flying,' he wrote to McGreevy. 'I hope I am not too old to take it up seriously nor too stupid about machines to qualify as a commercial pilot.' – Samuel Beckett *by Deirdre Bair*

Grey bleak final afternoon ladies and gentlemen this is your captain your cap welcoming you aboard the continuation of Flyways flight 185 from nothingness to New York's Laguardia non non non non non non nonstop to Chicago's Ohare and on from there in the passing grey afternoons to empty bleak eternal nothingness again with the Carey bus the credit-card machine the Friskem metal detector the boarding pass the in-flight magazine all returned to tiny bits of grit blowing across the steppe for ever

(*Pause.*)

Cruising along nicely now.

(*Pause.*)

Yes cruising along very nicely indeed if I do say so myself.

(*Long pause.*)

Twenty-two thousand feet.

(*Pause.*)

Extinguish the light extinguish the light I have extinguished the No Smoking light so you are free to move about the cabin have a good cry hang yourselves get an erection who knows however we do ask that while you're in your seats you keep your belts lightly fastened in case we encounter any choppy air or the end we've prayed for past time remembering our flying time from New York to Chicago is two hours and fifteen minutes the time of the dark journey of our existence is not revealed, you cry no you *pray* for a flight attendant you pray for a flight attendant a flight attendant comes now cry with reading material if you care to purchase a cocktail

(*Pause.*)

A cocktail?

(*Pause.*)

If you care to purchase a piece of carrot, a stinking turnip, a bit of grit our flight attendants will be along to see that you know how to move out of this airplane fast and use seat lower back cushion for flotation those of you on the right side of the aircraft ought to be able to see New York's Finger Lakes region that's Lake Canandaigua

closest to us those of you on the left side of the aircraft will only see
the vastness of eternal emptiness without end

(*Pause.*)

(*Long pause.*)

(*Very long pause.*)

(*Long pause of about an hour.*)

We're beginning our descent we're finished nearly finished soon
we will be finished we're beginning our descent our long descent
ahh descending beautifully to Chicago's Ohare Airport ORD
ORD ORD ORD seat backs and tray tables in their full upright
position for landing for ending flight attendants prepare for ending
it is ending the flight is ending please check the seat pocket in front
of you to see if you have all your belongings with you remain seated
and motionless until the ending until the finish until the aircraft has
come to a complete stop at the gate until the end

(*Pause.*)

When we deplane I'll weep for happiness.

IAN A. FRAZIER

Sir John Betjeman (1906–1984)

On the Derationing of Sweets

There's nougat at the Hendersons', the Hopes have got some fudge,
    And Pam has popped the pralines in the tool bag of her Rudge.
Voluptuous and tarmac-borne, she free-wheels through East
    Cheam,
    My caramelly angel girl, my luscious sweetmeat dream.

Down by-pass, heathland-hugging, coasts my freckled, blazered
    bliss.
    The long-desired puncture brings the peardrop-scented kiss,
And butterscotchy handclasps as we map our true love's course:
    Sweet the pangs of adolescence, sharp the prickles of the gorse.

At dusk, through built-up roadways, bird bath, loggia and gnome,
　To geysers, brunch, elevenses, the wonderland of home.
But who can think of Beauty or can care for things Above,
　When Oxshott's full of marzipan and hearts are full of love?

ARTHUR MARSHALL

Place Names of China

Bolding Vedas! Shanks New Nisa!
Trusty Lichfield swirls it down
To filter beds on Ruislip Marshes
From my loo in Kentish Town.

The Burlington! The Rochester!
Oh those names of childhood loos –
Nursie knocking at the door
'Have you done your Number Twos?'

Lady typist – office party –
Golly! All that gassy beer!
Tripping home down Hendon Parkway
To her Improved Windermere.

Chelsea buns and Lounge Bar pasties
All swilled down with Benskin's Pale,
Purified and cleansed by charcoal,
Fill the taps in Colindale.

Here I sit, alone and sixty,
Bald, and fat, and full of sin,
Cold the seat and loud the cistern,
As I read the Harpic tin.

ALAN BENNETT

Betjeman, 1984

I saw him in the Airstrip Gardens
  (Fahrenheit at 451)
Feeding automative orchids
  With a little plastic bun,
While above his brickwork cranium
  Burned the trapped and troubled sun.

'Where is Piper? Where is Pontefract?
  (Devil take my boiling pate!)
Where is Pam? and where's Myfanwy?
  Don't remind me of the date!
Can it be that I am *really*
  Knocking on for 78?

'In my splendid State Apartment
  Underneath a secret lock
Finger now forbidden treasures
  (Pray for me St Enodoc!);
TV plate and concrete lamp-post
  And a single nylon sock.

'Take your ease, pale-haired admirer,
  As I, half the century saner,
Pour a vintage Mazawattee
  Through the Marks and Spencer strainer
In a *genuine* British Railways
  (Luton made) cardboard container.

'Though they say my verse-compulsion
  Lacks an interstellar drive,
Reading Beverley and Daphne
  Keeps *my* sense of words alive.
Lord, but *how* much beauty was there
  Back in 1955!'

CHARLES CAUSLEY

Autumn

'Packing Susan off to Bedales
(Problem daughter, *entre nous*),
Touching up the sun-lounge paintwork,
Clearing spiders from the loo –

'Autumn's such a busy time, dear,
(Try this pippin – it's a beaut);
Madge is putting on a slide-show
At the Women's Institute.

'Gets quite nippy now, by teatime;
Mornings, you can see your breath . . .'
In the park, the smell of bonfires,
At The Home, the smell of death.

STANLEY J. SHARPLESS

At the Post Office

Fridays, when I draw my pension,
Thoughts I hardly dare to mention
Deep inside of me uncoil;
Through the grille I gaze so sweetly
At Miss Fanshawe, who – how neatly! –
Rubber-stamps my counterfoil.

Brisk the business, bright the glancing,
Slow the lengthy queue advancing
In our High Street GPO;
No room here for doubt or failure,
'What's the airmail to Australia?'
Trust my blue-eyed girl to know.

Senior citizen I may be,
But my Civil Service baby
Telescopes the years between;

As she hands the money to me
Half-forgotten lust runs through me –
Senex becomes seventeen.

STANLEY J. SHARPLESS

A Ticket-Collector's Love Song

The NUR Transport Review reported that some women wore revealing dresses to distract collectors and avoid paying their fare.

Miss J. Hunter Dunn, Miss J. Hunter Dunn,
Sidling past with your buttons undone,
What knockers you showed to the world and to me
When you came in from Ware on the 9.33!

The crowd surged around but I only had eyes
For the thrust of your chest and the white of your thighs;
Though nearing retirement, with two years to run,
I admit to my randiness, Joan Hunter Dunn.

My hand full of tickets, my heart full of joy,
How could I have guessed it was only a ploy?
Instead of collecting, I had a good look –
And probably broke every rule in the book.

Around us were tourists from France and Japan,
Within me a voice – 'You are only a man',
And there by the barrier hurrying through
Was wonderful, perfumy, bosomy you!

Oh! the sighs that I gave at the size of your bust,
Which made me abuse my position of trust!
And here I am reading Page 3 of the *Sun*
And dreaming, God help me, of Joan Hunter Dunn!

ROGER WODDIS

Louis MacNeice (1907–1963)

More Bagpipe Music

It's all go to Claridges, it's all go the champers,
The Glyndebourne music's such a drag, but there's always the
    Fortnum hampers;
We've a town and a country place, of course, where we keep our
    gees and doggies,
And we often weekend on the Continent in spite of the Krauts and
    Froggies.

Enoch Powell has got it right: deport the nigs and Pakkis,
The TUC's a bunch of Trots, and their leaders Moscow lackeys.
We'd give no dole to the unemployed, if they won't work they're
    lazy,
We've lots of City directorships, but of what we're rather hazy.

It's all go to hunt with the Quorn, it's all go to Ascot,
We've a brand-new Rolls we got as a perk, with our family crest as a
    mascot.
The Socialists tax us too much, we've always voted Tory
But we'll not say how we made our pile, for that's another story.

                                                    E. O. PARROTT

W. H. Auden (1907–1973)

Just a Smack at Auden

Waiting for the end, boys, waiting for the end.
What is there to be or do?
What's become of me or you?
Are we kind or are we true?
Sitting two and two, boys, waiting for the end.

Shall I build a tower, boys, knowing it will rend
Crack upon the hour, boys, waiting for the end?
Shall I pluck a flower, boys, shall I save or spend?
All turns sour, boys, waiting for the end.

Shall I send a wire, boys? Where is there to send?
All are under fire, boys, waiting for the end.
Shall I turn a sire, boys? Shall I choose a friend?
The fat is in the pyre, boys, waiting for the end.

Shall I make it clear, boys, for all to apprehend,
Those that will not hear, boys, waiting for the end,
Knowing it is near, boys, trying to pretend,
Sitting in cold fear, boys, waiting for the end?

Shall we send a cable, boys, accurately penned,
Knowing we are able, boys, waiting for the end,
Via the Tower of Babel, boys? Christ will not ascend.
He's hiding in his stable, boys, waiting for the end.

Shall we blow a bubble, boys, glittering to distend,
Hiding from our trouble, boys, waiting for the end?
When we build on rubble, boys, Nature will append
Double and redouble, boys, waiting for the end.

Shall we make a tale, boys, that things are sure to mend,
Playing bluff and hale, boys, waiting for the end?
It will be born stale, boys, stinking to offend,
Dying ere it fail, boys, waiting for the end.

Shall we go all wild, boys, waste and make them lend,
Playing at the child, boys, waiting for the end?
It has all been filed, boys, history has a trend,
Each of us enisled, boys, waiting for the end.

What was said by Marx, boys, what did he perpend?
No good being sparks, boys, waiting for the end.
Treason for the clerks, boys, curtains that descend,
Lights becoming darks, boys, waiting for the end.

Waiting for the end, boys, waiting for the end.
Not a chance of blend, boys, things have got to tend.
Think of those who vend, boys, think of how we wend,
Waiting for the end, boys, waiting for the end.

SIR WILLIAM EMPSON

Self-congratulatory Ode on Mr Auden's Election to the Professorship of Poetry at Oxford

He has come back at last, the boy with the inky fingers,
Who scrawled on the lavatory walls and frightened his granny
By roaring his inexplicable
Songs in the bathroom, grubby, embarrassing visitors,

Ran off to sea without warning or explanation,
Wrote long letters home in a mixture of languages,
Acquired an undoubtedly foreign
Accent, was given up for lost but can now cock a snook

At the smooth FO type and the bard-intoxicated professor
By sanction of his granny who taught him his tables,
Cuffed him and feared him and lost him, and now will be taught in
   her
Turn to suck eggs.

RONALD MASON

from The Tents of Wickedness: No Need to Cry

No need to cry '*Touché!*'
When scalped of your toupee.
All that's false must go.
Breast the future so:
Comrades marching bald
Of all illusion, galled
By nothing but a fattish
Sentimental fetish.

Beware the well-groomed prexy
Whose daughter wants your proxy;
Don't pay for those coiffures
Seen in rotogravures.
Beware the smiling briber.
Develop lots of fiber.
Plan on growing thinner
Of a reasonable dinner,
And leave the past to puke
Into its own peruke.

PETER DE VRIES

Ian Fleming (1908–1964)

from Bond Strikes Camp

Shadows of fog were tailing him through the windows of his Chelsea flat; the blonde had left a broken rosette of lipstick on the best Givan's pillowcase – he would have to consult last night's book-matches to find out where he had grabbed her. It was one bitch of a morning. And, of course, it turned out to be the day! For there was always one breakfast in the month when a very simple operation, the boiling of an egg so that the yolk should remain properly soft and the white precisely hard, seemed to defeat his devoted housekeeper, May. As he decapitated the fifth abort on its Wedgwood launching-pad he was tempted to crown her with the sixteen-inch pepper mill. Three minutes and fifty-five seconds later by his stopwatch and the sixth egg came up with all systems go. As he was about to press the thin finger of wholemeal toast into the prepared cavity the telephone rang. It was probably the blonde: 'Don't tell me: it all comes back – you're the new hat-check from the Moment of Truth,' he snarled into the receiver. But the voice which cut in was that of his secretary, Miss Ponsonby. 'He wants you now, smart pants, so step on the Pogo.'

Swearing pedantically, Bond pulled away from his uneaten egg and hurried from the flat to the wheel of his souped-up Pierce Arrow, a Thirty-one open tourer with two three-piece windscreens. A sulphurous black rain was falling and he nearly took the seat off a Beatnik as he swerved into Milner. It was that kind of a Christmas. Thirteen minutes later his lean body streaked from the tonneau-cover like a conger from its hole and he stood outside M.'s door with Lolita Ponsonby's great spaniel eyes gazing up at him in dog-like devotion.

'Sorry about the crossed line,' he told her. 'I'll sock you a lunch if they don't need you at Cruft's.' Then the green lights showed and he entered.

'Sit down, 007.' That was Grade C welcome indicating the gale warning. There had been several lately. But M. did not continue. He surveyed Bond with a cold, glassy stare, cleared his throat and suddenly lowered his eyes. His pipe rested unlit beside the tobacco in the familiar shell-cap. If such a thing had been possible, Bond would have sworn he was embarrassed. When at length he spoke, the voice was dry and impersonal. 'There are many things I have asked you to do, Bond; they have not always been pleasant but they have been in the course of duty. Supposing I were to ask you to do something which I have no right to demand and which I can justify only by appealing to principles outside your service obligations. I refer to your patriotism. You are patriotic, Bond?'

'Don't know, sir, I never read the small-print clauses.'

'Forgive the question, I'll put it another way. Do you think the end justifies the means?'

'I can attach no significance of any kind to such expressions.'

M. seemed to reflect. The mood of crisis deepened.

'Well, we must try again. If there were a particularly arduous task – and I called for a volunteer – who must have certain quali- fications – and only one person had those qualifications – and I asked him to volunteer. What would you say?'

'I'd say stop beating about the bush, sir.'

'I'm afraid we haven't even started.'

'Sir?'

'Do you play chess, Bond?'

'My salary won't run to it.'

'But you are familiar with the game?'

'Tolerably.' As if aware that he was in the stronger position, Bond was edging towards insolence.

'It has, of course, been thoroughly modernized; all the adventure has been taken out of it; but the opening gambits in which a piece used to be sacrificed for the sake of early development proved unsound and were therefore abandoned. But it is so long since they have been tried that many players are unfamiliar with the pitfalls and it is sometimes possible to obtain an advantage by taking a risk. In our profession, if it be a profession, we keep a record of these forgotten traps. Ever heard of Mata Hari?'

'The beautiful spy?' Bond's voice held derision. The school prefect sulking before his housemaster.

'She was very successful. It was a long time ago.' M. still sounded meek and deprecating.

'I seem to remember reading the other day that a concealed microphone had replaced the *femme fatale*.'

'Precisely. So there is still a chance for the *femme fatale*.'

'I have yet to meet her.'

'You will. You are aware there is a Russian military mission visiting this country?'

Bond let that one go into the net.

'They have sent over among others an elderly general. He looks like a general, he may well have been a general, he is certainly a very high echelon in the KGB. Security is his speciality; rocketry, nerve gases, germ warfare – all the usual hobbies.' M. paused. 'And one rather unusual one.'

Bond waited, like an old pike watching the bait come down.

'Yes. He likes to go to night clubs, get drunk, throw his money about and bring people back to his hotel. All rather old-fashioned.'

'And not very unusual.'

'Ah.' M. looked embarrassed again. 'I'm just coming to that. We happen to know quite a bit about this chap, General Count Apraxin. His family were pretty well known under the old dispensation though his father was one of the first to join the party; we think he may be a bit of a throwback. Not politically, of course. He's tough as they come. I needn't tell you Section A make a study of the kind of greens the big shots go in for. Sometimes we know more about what these people are like between the sheets than they do themselves; it's a dirty business. Well, the General is mad about drag.'

'Drag, sir?'

M. winced. 'I'm sorry about this part, Bond. He's "*so*" – "*uno di quelli*" – "one of those" – a sodomite.'

Bond detected a glint of distaste in the cold blue eyes.

'In my young days,' M. went on, 'fellows like that shot themselves. Now their names are up for every club. Particularly in London. Do you know what sort of a reputation this city has abroad?' Bond waited. 'Well, it stinks. These foreigners come here, drop notes of assignation into sentries' top-boots, pin fivers on to guardsmen's bearskins. The Tins are livid.'

'And General Apraxin?' Bond decided to cut short the Wolfenden.

'One of the worst. I told you he likes drag. That's – er – men dressed up as women.'

'Well, you tell me he's found the right place. But I don't quite see where we come in.'

M. cleared his throat. 'There's just a possibility, mind, it's only a possibility, that even a top KGB might be taken off guard – if he found the company congenial – perhaps so congenial that it appealed to some secret wish of his imagination – and if he talked at all (mind

288

you, he is generally absolutely silent), well then anything he said might be of the greatest value – anything – it might be a lead on what he's really here for. You will be drawing a bow at a venture. You will be working in the dark.'

'Me, sir?'

M. rapped out the words like a command. '007, I want you to do this thing. I want you to let our people rig you up as a moppet and send you to a special sort of club and I want you to allow yourself to be approached by General Apraxin and sit at his table and if he asks you back to his hotel I want you to accompany him and any suggestion he makes I request you to fall in with to the limit your conscience permits. And may your patriotism be your conscience, as it is mine.'

It was a very odd speech for M. Bond studied his fingernails. 'And if the pace gets too hot?'

'Then you must pull out – but remember, T. E. Lawrence put up with the final indignity. I knew him well, but knowing even that, I never dared to call him by his Christian name.'

Bond reflected. It was clear that M. was deeply concerned. Besides, the General might never turn up. 'I'll try anything once, sir.'

'Good man.' M. seemed to grow visibly younger.

'As long as I'm not expected to shake a powder into his drink and run away with his wallet.'

'Oh, I don't think it will come to that. If you don't like the look of things, just plead a headache; he'll be terrified of any publicity. It was all Section A could do to slip him a card for this club.'

'What's its name?'

M. pursed his lips. 'The Kitchener. In Lower Belgrave Mews. Be there about eleven o'clock and just sit around. We've signed you in as "Gerda".'

'And my – disguise?'

'We're sending you off to a specialist in that kind of thing – he thinks you want it for some Christmas "do". Here's the address.'

'One more question, sir. I have no wish to weary you with details of my private life but I can assure you I've never dressed up in "drag" as you call it since I played Katisha in *The Mikado* at my prep school. I shan't look right, I shan't move right, I shan't talk right; I shall feel about as convincing arsing about as a night-club hostess as Randolph Churchill.'

M. gazed at him blankly and again Bond noticed his expression of weariness, even of repulsion. 'Yes, 007, you will do all of those things and I am afraid that is precisely what will get him.'

Bond turned angrily but M.'s face was already buried in his signals. This man who had sent so many to their deaths was still alive and now the dedicated bachelor who had never looked at a woman except to estimate her security risk was packing him off with the same cold indifference into a den of slimy creatures. He walked out of the room and was striding past Miss Ponsonby when she stopped him. 'No time for that lunch, I'm afraid. You're wanted in Armoury.'

The Armoury in the basement held many happy memories for Bond. It represented the first moments of a new adventure, the excitement of being back on a job. There were the revolvers and the Tommy guns, the Smith and Wessons, Colts, Lugers, Berettas, killer weapons of every class or nationality; blow-pipes, boomerangs, cyanide fountain-pens, Commando daggers and the familiar heap of aqualungs, now more or less standard equipment. He heard the instructor's voice. 'Grind your boot down his shin and crush his instep. Wrench off his testicles with yer free hand and with the fingers held stiffly in the V-sign gouge out his eyes with the other.'

He felt a wave of home-sickness.

CYRIL CONNOLLY

Lawrence Durrell (1912–   )

from Ivy

Aleicester, the poet, has at last finished the mighty palindrome that has entirely engaged his attention for the past eight years. Cloya brought it to me at dawn last Tuesday and I read it through in six hours, all the way from its brave, Homeric opening statement, 'T. Eliot, top bard, notes putrid tang,' to the great dying fall of its final line, '. . . Gnat-dirt upset on drab pot toilet.' Cloya tells me it will probably never be published; Aleicester, half mad with his vision, has already wrangled with his publisher, claiming that since the work can be read backward as well as forward he must receive double royalties. Ironic end to one so talented, so bored.

Did I say 'too-Western littoral' earlier? Odd! Just this morning I received another communication from Pinchbeck, the novelist, in which he urges me to move eastward. Near the end of this typically assertive document – a high-heaped interlinear correcting certain literate but misconceived comments I had scrawled in the margins of a fugitive work by Rhodmek Kun, the old bard of this narrow, fluminose island – he writes: 'Novelists, like horticulturists, must find the proper climate for their little crop of hybrid conceits. If you persist in planting your lush tropical blooms by the sidewalks of a Hyperborean stone city, you will not be entitled to the luxury of surprise or hurt when preoccupied residents turn coldly away from your finest blossoms muttering, "They don't even look real." Your own verb-garden, your overmulched nouns, require a feverish Levantine sun, the swollen profligacies of some Eastern delta. Plant your flowers there – in Smyrna, Aleppo, or Alexandria – let them burgeon in all their premeditated brilliance, and *then* watch the tourists trample your borders! See them sniff, note the shocked delight in their eyes as they ogle each purple stalk, each velvet petal, each naughty stamen, and listen to them as they exclaim, "How lovely, how wicked, how *true*!" '

Pinchbeck is listenable, of course, but I must confess that I suspect him of jealousy. For one thing, he writes so much like me – implacably Gongoresque, logorrheac to a fault. And then, Copernicus has told me that Pinchbeck once indulged in a bitter public outburst against my concept of the novel as a five-sided continuum – the quincunx book, with four characters (or four volumes) spinning in orbit about the fixed centre dot of events, like a die flung down on the green baize table of truth.

I must leave now; she will be waiting. The skin over my temples feels tautly stretched – a certain warning of the onset of *cafard*. It takes me forever to get going these days; one might even suspect me of wishing to inflate the meaning of each action, however trivial or fascinating, through cunctation and quiddity.

Out, then, again into the streets. I turn westward, toward the sun, stumping bravely toward Dr Balsamic's antiseptic couloirs. Micasheen from the minarets of the Squibb Building. Below the conflagration of afternoon sky, below the great Weehawken Corniche, the seared, exhausted traffic-swarm, thrilling the belly with the blare of its impatient horns. Squadrons, platoons, entire divisions of pedestrians, package-bearing, newspapered, come clicking toward me, and I notice again how blurred, how impalpable they all seem in the ambient mistral that blows across this city at all seasons from the slopes of Mt Simile. On the corner, Gepetto, the bearded convert, winks to me as he hurries past on his way to evensong – the Copt on the beat.

I come at last to the address, pass under the chaste, fly-specked sign ARISTOTLE BALSAMIC, D.V.M., and step into the white-walled foyer and the clean, masochistic scent of iodoform. The Dravidian receptionist ushers me into Balsamic's empty consulting room, where I sit briefly, listening to the yelps and bayings of hell that fall faintly here upon my abashed ears. Palpitant, I hear a step and a shuffle without, and they enter, Balsamic resembling a sleepy-eyed snowy owl in his sterile gown, and Ivy almost hidden behind him, her head low.

No bandage. I had expected bandages. My waif is thinner, etiolated by her experience, but when she sees me her gazelle eyes light up bravely. But she does not throw herself into my arms in her customary abandoned *abbraccio*. It is as I had known it would be: forgiveness was too much to expect.

I must speak. 'How is she, Doctor?'

'Fine,' Balsamic says. 'No complications. You can take her home now.'

'But then what?' I cry out. 'What will she think of me for putting her through all this? I mean, what about the *spirit*, the inner maelstrom? Isn't there danger of post-operative synecdoche?'

Balsamic regards me sceptically, looking like – well, like a sceptical doctor. 'Listen,' he says wearily, 'it was perfectly routine. It's normal to spay a dog of her age. I recommended it, and I'm sure I was right.'

I take the leash from him and make one more effort. 'Doesn't it mean *anything* to her?'

'Not a blessed thing. Oh, if she seems to have any trouble sleeping tonight, you might slip her a Bufferin, but that's all. In a few days she'll have forgotten all about this.' He must perceive some vestigial shimmer – could it be disappointment? – in my eyes, for he steps forward and places a friendly, scrubbed, Philistine hand on my arm. 'Look, fella,' he says in his emollient baritone, 'you writers, particularly you vocabulary-enrichers, ought to go easy on yourselves. All this high-class suffering and speculating, I mean. You're so damned sure that everybody is chock-full of passion and guilt and memory and all like that, when most of the time – almost all the time, if you ask me – they're not thinking of anything but their next can of Ken-L-Ration. Keep that in mind – OK?'

I nod, and Ivy and I take our leave. Outside, darkness has veiled the aged face of the courtesan streets, and the buildings above us cast down an autumnal pollen of yellow lights. The leash slack between us, we turn automatically and prophetically toward the East, each wincing faintly from our interior wounds. We are both exhausted, and no wonder.

ROGER ANGELL

from Voluptia

In my mind, I was thinking. Alexandria, Queen of Cities, gathered round me as if it were a violet dusk. Mauve clouds like sheered seaweed filtered across the sky. Somewhere, over boxes of nougat, ambassadors wrangled. I scratched a lovebite on my shoulder and gazed down at my pallid body, clad in its tartan underdrawers, stretched out before me, a long, sad groan of fate. Oh, how lonely I felt. I called Ali, in my best Greek, to bring me a nectarine of Scythian *krash*. I was so subtracted I forgot he was deaf, and probably knew no Greek anyway. But he KNEW, even as I held up a finger which hung in the velvet air like a tendril of verbena.

Then Voluptia was there. She laid a hand over my ears, and whispered softly. I could not hear her. I gazed upon her dank lips, rubbed with old kisses, those obfuscating osculations suspended there, recalled on the instant she reappeared. That her words were endearments of love (L–O–V–E) I was sure. Then, with a brisk chattering snatch of laughter, she sat: as delicately as a mushroom on the green sward.

'Darley!' she whispered.

'Voluptia!' I murmured.

'Darley!' she said.

Then I noticed she had lost her nose! I stared spellbound at the hole like a fox's hide which lay gaping between her eyes. A long moment wound itself way; I knew she would tell me. 'I've had a tiresome day,' she began. Ali came in with my *krash*, and I signalled one for her in my second-best Greek.

'First,' she whispered, 'let us drink to . . . love!'

'Life!' I said.

She arranged herself into a pattern of Byzantine order, her clothes fighting for their colour with the grass. 'I lost an ear this morning,' she muttered at last. 'Hamid cut it off in pique. Then the left eye Memlik dashed out at lunchtime, because I wouldn't take him on Mountolive's spider-shoot.' But it was still the nose that took me by surprise. I looked at her, trying to fathom the labyrinths of her silence. What can I give you, I cogitated with myself, but sympathy? (As Pursewarden – the devil – wrote: TO ALL WHO SUFFER SHALL COME . . . SUFFERING.)

The heat popped and eddied in my eardrum; I watched lazily as a bead of sweat formed on the skin of my baggy, shapeless hand. 'Let us make love,' I outspake at last, 'even on a punt, even on Mareotis, which by now must be the colour of gunmetal, the texture of boiled offal. Now!' I feared that she would feel unwanted.

'No,' she responded, vivid in grass, 'I must tell you the story, and without obfuscation. There are three versions so far, as many as there are persons, and there might be more if we wait. If we have time to wait. You see, it is so cruel, not really knowing WHY!'

'Yes,' I muttered. My heart was drenched in brilliants of violet love. But before she could even begin her first explanation, there was the sound of footfalls, many footfalls. Scobie dashed in on us, his glass lips blubbering. Behind, the soft-footed Ali beat out his lighter yet fundamentally arrogant note. He stood protective as Scobie, disagreeably abnormal, spoke in a tottering voice.

'Sorry, Darley,' he said, avoiding looking directly at the nipples on my chest, 'but I've got to cart Voluptia off to chokey. She's been interfering down in the circumcision booths. There've been complaints.'

Voluptia, to give credit, resisted.

'YA SCOBIE,' I yelled, 'are you sure you're not under the influence?' After a moment he nodded, closing his eyes. Then musingly he *loquitur*: 'Sometimes the mind strays further than life allows. It is easy to excuse, but one's duty is in the end to judge. Alas, our pitiless city demands . . .'

MALCOLM BRADBURY

294

Dylan Thomas (1914–1953)

Under Broadcasting House

FIRST VOICE: To begin at the beginning of the anniversary end. It is autumn, sunless day in the big city, car-filled and negro-black. Listen. It is midday moving in the streets, in the air-waving, script-scattered Portland Place, under Broadcasting House. Look, as a dozen desk-bound directors

SECOND VOICE: Lift a hang-over from the beer-spilled blotter and sigh to the world at large

DIRECTORS: How glad I am that I discovered Dylan.

FIRST VOICE: And Mrs Jenkins from Sea View Terrace, Laugharne, kicks the cat, glares at the transistor and mutters

MRS JENKINS: Dylan who?

FIRST VOICE: There's a hotch-potch of verses from the hum-drumming records of the medium-wave, cashing-in of compères, killings, quick and easy, poetry pumping from the clapped-out set, carry on Llareggub. Words are worshipped, quotes quoted, interviews granted, memoirs sold: wives blush, sons wince and tills ring.

SECOND VOICE: Come now, to the drinks-all-round, spruced-up, juiced-up lounge bar in He-Lived-Here Laugharne, where the locals jostle and jeer at a Cadillac, crammed with keepsakes and Americans.

FIRST LOCAL: I don't know where we'd be without Dylan.

SECOND LOCAL: We are without him, Dai. I don't know where we'd be with him.

FIRST VOICE: And Mrs Jenkins, in Sea View Terrace, kicks the transistor, opens the Kattomeat and mutters

MRS JENKINS: Oh, *that* Dylan! If only I'd realised at the time I might have spoken to him.

SECOND VOICE: While a ghost from the W1A 1 double A'd Broadcasting House gasps into the ether.

SECRETARY: Oh, Dylan! We all loved you. You did go off the rails a bit, though. Towards the end.

FIRST VOICE: The full-to-the-brim day dims. The candled cakes for the twenty-five dead years are blown out. Mementoes are tidied and tucked away down Memory Lane, tills cashed up,

295

takings checked, Welsh accents dropped, and the big, soft city hardens at the edges as night falls under Broadcasting House.

RICHARD QUICK

Adventures in the Fur Game

. . . The stairs creaked, full of protesting whispers as we stumbled up to the bedroom. Dad flung open the door with a window-rattling, wash-basin shout of surprise. His bed, normally white and smooth as blancoed snow was all rough and tumbled like sea waves. The sun shone through the sea-spying windows and mottled his seething snout. 'That old she-goat next door has been here!' he thundered.

'What! Mrs Probert? Never,' said Mum. 'It's some no-good out-of-work boyos. You've seen them, propping up the morning outside the Sailors' Arms.' Then Mum saw her own blown-about, sea-slapped bed. 'It's envy! That's what it is. Envy of the beargeoisie!' She picked up a photograph of me as a baby gazing bewildered and blue-eyed at the dicky-bird. 'At least they left my little bear behind,' she said.

'I wouldn't say your behind was little!' said Father with his shovelling sand laugh.

'I'll push that laugh down your throat till your tail drops off!' Mother said. 'We have been broken into, burgled, and all you can do is joke like a jackass!'

But I looked at my own bed. And there she was – the lovely girl of my dreams! Her lovely locks lingered gold-spun over the coverlet. Not with the brassy boldness of a Polly Garter, but like the sea where it foams like a flame at sunset.

For a moment I stared at her, as silent as Sunday, till opening her eyes, she gave a startled cry. She was out of the bed like a bolt, through the open door and down the stairs.

'Stop thief!' cried Father.

'Come back, Teddy! You're not to chase her!' Mother called out to me. But dazzled by her beauty I stumbled after her, a blind bear in the sun.

She waited a moment at the front door. 'I only came to find my

lost Teddy bear,' she said. The sun hummed down through the
cotton flowers of her dress to the bell of her heart.

'Where are you from?' I asked her. She did not wait, but just said,
'Goodbye!' and then ran along the cobbled street and into the wood.
I followed her. She raced among the trees, over the dewy hills, from
silence into the sound of the sea.

'Come back! Come back!' I called. 'I'm the Teddy you are looking
for.' But she ran on, over the sand, past the bobbing boats and the
stone-warmed seats where the fishermen spit and spin out the day. I
lost her among the sand dunes. The breezes drew long breaths. Oh,
where is she now? 'It's a once upon a time tale,' whispered the waters.
'But not this time. You must go back, Bear.'

So sadly I went back in the dying of the day. 'I'm head over
bells in love with her,' I told Mother. 'I shall marry her when I
find her.'

'Marry her! Impossible! You must tell Teddy the facts of life,
Father!'

Father grunted. 'The facts are son – you could never marry her.
You see, she could never bear a bear.'

'She would be unbearable,' Mother said.

When I finally understood the pain was as sharp as sciatica. But
in a once upon a time tale . . . Anyway, I still visit the sand dunes on
lulling afternoons where the sea laps and idles in, dreaming of the
day she may come again looking for her Teddy. Then at long last I
shall stroke her golden hair and lay my head on her lovely red-
berried breast.

P. W. R. FOOT

Henry Reed (1914–   )

The Mending of Fuses

Tonight we have mending of fuses. Yesterday
We had cleaning of wastepipes. And tomorrow morning
We shall have horrors we dare not imagine. But tonight,

Tonight we have mending of fuses. For convenience fuse boxes
Are located in the darkest and most inaccessible
Corners of the domicile. Groping among spiders' webs
I know, whichever I choose first, the one wanted will be last.
To effect fuse-mending properly, one needs fuse wire.
We ought to have had some somewhere, but would have saved an
    hour
If we had borrowed from next door in the first place.
Tonight, after the flash, we shall have mending of fuses again
After the mending of plugs, which we could do
If we could remember the wiring, which we could do
If we could find the diagram from the Electricity Board.
Tomorrow we shall have mending of fuses again;
For tonight we shall make do with candles.

E. O. PARROTT

Charles Causley (1917–   )

Book Review

Longest and much the dearest –
The price of books benumbs –
With a slap of sail and a following gale
The rhymer Causley comes.

Now Causley comes from Cornwall,
And, brother, how it shows.
The harbour bell and that fishy smell
Assault both ears and nose.

But Causley's balladeering
Is good for youth to gnaw on
(In fact, to be frank, it's a Doggerel Bank
That any kid can draw on).

He uses simply, sociably,
The skill he's been allotted;
And that's a start. Because in art
Not all the cream is clotted.

RUSSELL DAVIES

Muriel Spark (1918–   )

Last Things

'I hope you are both keeping an extremely careful eye on the weather,' says Sister Felicity, who is small and fat, with a shrewd mouth, 'It is perhaps the commonest way available of procuring our downfall.'

'I can't think of any reason why it should be,' says Sister Mercy, who is famous for being stupid, and for getting the weaker lines of dialogue, and who will die, in distressing circumstances, rather closer to the beginning of this story than any of the others.

'Felicity is right, of course,' says Sister Georgina, still one of the novices, but taken up by Sister Felicity for her cunning: she is reputed to have worked for the Political Intelligence Department of a certain Foreign Office during the war. 'It is a question of sustaining an adequate level of probability. Even a simple change of barometric pressure can lead with unbroken logic to a chill, and a chill to bronchial pneumonia, which in turn can have fatal consequences without disturbing at all what people are pleased to think of as the normal order of things.'

'That is why Sister Georgina urged you to put on your thickest shoes,' says Sister Felicity, walking on with her quite long stride.

The three nuns, black like crows in the habit of their order, walk, on the grass, under the trees, up and down, round and round, in the private and unseen grounds of this rigorous convent, notable for its chastity, in an unnamed northern country. It is, for the moment, a nice day. The sun is shining in an apparently pleasant way on the grass, on the leaves of the trees, and the barometric pressure, while subject to sudden fluctuation in these parts, is recorded as steady and fair in the newspapers that will, on the following day, have so much to report, in long black columns of type, about these lawns, these trees, this famous and rigorous convent. Inside the cold stone buildings, just visible over the wall, the other nuns are even now performing the appropriate observances. The Prioress, in her white habit, is looking at her watch and noting, so that she will be able to report tomorrow, when it all comes out, the extent of Felicity's absence. But, at this moment, she is not alarmed. Felicity's absences are famous. She has been at this convent longer than any other nun, and her shrewd tongue and her authoritative manners have won her exceptional privileges, privileges now as ritualized, in their way, as the Vespers and the Complines, the duties and observances, that the reporters will record for their columns, the television crews film for their audiences, in the weeks of publicity that are to follow.

'The real torment', says Sister Georgina, drawing Mercy away from a large puddle which has appeared before them in the path, 'is to know that there is a hand at work, yet not to know where and when it will choose to reveal itself.'

'I don't think I want anything more to do with this plot,' says Sister Mercy suddenly, putting her hands to her face, and bursting into tears. 'I'm not even sure there is a plot,' she cries, looking at the other two.

Sister Felicity stops abruptly, and looks at Mercy, appraising her with her judging brow. 'I'm sorry, my dear,' she says, 'I am afraid you have very little choice. It is the way of things to be necessary, when *we* wish them to be contingent. But this you know, from your faith. There is little any of us can do about it, except take every intelligent precaution. That is why Sister Georgina has brought a sunshade, as I, you see, have brought my umbrella. Of course,' she adds, 'the best thing of all is just not to be her type.'

A small white cloud appears in the blue sky above the trees in the convent garden.

'I think Felicity should notice this cloud,' says Georgina.

'I have already noticed it, my dear,' says Felicity, walking round and round, up and down.

'If one were to leave and go somewhere else under another name,' says Mercy.

'I very much doubt if that would work, except in the most exceptional circumstances,' says Felicity.

'But what circumstances?' cries Mercy.

'If, perhaps, one were being saved for something,' says Felicity. 'You must understand, Mercy, I have been in a novel before. I know what it's like. It is extremely uncomfortable, unless one manages to stay entirely peripheral to the main line of the action, and not to draw attention to oneself in any way. I have always thought', she adds, drawing Sister Georgina from the vicinity of a large overhanging branch on an old tree, 'that the best way is to be a member of the servant classes, or to be asleep in another room most of the time.'

'It *has* been done,' says Sister Georgina. 'There have been some who have escaped. One was called Golly Mackintosh, who conducted herself with very sensible restraint, I thought, in remaining out of Italy entirely over the period when that English film actress had such a bad time.'

'Which actress was that?' asks Mercy.

'Felicity will know her name,' says Georgina. 'She is stupendously well read.'

'Annabel Christopher,' says Sister Felicity. 'There was also a sickly looking man in a plane and a hotel who was wise enough to confine himself to the minimum of conversation with Lise.'

'Who is Lise?' asks Sister Mercy.

'She is in another by the same hand,' says Sister Georgina. 'A woman of great linguistic abilities, but I'm afraid the effect of that sort of cleverness is only to get oneself noticed.'

'I think it would be unwise to say much in front of Mercy about what happened to Lise,' says Felicity. 'I fear they are much of a type. Am I mistaken, or is that cloud growing darker? I'm sure we'd be wise to return as quickly as we can to our offices.'

Under the trees, at the very end of the garden, the three nuns turn. 'I wish we could get ourselves into the hands of Mr Fowles,' says Sister Mercy, as they walk back in their dark habits. 'He's much kinder, and allows his people an extraordinary freedom of choice.'

'We understand your feelings,' says Sister Georgina, 'but it's a very secular judgement. In any case, you'd find with him that what's sauce for the goose is sauce for the gander, if you understand me.'

'I think not,' says Mercy.

'One would almost certainly find oneself being rogered by one of his libidinous heroes,' says Felicity. 'At least our context here is not particularly Freudian.'

'It could be interesting,' says Mercy.

'I have never myself taken any pleasure in the sex part,' says Georgina. 'It is all right at the time, but not afterwards.'

'I think I could put up with it,' says Mercy. 'I expect one could enjoy it a great deal, if one was prepared to become famous at it.'

There is a sudden burst of lightning from the darkening cloud above the trees, causing Mercy to fall inert to the ground. The other two nuns, in their black habits, kneel beside her. In a moment they rise, their faces solemn. 'It was lucky she murmured something sensitive just before she passed on,' says Georgina, looking down on the recumbent body, which before the night will lie in the chapel of the convent, the composed and stupid face staring sightlessly up at the nuns who file by and, later, at the police inspector who finally orders the autopsy.

'I am afraid we were not paying sufficient attention,' says Felicity. 'We had dropped our guard.'

Georgina breathes hard, as if fighting off inevitable tears. 'It is not very kind of Miss Spark,' she says. 'And it is hardly as if Mercy were a full protagonist.'

'Come,' says Felicity, 'I think we should sit over there by the wall and be quiet for a while. If there were no dialogue, there could be nothing to incense her.'

The two nuns, in their black habits, walk to a corner of the garden that is treeless and, putting down the sunshade, putting down the umbrella, they seat themselves, backs against the wall, at a place that, in tomorrow's papers, will be marked with a stark X. They look across the bright trimmed green of the turf, beyond the crumpled black corpse, to the columns of trees, the once again blue sky. In the blue of the sky appears a white plume rather like a feather, the trail of an aeroplane that carries many travellers from homes to meetings, from holidays to homes, travellers who will read with surprise in their next day's journals of the events that unfolded, apparently without connection, below them.

'Even she could hardly want to push coincidence too far,' says Georgina, inspecting the plane with some anxiety. 'Surely her critics would begin to talk.'

Felicity, too, looks at the plane. 'I think you may be right to see a hand,' she says. 'And I am afraid the critics themselves are not entirely innocent in these matters.'

'I had not known there could be others,' says Georgina.

'You have not heard of a Professor Kermode?'

'I had not thought of him in this connection,' says Sister Georgina. 'I thought he was usually in America.'

'The Atlantic may be a substantial stretch of water, Georgina,' says Felicity, 'but it is not an outright barrier to intellectual intercourse. I think we should go in.'

But Sister Georgina is still looking at the plane, with its many travellers, and glimpsing, with a growing horror, the silvery piece of metal, a part of a wing perhaps, a piece of a wheel, that has detached itself from it and, twirling, changing in shape but not in direction, angles down through the air towards the treeless corner of the garden. She rises and runs, her gaze fixed in the air. The aeroplane part whistles in its descent and falls harmlessly into an adjoining field. Felicity rises, in her black habit, and runs to Georgina who, looking upward, has stumbled over a croquet hoop, inadvertently left in the grass, and fallen to the ground. 'You were lucky, Georgina,' she says. 'You might well have been dead.' But a closer inspection reveals the truth; the fall has clearly been a heavy one, for Georgina, in fact, is.

For a moment Sister Felicity stands there, in her dark habit. She looks at the two crumpled bodies that lie in the grass, in spots which, tomorrow, will be staked around, and examined intently by many policemen. Then, in a sudden movement, she disappears behind an adjacent bush. 'She's caught me,' she shouts, in seven languages. There is a sound as of cloth ripping: a white coif flies above the bush and falls some distance away on the grass. A short while after a figure appears from behind the bush, in familiar street clothes, a dress of slightly more than miniskirt length. The shoes are perhaps heavy, and the blackness of the material of the dress duller than would suit most people's tastes. The figure rapidly crosses the grass of the convent garden, walking not towards the buildings but away from them, towards the high wall that shuts out the diurnal world beyond. And now the figure reaches this high stone wall, climbing it with agility and some speed. It gives a last glance to the garden that will be in so many papers, and then disappears from sight.

Later Felicity will do many things. She will fly to Africa, to Canada, to South America. She will hunt tiger in India, and take a small canoe down the Amazon river, through disease-infested waters and snake-inhabited swamps. She will climb precipitous mountains in the Tyrol, where sheer drops overlook green and church-filled valleys far below. She will die, in New York City, in the year 2024, at the age of ninety-eight, of benign old age. She will lie in bed at the last, and look up, and say: 'What did you want of me? What have you been waiting for all this time?' But I don't feel that it's my business to go around answering questions like that.

MALCOLM BRADBURY

J. D. Salinger (1919–   )

Review

I can't help thinking – and I've been lying here in the bath for three solid (more accurately, fluid) hours – that Mr Buddy Glass Salinger is altogether too close to his subject. Which – or rather who, it being his brother Seymour – rightly, as you'll agree, doesn't appear in these pages. But what about Paula Kyte? Paula, I allow, wasn't one of the Glass children, she never (so far as my admittedly lacunal knowledge goes) was panelled on *It's a Wise Child*, indeed – not to cut a short story anywhere near long enough, *New Yorker* rates being what they are – she doesn't exist, never did exist, probably (though this begs the reincarnation question) never will exist. Why isn't *she* mentioned? (I pause to reach myself a cooling drink from the conveniently positioned *tabouret* and take a drag on my cigar.) One mustn't be too goddam simple. Or there's Botticelli's grapes. To the best of my recollection, Seymour never, on any ascertainable chronological occasion, referred to them, either directly or indirectly, probably never once thought about them, perhaps had never even heard of them. *There's* a starting point!

J. A. LINDON

Iris Murdoch (1919–   )

from The Sublime and the Ridiculous

'Flavia says that Hugo tells her that Augustina is in love with Fred.'

Sir Alex Mountaubon stood with his wife Lavinia in one of the deeply recessed mullion windows of the long gallery at Bishop's Breeches, looking out at the topiary peacocks on the terrace beyond. In front of them the fountain, topped with statuary in which a naked Mars played joyously with a willing Venus, gently coruscated, its tinkle audible through the open windows. The scene before them was of order and peace. They could look down the park at the mile-long drive of lindens, the colour of jaundice; to one side, away from its necessary order, stood one dark and contingent cedar tree. Beneath it their older daughter, Flavia, could be seen from the window, sitting on a white wooden seat, in her unutterable otherness, her pet marmoset on her shoulder, her cap of auburn hair shining like burnished gold on her head. Nearer to the house, in the rose garden, their younger daughter, seven-year-old Perdita, strange, mysterious and self-absorbed as usual, was beheading a litter of puppies with unexpectedly muscular and adult twists of her slender arm. Her cap of golden hair shone like burnished auburn on her head.

Alex turned, catching sight of himself in the big, gilt, rather battered cupid-encrusted mirror that soared over the mantel. Mortality was there in the darkened eyes, but most of what he saw there, the solid, round face of a man of principle, pleased him exceedingly. His book, a philosophical study of Niceness, was almost complete; in its writing, Lavinia, his second wife, had proved the perfect helpmeet and companion. No one lay dying upstairs. He looked around at the familiar objects, the Titians and Tintorettos, glowing in their serried ranks with jewelled beneficence, the twined, golden forms of bodies twisted together suggesting a radiant vision of another world. In cases stood the Sung cups, the Ting plates, the Tang vases, the Ming statuettes, the Ching saucers; these last must, almost certainly, go.

'Who says whom tells her that who is in love with whom?'

Lavinia, her arms full of lilies, did not turn. 'Flavia,' she said.

'And are they?'

'They think so. I don't think they quite know.'

'But at least we know. About us,' said Alex lovingly. He looked out of the window and saw Perdita staring strangely up at the house; and suddenly, involuntarily, he recalled again that experience of utter freedom he had known for the first time when he and Moira LeBenedictus had lain naked together in the Reading Room of the British Museum, after hours of course; he, as a senior civil servant, had been entitled to a key. Other moments came back: Moira walking through Harrods without her shoes, Moira on the night they had boxed together on the roof of St Paul's Cathedral, Moira threatening him in the Tottenham Hotspurs football ground at midnight with her whaler's harpoon.

Two miles away, in the bathroom at his house, Buttocks, Sir Hugo Occam laid down his razor. He walked through into the bedroom where Moira LeBenedictus lay. She was his good towards which he magnetically swung. She lay on the bed, gathering her hair together into a cap of black.

'Are we acting rightly?'

'I think we are,' she said.

'Oh, Moira.'

'Come, come, Hugo,' she said. From the alcove, Leo Chatteris, a spoiled priest, long in love with Moira, watched them in protective benediction. Could he surrender her? The pain was so much he knew it was right . . .

MALCOLM BRADBURY

Kingsley Amis (1922–   )

What about You?

When Mrs Taflan Gruffyd Lewis left Dai's flat
She gave her coiffe a pat

Having straightened carefully those nylon seams
Adopted to fulfil Dai's wicked dreams.
Evans didn't like tights.
He liked plump white thighs pulsing under thin skirts in packed pubs
    on warm nights.

That's that, then, thought Evans, hearing her Jag start,
And test-flew a fart.
Stuffing the wives of these industrial shags may be all
Very well, and *this* one was an embassy bar-room brawl
With Madame Nhu.
Grade A. But give them that fatal twelfth inch and they'll soon take
    their cue

To grab a yard of your large intestine or include your glans
Penis in their plans
For that Rich, Full Emotional Life you'd thus far ducked
So successfully.
Yes, Evans was feeling . . . Mucked
-up sheets recalled their scrap.
Thinking barded thoughts in stanza form after shafting's a right
    sweat. Time for a nap.

EDWARD PYGGE

Remember Lot's Wife

Sometimes in later years
    dining with bosom pals
Lot felt a nervous wreck
    passing the salt,
But on the evidence
    (Genesis 19 *et seq.*)
Mrs Lot's tragic end
    wasn't his fault.

Poor sod was queer of course,
   shouldn't have married her,
Sex-starved and sore-eyed
   she looked back in tears,
Nothing but ashes and
   sodium chloride,
Thank God I'm hetero;
   whiskey please; cheers.

STANLEY J. SHARPLESS

Philip Larkin (1922–1985)

After the Library

After the library and tea (tired cakes in plastic wraps)
I pad the dappled park I once forsook.
The scented summer wind whirls dust and scraps
Against the thighs of mini-skirted girls,
Exposing nylon flimsies, lemon, rose;
Cheap thrills, you might suppose,
To one who, life half-gone, bends to a book.

But I was always easily bored, withdrawn:
The gilt-edged promises that life unfurls
Like paper flowers are flawed. A broken chime
Of fading laughter drifts up from the lawn.
Soon the dark-visaged keeper will call time.

DOUGLAS GIBSON

Mr Strugnell

'This was Mr Strugnell's room,' she'll say –
And look down at the lumpy, single bed.
'He stayed here up until he went away
And kept his bicycle out in that shed.

'He had a job in Norwood library –
He was a quiet sort who liked to read –
Dick Francis mostly, and some poetry –
He liked John Betjeman very much indeed

'But not Pam Ayres or even Patience Strong –
He'd change the subject if I mentioned them,
Or say, "It's time for me to run along –
Your taste's too highbrow for me, Mrs M."

'And up he'd go and listen to that jazz.
I don't mind telling you it was a bore –
Few things in this house have been tiresome as
The sound of his foot tapping on the floor.

'He didn't seem the sort for being free
With girls or going out and having fun.
He had a funny turn in 'sixty-three
And ran round shouting "Yippee! It's begun!"

'I don't know what he meant, but after that
He had a different look, much more relaxed.
Some nights he'd come in late, too tired to chat,
As if he had been somewhat overtaxed.

'And now he's gone. He said he found Tulse Hill
Too stimulating – wanted somewhere dull.
At last he's found a place that fits the bill –
Enjoying perfect boredom up in Hull.'

WENDY COPE

Second-hand Car Dealer

I'm not a man to muck about,
And you're a decent sort of chap,
So I won't talk a load of crap,
This old jalopy's up the spout.

The engine runs by fits and starts,
You would do better with a bike,
The body, well – it's had it – like
A superannuated tart's.

If you decide to have a bash
You may end up in kingdom come;
You think I've got a nerve, then, chum?
I need the cash, the cash, the cash.

STANLEY J. SHARPLESS

John Wain (1925–)

Keeping up with Kingsley

Ah well! It's good to be rid of all the strain.
It's such a pain to turn the drivel out.
(*And* to keep up with Kingsley and John Braine!)

Of course, they never saw what I was about:
Emancipation from the printed page . . .!
How's that for a way to still the doubter's doubt,
A slogan for the post-McLuhan age?

Poems should be read out loud. Mine too!
                                        But man
You'd think they'd let you make a living wage.

A *Word Carved on a Sill*. We do what we can.
OK, I was wrong to back the Empson horse:
I couldn't even get the stuff to scan;

Words never let you conquer them by force.
But certain possibilities remain.
I'll make a new anthology. And of course
I'll have to take up lecturing again.

COLIN FALCK

Anon (Romantic Ballad)

I Hold Your Hand in Mine

I hold your hand in mine, dear,
I press it to my lips.
I take a healthy bite from
Your dainty fingertips.

My joy would be complete, dear,
If you were only here,
But still I keep your hand as
A precious souvenir.

The night you died I cut it off,
I really don't know why.
For now each time I kiss it, I
Get bloodstains on my tie.

I'm sorry now I killed you, for
Our love was something fine,
And till they come to get me, I
Shall hold your hand in mine.

TOM LEHRER

Anon (Negro Spiritual)

The Heavenly Fish Queue

When Ah rides in ma chariot to de sky
  (Yes, mam, Ah's tellin' you!)
Dis pore ol' nigger wid der fish to buy
  Will be right in de front ob de queue,

(Yes, Lawd, right in de front ob de queue.)

Till de Hebenly fish-shop opens wide,
  Wid paint all fresh an' new,
Dere'll be golden seats fo' de folk outside,
  An' I'll set in de front ob de queue.

(Yes, Lawd, right in de front ob de queue.)

Dere'll be cawfee an' doughnuts handed out
  In cups an' plates bright blue;
An' de angel ob de Lawd gonna sing an' shout:
  'Take 'em fust to de front ob de queue.'

(Yes, Lawd, right in de front ob de queue.)

When de rich white folks done telephone,
  De Lawd – Ah tells yo' true –

He will laugh an' say de best fish hab gone
　To de nigger in de front ob de queue.

(Yes, Lawd, right in de front ob de queue.)

ALLAN M. LAING

Allen Ginsberg (1926–　　)

Squeal

I saw the best minds of my generation
Destroyed – Marvin
Who spat out poems; Potrzebie
Who coagulated a new bop literature in fifteen
Novels; Alvin
Who in his as yet unwritten autobiography
Gave Brooklyn an original *lex loci*.
They came from all over, from the pool room,

The bargain basement, the rod,
From Whitman, from Parkersburg, from Rimbaud
New Mexico, but mostly
They came from colleges, ejected
For drawing obscene diagrams of the Future.

They came here to LA,
Flexing their members, growing hair,
Planning immense unlimited poems,
More novels, more poems, more autobiographies.

It's love I'm talking about, you dirty bastards!
Love in the bushes, love in the freight car!
I saw them fornicating and being fornicated,
Saying to Hell with you!

America.
America is full of Babbitts.
America is run by money.

What was it Walt said? Go West!
But the important thing is the return ticket.
The road to publicity runs by Monterey.
I saw the best minds of my generation
Reading their poems to Vassar girls,
Being interviewed by *Mademoiselle*.
Having their publicity handled by professionals.
When can I go into an editorial office
And have my stuff published because I'm weird?
I could go on writing like this forever . . .

LOUIS SIMPSON

Alan Sillitoe (1928–   )

from Room at the Bottom

The huge green Nottingham trolley-bus circumnavigated the roundabout of Canning Circus, its rod-like poles hissing as they crossed the centripetal nexus of overhead wires, and pulled up at the stop. A group of lads from the factory, on good money nowadays, got off, laughing, shouting and saying their tatas. Eustace Seaton stared wistfully at them and then stepped on, with great arm-swinging strides, up the gradient of the Derby road, only wishing he could afford the fourpenny fare into Radford. A javelin wind was daggering into him, and an evening rain made an oily shine on the pavements. Home seemed miles off, but Eustace stumped on, his feet feeling like great lumps of pig-iron at the bottom of his legs. He walked past pub doors out of which came draughts of beer and smoke smells, but with his pockets as empty as boggery it was no use thinking of stopping. Under the street lamps drunks mumbled in the gutters, celebrating the start of the weekend binge, and swaddies walked in and out of the pawnshops. It was a tiring, uphill walk, but at last Eustace knew that he was getting there when he saw that the policemen were at last walking about in pairs. 'Hey up, goodnight, lads,' he said, as he passed a couple; it gave him a happy feeling to know that he lived in a stable, responsible society where, impartially, the interests of all good men were so carefully protected.

Now he was there. He walked down the street of back-to-backs, feeling round him the life he knew so well. The roofs of the outside lavatories were flushed red in the post-meridional glow of the setting sun; the fog-dragon of night was beginning to slink between the steaming chimney-pots. Kids he had been at school with, swum in the canal with, now on the machines at Player's and the Raleigh, were unloading crates of pinched fags and tools from the sidecars of motor-bikes. The family on the corner, two years in arrears on the rent, were doing another flit, all their furniture, and several other people's besides, stacked up on creaking barrows, while a crowd of ragged-arsed kids tagged behind. On every doorstep housewives threw plates at hire-purchase collectors, and the white faces of the army deserters peered up at him through cellar gratings.

He turned along the twitchell towards the back door, and clobbered through the yard. His brother Arthur was sitting at the open back bedroom window, rifle in hand, taking pot shots between the houses at the distant figures of bailiffs as they passed back and forth on the Derby Road, an everlasting source of annoyance to the Seatons. 'Hey up, me owd duck,' he shouted as Eustace came along the twitchell, vomiting into a convenient jug; Eustace suppressed a frisson of irritation at the uncouthness of his kinsman.

'Bagged owt?' asked Eustace.

'Nowt,' said Arthur. ' 'Ere, there's that owd biddy down t'twitchell as towd on me to the bobs. I'll notch her in the buttock.' Leaving his brother to it, Eustace stuck his head in through the back door that led into the tiny kitchen, overheated by the large fire used for mashing tea and making dough for wads. Whenever he did this, he was always struck by the way the Gissing-like naturalism of the ambience was mitigated by a Lawrentian vitality; he felt that again now. Vera Seaton stood at the table, scraping jam on to a buttie.

'Hello, our mam,' said Eustace.

'Look, 'ere 'e is, then, daren't show 'is bleddy face round t'door,' said Vera Seaton. 'Where in the name of boggery 'ave yo' bin, then, eh?'

'Well, our mam,' said Eustace, 'I 'ardly like to say. I've been up the university, and they've accepted me to tek a degree i' classics, our mam.'

Vera looked at him scornfully. 'This is a fine bleddy thing, this is, innit, then?' she said. 'I don't know what Seaton'll say. I expect 'e'll bat your bleddy tab for yo'. We've never 'ad a bleddy layabout in the family before.'

' 'Ow is our dad, our mam?' asked Eustace, easing off his steaming shoes.

' 'E's in a real lather, and no mistake. Our Brian's come 'ome from Swansea and 'e's brought a black lass with 'im. Seaton towd her she'd 'ave to sleep up in t'loft wi' the deserters 'cos she's so mucky. You'd better tek care what you say, our Eustace, if yo' want my opinion.'

There was a thunder of footsteps on the stairs, and the door from the hall shot violently open. Seaton stood there in his braces, breathing heavily, his face inflamed to the colour of puce. It was at once apparent to Eustace, a delicate lad, always sensitive to atmosphere, that his father was, as so often, a trifle out of sorts.

' 'Ere, was it your 'eavy boots woke me up, then, when I'm trying to get a bit of shut-eye?' he asked thick-voiced in the doorway.

'They can't have bin, our dad,' said Eustace. 'They've never bin upstairs.'

'Don't yo' cheek me, yer young bogger-lugs,' exclaimed Seaton. 'And look at that bleddy clock. What time do yo' call this, then? Fine bleddy time to come 'ome, innit? We've bin sitting 'ere for 'alf an hour, peein' ussens to 'ave us snap, and yo' comin' in this late.'

'Well, I'm sorry, our dad,' said Eustace, 'but I 'adn't no money left for the trackless, cos I'd spent it all buyin' these books about Spinoza and Descartes and 'umanistic rationalism, our dad, and so I 'ad to leg it 'ome, and it took me a long time.'

'Leg it 'ome?' Seaton dissolved into black anger. 'Yer silly loon-faced young mardarsed bogger, I've towd yo' once if I've towd yer fifty times, get on the bleddy trolley and when they want the fare, tell 'em yo're under five.'

'But, our dad, I'm eighteen.'

'Well, tell 'em it's the bomb, sharpshit; tell 'em you're a mutation. Yo' bleddy look like one to me.'

'I don't like telling lies, our dad.'

'Well, yo' gret soft thing,' said Seaton. 'Yo' allus was the mardarse.

Right from a nipper. When all the others wor on probation for nickin', all yo' wanted to do with yer bleddy sen was go to the grammar school and read Theocritus on pastoral.'

MALCOLM BRADBURY

Peter Porter (1929–)

E Pericoloso Sporgersi

But a modulation to D flat minor
argues for pronouns of a different kind:
the consideration of history as syntax
or a slow dance of nomadic stones.
No wonder that the flight of the pigeon
over the Piazza Cortina at sunset
becomes a gesture of the purest angst.

Pastruccio knew what to make of such
gratuitous moments, the refractions
of inveterate light. In a garden
of non sequiturs the silkworm dozes,
ignorant of Spinoza and unworried
by sex or the darkening obscurity
of sonorous sentences like these.

My cat piddles on the carpet and yawns.
Art, he reflects, is rivalled only
by a cargo of absolutes sailing northward
to Goethe's incomparable parakeet.
The gods dream dictionaries and sonatinas.
Beyond the window their shadows lengthen,
aspiring to the stature of a late quartet.

WENDY COPE

Ted Hughes (1930–   )

Budgie Finds His Voice

from The Life and Songs of the Budgie *by Jake Strugnell*

God decided he was tired
Of his spinning toys.
They wobbled and grew still.

When the sun was lifted away
Like an orange lifted from a fruit-bowl

And darkness, blacker
Than an oil-slick
Covered everything forever

And the last ear left on earth
Lay on the beach,
Deaf as a shell

And the land froze
And the sea froze

'Who's a pretty boy then?' Budgie cried.

WENDY COPE

Looking in the Mirror

My eyebrows are as thick as thieves.
They hang like shags of tobacco
Above a nose like a wedge, a doorstop.
They could probably get knotted.

A chin juts out. A blunt,
Almost pointless boulder of bone,
Stuck out stern from the face.
The lips are as grim as poachers'.

Curving quietly, up to no good.
The furrow between them is rough:
They seem to snag on laughter.
Nothing much given away here.

And the hair, thick as quills
From which feathers are stripped:
Swept back by an oily rake
There is great weight on my forehead.

BILL GREENWELL

Slug Resting

I lie in the middle of the path, my eyes closed.
Inaction. No warning fear
Between my wet head and wet tail:
Or in sleep rehearse nibbles and chew.

The convenience of the smooth path!
The greens are lined up for my digestion.
It took the whole of one lettuce
to produce my body. Now my guts

hold a lettuce and dissolve it all
slowly. I eat where I please
in the allotment of earth.
My manners are nibbling at leaves.

For the one trail of my slime is a zigzag
Through the rows of the growing.
No pellets deter me.
There is no backbone in my body.

A foot is above me.
Something has changed since I began.
I am getting the boot.
The path is printed.

ANDREW STIBBS

Harold Pinter (1930–   )

A Bear Called Paddington

HENRY BROWN: Where you from?

BEAR: Peru.

HENRY BROWN: I knew a bear once. He came from Peru. Well, just out of Peru, it was. Yes. He had a llama, this Peruvian bear, a terrific spitter, what a spitter. (*Pause.*) What part of Peru, then?

BEAR: Darkest.

HENRY BROWN: Darkest. (*Pause.*) Dark . . . est. (*Pause.*) How much more marmalade you thinking of scoffing, then?

BEAR: Just . . . a few jars.

HENRY BROWN: You know, I bet you're a devil for buns. Sticky ones? Yes. You probably had more cream buns than a Lima llama on Bank Holiday.

JUDY: Cut it out, Dad.

HENRY BROWN: Cut it out, what d'you mean? He comes here, label round his neck, big label, says he's got an Aunt Lucy, what about Aunt Lucy, then? Come on, where's this Aunt Lucy? She was a goer, I can tell. (*Pause.*) This isn't Peru, you woolly git. It's Paddington.

BEAR: Paddington. That's . . . that's a good name.

BILL GREENWELL

George Macbeth (1932–   )

from Peregrine Prykke's Pilgrimage

The blood has soaked the bone which hides the stone
The rat excreted in the telephone.
Fellating stone and bone I taste the blood
Which laps around my pelvis like a flood.
I feel a painful pressure in my groin
On either side of which I have a loin.
My loins are groined, my stone's a bloody bone:
I'll have to learn to leave myself alone.

CLIVE JAMES

Athol Fugard (1932–   )

The Wind in the Willows

TOAD: Some time I've had. I've been in gaol. I got thrown in the
river. I lost my wallet but I took a horse and sold it so I tell you
I made the white man look a bloody fool, ja.

RAT: It's you is a bloody fool, man. You lost a wallet and in it your
pass I bet. That little book, eh?

TOAD: So I'll get another.

RAT: You think it's bloody easy, man? You think you'll find another
one like shit in the street? You're in big trouble, man. And
you're wearing a washerwoman's dress. You know what they'll
do to you for immorality if they catch you? You'll go to prison –
ja, maybe to Robben Island.

TOAD: I'd die there.

RAT: You don't want to die?

TOAD: I don't want to die.

RAT: Then I tell you, man, start running now and if the white
weasels catch you keep smiling and say 'Yes, baas' to everything.

KEN RUDGE

Craig Raine (1944–)

Birth

This child emerges slowly
like a raisin from a dead man's mouth,

Wailing like a banshee on hot bricks.
The attendants stiffen

like hatstands. Their rubber gloves
stick to their hands like cellophane

on a long-lost lollipop.
The umbilical cord, a twist of pink liquorice,

is snipped by the haberdasher's scissors.
My tears are hailstones
hitting the instrument tray like stray silver bullets.
In the distance, my wife

wraps the baby to her like lambswool
discovered in a forgotten bottom drawer.

This child is still sticky:
it has swum five Channels, freshly greased.

BILL GREENWELL

Birthday

Your birthday is a pockmarked face
from a line of willing suspects, cleanly shaven

in a scrubland of beards: Your place
is to stand, unruffled, like a solitary raven,

croaking thanks upon a vanity case
of bound and manacled gifts, as quietly craven

as a captured triple-agent. This space,
spotlit as for some private matinée, is your haven.

BILL GREENWELL

The Lavatory Attendant

Slumped on a chair, his body is an S
That wants to be a minus sign.

His face is overripe Wensleydale
Going blue at the edges.

In overall of sacerdotal white
He guards a row of fonts

With lids like eye-patches. Snapped shut
They are castanets. All day he hears

Short-lived Niagaras, the clank
And gurgle of canescent cisterns.

When evening comes he sluices a thin tide
Across sand-coloured lino

Turns Medusa on her head
And wipes the floor with her.

WENDY COPE

Pam Ayres (1947–   )

Post-natal Pome

The midwife shouts, 'Push 'arder!
I can see 'is little 'ead!'
Me 'usband says all trembly like,
'I should 'ave stayed in bed!'
I give 'is 'and a squeeze and says,
'Don't fret me 'oney bun!
It's woman's lot to bear the pain,
And man's to 'ave the fun!'
'Is face goes sort of whitish,
And 'is knees begin to knock,
I beg the nurse to bring more gas,
To ease 'is state of shock;
And when at last the baby comes,
I does the job real neat –
While the midwife 'elps me 'usband,
Who 'as fainted at 'er feet.

TIM HOPKINS

VARIATIONS

from The Muse among the Motorists

RUDYARD KIPLING

SEPULCHRAL
(*from the Greek anthologies*)

Swifter than aught 'neath the sun the car of Simonides moved him.
Two things he could not out-run – Death and a Woman who loved
  him.

ARTERIAL
(*Early Chinese*)

I

Frost upon small rain – the ebony-lacquered avenue
  Reflecting lamps as a pool shows goldfish.
The sight suddenly emptied out of the young man's eyes
  Entering upon it sideways.

II

In youth, by hazard, I killed an old man.
  In age I maimed a little child.
Dead leaves under foot reproach not:
But the lop-sided cherry-branch – whenever the sun rises,
  How black a shadow!

THE ADVERTISEMENT
(*in the manner of the earlier English*)

Whether to wend through straight streets strictly,
Trimly by towns perfectly paved;
Or after office, as fitteth thy fancy,

Faring with friends far among fields;
There is none other equal in action,
Sith she is silent, nimble, unnoisome,
Lordly of leather, gaudily gilded,
Burgeoning brightly in a brass bonnet,
Certain to steer well between wains.

THE JUSTICE'S TALE
(*Chaucer*)

With them there rode a lustie Engineere
Wel skilled to handel everich waie her geere,
Hee was soe wise ne man colde showe him naught
And out of Paris was hys learnynge brought.
Frontlings mid brazen wheeles and wandes he sat,
And on hys heade he bare an leathern hat.
Hee was soe certaine of his gouvernance,
That, by the Road, he tooke everie chaunce.
For simple people and for lordlings eke
Hee wolde not bate a del but onlie squeeke
Behinde their backés on an horné hie
Until they crope into a piggestie.
He was more wood than bull in china-shoppe,
And yet for cowes and doggés wolde hee stop,
Not out of Marcie but for Preudence-sake –
Than hys dependaunce ever was hys brake.

TO A LADY, PERSUADING HER TO A CAR
(*Ben Jonson*)

Love's fiery chariot, Delia, take
Which Vulcan wrought for Venus' sake.
Wings shall not waft thee, but a flame
Hot as my heart – as nobly tame:
Lit by a spark, less bright, more wise
Than linkèd lightnings of thine eyes!
Seated and ready to be drawn
Come not in muslins, lace or lawn,
But, for thy thrice imperial worth,

Take all the sables of the North,
With frozen diamonds belted on,
To face extreme Euroclydon!
Thus in our thund'ring toy we'll prove
Which is more blind, the Law or Love;
And may the jealous Gods prevent
Our fierce and uncontrouled descent!

THE PROGRESS OF THE SPARK
(XVIth Circuit)
(*Donne*)

This spark now set, retarded, yet forbears
To hold her light however so he swears
That turns a metalled crank and, leather-cloked,
With some small hammers tappeth hither and yon;
Peering as when she showeth and when is gone;
For wait he must till the vext Power's evoked
That's one with the lightnings. Wait in the showers soaked;
Or by the road-side sunned. She'll not progress.
Poor soul, here taught how great things may be less
Be stayed, to file contacts doth himself address!

WHEN THE JOURNEY WAS INTENDED TO THE CITY
(*Milton*)

When that with meat and drink they had fulfilled
Not temperately but like him conceived
In monstrous jest at Meudon, whose regale
Stands for exemplar of Gargantuan greed,
Beneath new firmaments and stars astray,
Circumvoluminant; nor had they felt
Neither the passage nor the sad effect
Of many cups partaken, till that frost
Wrought on them hideous, and their minds deceived.
Thus choosing from a progeny of roads,
That seemed but were not, one most reasonable,
Of purest moonlight fashioned on a wall,
Thither they urged their chariot whom that flint
Buttressed received, itself unscathed – not they.

TO MOTORISTS
(*Herrick*)

Since ye distemper and defile
Sweet Herè by the measured mile,
Nor aught on jocund highways heed
Except the evidence of speed;
And bear about your dreadful task
Faces beshrouded 'neath a mask;
Great goblin eyes and gluey hands
And souls enslaved to gears and bands;
Here shall no graver curse be said
Than, though y'are quick, that ye are dead!

THE TOUR
(*Byron*)

Thirteen as twelve my Murray always took –
   He was a publisher. The new Police
Have neater ways of bringing men to book,
   So Juan found himself before J.P.'s
Accused of storming through that placid nook
   At practically any pace you please.
The Dogberry, and the Waterbury, made
It fifty mile – five pounds. And Juan paid!

THE IDIOT BOY
(*Wordsworth*)

He wandered down the mountain grade
   Beyond the speed assigned –
A youth whom Justice often stayed
   And generally fined.

He went alone, that none might know
   If he could drive or steer.
Now he is in the ditch, and Oh!
   The differential gear!

CONTRADICTIONS
(Longfellow)

The drowsy carrier sways
  To the drowsy horses' tramp.
His axles winnow the sprays
Of the hedge where the rabbit plays
  In the light of his single lamp.

He hears a roar behind,
  A howl, a hoot, and a yell,
A headlight strikes him blind
And a stench o'erpowers the wind
  Like a blast from the mouth of Hell.

He mends his swingle-bar,
  And loud his curses ring;
But a mother watching afar
Hears the hum of the doctor's car
  Like the beat of an angel's wing!

So, to the poet's mood,
  Motor or carrier's van,
Properly understood,
Are neither evil nor good –
  Ormuzd nor Ahriman!

FASTNESS
(Tennyson)

This is the end whereto men toiled
  Before thy coachman guessed his fate, –
  How thou shouldst leave thy 'scutcheoned gate
On that new wheel which is the oiled –

To see the England Shakespeare saw
  (Oh, Earth, 'tis long since Shallow died!
  Yet by yon farrowed sow may hide
Some blue deep minion of the Law) –

329

To range from Ashby-de-la-Zouch
  By Lyonnesse to Locksley Hall,
  Or haply, nearer home, appal
Thy father's sister's staid barouche.

THE BEGINNER
(After he has been extemporizing on an instrument
not of his own invention)
(*Browning*)

Lo! what is this that I make – sudden, supreme, unrehearsed –
  This that my clutch in the crowd pressed at a venture has raised?
Forward and onward I sprang when I thought (as I ought) I
    reversed,
  And a cab like a martagon opes and I sit in the wreckage dazed.
And someone is taking my name, and the driver is rending the air.
  With cries for my blood and my gold, and a snickering newsboy
    brings
My cap, wheel-pashed from the kerb. I must run her home for repair,
  Where she leers with her bonnet awry – flat on the nether springs!

THE DYING CHAUFFEUR
(*Adam Lindsay Gordon*)

Wheel me gently to the garage, since my car and I must part –
  No more for me the record and the run.
That cursed left-hand cylinder the doctors call my heart
  Is pinking past redemption – I am done.
They'll never strike a mixture that'll help me pull my load.
  My gears are stripped – I cannot set my brakes.
I am entered for the finals down the timeless untimed Road
  To the Maker of the makers of all makes!

A CHILD'S GARDEN
(*R. L. Stevenson*)

Now there is nothing wrong with me
Except – I think it's called T.B.

And that is why I have to lay
Out in the garden all the day.

Our garden is not very wide,
And cars go by on either side,
And make an angry-hooty noise
That rather startles little boys.

But worst of all is when they take
Me out in cars that growl and shake,
With charabancs so dreadful-near
I have to shut my eyes for fear.

But when I'm on my back again,
I watch the Croydon aeroplane
That flies across to France, and sings
Like hitting thick piano-strings.

When I am strong enough to do
The things I'm truly wishful to,
I'll never use a car or train
But always have an aeroplane;

And just go zooming round and round,
And frighten Nursey with the sound,
And see the angel-side of clouds,
And spit on all those motor-crowds!

THE MORAL
(*Rudyard Kipling*)

You mustn't groom an Arab with a file,
   You hadn't ought to tension-spring a mule.
You couldn't push a brumby fifty mile
   And drop him in a boiler-shed to cool.
I'll sling you through six counties in a day.
   I'll hike you up a grade of one in ten.
I am Duty, Law and Order under way,
   I'm the Mentor of banana-fingered men!

I will make you know your left hand from your right.
  I will teach you not to drink about your biz.
I'm the only temperance advocate in sight!
  I am all the Education Act there is!

Old King Cole – Variations of an Air

G. K. CHESTERTON
Composed on having to appear in a pageant as Old King Cole

Tennyson

Cole, that unwearied prince of Colchester,
Growing more gay with age, and with long days
Deeper in laughter and desire of life,
As that Virginian climber on our walls
Flames scarlet with the fading of the year,
Called for his wassail and that other weed
Virginian also, from the western woods
Where English Raleigh checked the boast of Spain,
And lighting joy with joy, and piling up
Pleasure as crown for pleasure, bade men bring
Those three, the minstrels whose emblazoned coats
Shone with the oyster-shells of Colchester;
And these three played, and playing grew more fain
Of mirth and music; till the heathen came,
And the King slept beside the northern sea.

W. B. Yeats

Of an old King in a story
  From the grey sea-folk I have heard,
Whose heart was no more broken
  Than the wings of a bird.

As soon as the moon was silver
  And the thin stars began,

He took his pipe and his tankard,
  Like an old peasant man.

And three tall shadows were with him
  And came at his command;
And played before him for ever
  The fiddles of fairyland.

And he died in the young summer
  Of the world's desire;
Before our hearts were broken
  Like sticks in a fire.

Robert Browning

Who smoke-snorts toasts o' My Lady Nicotine,
Kicks stuffing out of Pussyfoot, bids his trio
Stick up their Stradivarii (that's the plural)
Or near enough, my fatheads; *nimium*
Vincina Cremonæ (that's a bit too near).
Is there some stockfish fails to understand?
Catch hold o' the notion, bellow and blurt back 'Cole'?
Must I bawl lessons from a horn-book, howl,
Cat-call the cat-gut 'fiddles'? Fiddlesticks!

Walt Whitman

Me clairvoyant,
Me conscious of you, old camarado,
Needing no telescope, lorgnette, field-glass, opera-glass, myopic
  pince-nez,
Me piercing two thousand years with eye naked and not ashamed;
The crown cannot hide you from me;
Musty old feudal-heraldic trappings cannot hide you from me,
I perceive that you drink.
(I am drinking with you. I am as drunk as you are.)
I see you are inhaling tobacco, puffing, smoking, spitting
(I do not object to your spitting);
You prophetic of American largeness,

You anticipating the broad masculine manners of these States;
I see in you also there are movements, tremors, tears, desire for the
  melodious,
I salute your three violinists, endlessly making vibrations,
Rigid, relentless, capable of going on for ever;
They play my accompaniment; but I shall take no notice of any
  accompaniment;
I myself am a complete orchestra.
So long.

Swinburne

In the time of old sin without sadness
  And golden with wastage of gold
Like the gods that grow old in their gladness
  Was the king that was glad, growing old;
And with sound of loud lyres from his palace
  The voice of his oracles spoke,
And the lips that were red from his chalice
  Were splendid with smoke.
When the weed was as flame for a token
  And the wine was as blood for a sign;
And upheld in his hands and unbroken
  The fountains of fire and of wine.
And a song without speech, without singer,
  Stung the soul of a thousand in three
As the flesh of the earth has to sting her,
  The soul of the sea.

Salad

MORTIMER COLLINS

Swinburne

O cool in the summer is salad,
  And warm in the winter is love;
And a poet shall sing you a ballad
  Delicious thereon and thereof.

A singer am I, if no sinner,
  My Muse has a marvellous wing,
And I willingly worship at dinner
  The Sirens of Spring.

Take endive . . . like love it is bitter;
  Take beet . . . for like love it is red;
Crisp leaf of the lettuce shall glitter,
  And cress from the rivulet's bed;
Anchovies foam-born, like the Lady
  Whose beauty has maddened this bard;
And olives, from groves that are shady;
  And eggs – boil 'em hard.

Browning

Waitress, with eyes so marvellous black
  And the blackest possible lustrous gay tress,
This is the month of the Zodiac
  When I want a pretty deft-handed waitress.
Bring a china-bowl, you merry young soul;
  Bring anything green, from worsted to celery;
Bring pure olive-oil, from Italy's soil . . .
  Then your china-bowl we'll well array.
When the time arrives chip choicest chives,
  And administer quietly chili and capsicum . . .
(Young girls do not quite know what's what
  Till as a Poet into their laps I come).
Then a lobster fresh as fresh can be
  (When it screams in the pot I feel a murderer);
After which I fancy we
  Shall want a few bottles of Heidsieck or Roederer.

Tennyson

King Arthur, growing very tired indeed
Of wild Tintagel, now that Lancelot
Had gone to Jersey or to Jericho,
And there was nobody to make a rhyme,

And Cornish girls were christened Jennifer,
And the Round Table had grown rickety,
Said unto Merlin (who had been asleep
For a few centuries in Broceliande,
But woke, and had a bath, and felt refreshed):
'What shall I do to pull myself together?'
Quoth Merlin: 'Salad is the very thing,
And you can get it at the "Cheshire Cheese".'
King Arthur went there: *verily*, I believe
That he has dined there every day since then.
Have you not marked the portly gentleman
In his cool corner, with his plate of greens?
The great Knight Lancelot prefers the 'Cock',
Where port is excellent (in pints), and waiters
Are portlier than kings, and steaks are tender,
And poets have been known to meditate . . .
Ox-fed orating ominous octastichs.

The Poets at Tea

BARRY PAIN

I   *Macaulay, who made it*

Pour, varlet, pour the water,
    The water steaming hot!
  A spoonful for each man of us,
  Another for the pot!
We shall not drink from amber,
  Nor Capuan slave shall mix
For us the snows of Athos
  With port at thirty-six;
Whiter than snow the crystals,
  Grown sweet 'neath tropic fires,
More rich the herbs of China's field,
The pasture-lands more fragrance yield;
For ever let Britannia wield
  The tea-pot of her sires!

2 *Tennyson, who took it hot*

I think that I am drawing to an end:
For on a sudden came a gasp for breath,
And stretching of the hands, and blinded eyes,
And a great darkness falling on my soul.
O Hallelujah! . . . Kindly pass the milk.

3 *Swinburne, who let it get cold*

As the sin that was sweet in the sinning
  Is foul in the ending thereof,
As the heat of the summer's beginning
  Is past in the winter of love:
O purity, painful and pleading!
  O coldness, ineffably gray!
Oh, hear us, our handmaid unheeding,
  And take it away!

4 *Cowper, who thoroughly enjoyed it*

The cosy fire is bright and gay,
The merry kettle boils away
  And hums a cheerful song.
I sing the saucer and the cup;
Pray, Mary, fill the tea-pot up,
  And do not make it strong.

5 *Browning, who treated it allegorically*

Tut! Bah! We take as another case –
  Pass the bills on the pills on the window-sill; notice the capsule.
(A sick man's fancy, no doubt, but I place
  Reliance on trade-marks, Sir) – so perhaps you'll
Excuse the digression – this cup which I hold
  Light-poised – Bah, it's spilt in the bed! – well, let's on go –
Held Bohea and sugar, Sir; if you were told
  The sugar was salt, would the Bohea be Congo?

'Come, little cottage girl, you seem
    To want my cup of tea;
And will you take a little cream?
    Now tell the truth to me.'

She had a rustic, woodland grin,
    Her cheek was soft as silk,
And she replied: 'Sir, please put in
    A little drop of milk.'

'Why, what put milk into your head?
    'Tis cream my cows supply';
And five times to the child I said:
    'Why, pig-head, tell me, why?'

'You call me pig-head,' she replied;
    'My proper name is Ruth.
I called that milk' – she blushed with pride –
    'You bade me speak the truth.'

7   *Poe, who got excited over it*

Here's a mellow cup of tea, golden tea!
What a world of rapturous thought its fragrance brings to me!
    Oh, from out the silver cells
    How it wells!
    How it smells!
Keeping tune, tune, tune
To the tintinnabulation of the spoon.
And the kettle on the fire
Boils its spout off with desire,
With a desperate desire
And a crystalline endeavour
Now, now to sit, or never,
On the top of the pale-faced moon,
But he always came home to tea, tea, tea, tea, tea,
    Tea to the n——th.

8 *Rossetti, who took six cups of it*

The lilies lie in my lady's bower
(O weary mother, drive the cows to roost),
They faintly droop for a little hour;
My lady's head droops like a flower.
She took the porcelain in her hand
(O weary mother, drive the cows to roost),
She poured; I drank at her command;
Drank deep, and now – you understand!
(O weary mother, drive the cows to roost.)

9 *Burns, who liked it adulterated*

Weel, gin ye speir, I'm no inclined,
Whusky or tay – to state my mind,
   For ane or ither;
For, gin I tak the first, I'm fou,
And gin the next, I'm dull as you,
   Mix a' thegither.

10 *Walt Whitman, who didn't stay more than a minute*

One cup for my self-hood
Many for you. *Allons, camerados*, we will drink together,
O hand-in-hand! That tea-spoon, please, when you've done with it.
What butter-colour'd hair you've got. I don't want to be personal.
All right, then, you needn't. You're a stale-cadaver.
Eighteen-pence if the bottles are returned.
Allons, from all bat-eyed formula.

Right of Reply: Rejoinders to Poets from the Subjects of their Verses

A Toad on Philip Larkin

Why should I let this bald berk
Make me a label?
Aren't there enough tropes for *work*,
Without using libel?

Toads to the toadist poets
Are pustules of poison,
Writhing all over with gnarled warts,
That give you a *frisson*.

Writers with axes to grind
Never get it right.
They won't even peer in a pond,
To set themselves straight.

Just think of old Larkin's sheer folly
As he rambles and stutters:
Slow-witted, short-sighted and scaly,
Like some bloody tortoise.

                BASIL RANSOME-DAVIES

The Lamb on William Blake

Come off it, Blake, look at the facts of life –
An old ram made me with his woolly wife;
And if some human calls himself a lamb
And meek and mild, I think it's just a sham.
For Jesus, just like you, had tastes carnivorous –
From him and all your kind, Buddha deliver us!

                FIONA PITT-KETHLEY

The Pig on Ted Hughes

The man stood with his biro poised.
He was paid, they said, as much as three men.
His jutting jaw, thick furrowed eyebrows.
These jotters stand right out.

His gait and native Yorkshire grit
Seemed to me a bloody cheek.
I was just a dead porker, not yet sliced.
And he wanted his pound of flesh.

He clocked me one with his fist.
It did not seem to bother him,
Smacking my crackling. His kind
Are always coining it with animals.

Even bacon deserves a bit of respect.
That includes bluff, gruff Northern sorts.
This git in the old leather jacket,
How would he like to be soused in hot water?

BILL GREENWELL

The Snake on D. H. Lawrence

I knew his sort – a poet.
The dark-haired ones are all right, mild drinkers perhaps,
But the red-heads are liable to fly off the handle.
He puts the whole length of my back up, standing there
Like a stick of rock.
I could tell what he was thinking – they're all the SAME.
I reminded him of his penis.
So I thought, right mate, you can just wait till I've had my fill.
What a nerve! To think that the whole point of my existence
Is just to be a piece of his foetid imagery!
I was just framing in my mind some neat metaphor for him,
When he hurled a lump of wood at me.
Therefore I relieved myself in the trough and left.

N. J. WARBURTON

'Four-Feet' on Rudyard Kipling

I have done mostly what most dogs do,
And slept by my Master's bed;
But I can't abide (and I tell it true)
Two-Feet striding ahead.

Whenever my nose finds something new,
Or sniffs at a bird that's dead,
Two-Feet whinges, 'Oh, leave that, do!'
And tugs on my leash ahead.

If I wasn't as into Self as you,
And didn't need to be fed,
I'd lift my leg just an inch or two
On Two-Feet marching ahead.

ROGER WODDIS

A Shropshire Lad to A. E. Housman

By vale and copse, by field and hedge,
  From fair to market-place,
From Bredon Hill to Wenlock Edge
  I've been your beast of chase!
You've clapped me into Shrewesbury Gaol
  And slept me with the brave:
You've dragged me from my pot of ale
  To dig my distant grave.

For me you've found six feet of ground
  As soldier, drunk or dry,
Till there was never, I'll be bound,
  So tired a lad as I.
You've haunted me and daunted me
  On every road I've trod;
You've shipped me hence for thirteen-pence:
  I've had enough, by God!

PENDEXTRE

342

The Fair Youth Responds to William Shakespeare

Poor Will, the mentor of my youthful mirth,
Foiled by that maze of love where all men stray,
What are thy musings and mischances worth?
Why dost thou still pursue a winding way?
'Tis not the winter of thy discontent
Shall force untimely fruit from my fair spring,
Nor music-maker's fond arbitrement
Draw forth the song that thou wouldst have me sing.
Forbear, good friend, the boast of conquered time
And vain ambition for immortal days;
When thou art dead, who shall rehearse the rhyme
That decked my lasting monument with praise?
    Those flowers shall fade, while I stand fast in fame,
    And Shakespeare's sonnets die with Shakespeare's name.

MARY HOLTBY

Porphyria to Robert Browning

That's my last lover there upon the wall,
In Winterhalter's hand, or is it Landseer's?
Hey, ho! *De minimis non curat lex.*
(See how I quote to spin the matter out)
Nay, nay, but there upon the wall see plain
My fifteenth lover, Browning or some such.
My husband thrashed him, through no wish of mine;
My thoughts were then on Alfred Tennyson.
I told him this, which turned his mind adrift.
One rainy night he seized my switch of hair,
Throttled the bedpost, and sat seven hours
Clucking and cooing drivel to his toes,
Happy, until my husband oped the door;
Oh, then 'twas ancient Harold and the whip.

I saw his poem after, silly lad;
I think he knew not rump from elbow-joints.

PAUL GRIFFIN

The Nymph's Reply to Christopher Marlowe's Passionate Shepherd

If all the world and love were young,
And truth in every shepherd's tongue,
These pretty pleasures might me move,
To live with thee, and be thy love.

Time drives the flocks from field to fold
When rivers rage, and rocks grow cold,
And Philomel becometh dumb;
The rest complain of cares to come.

The flowers do fade, and wanton fields
To wayward winter reckoning yields;
A honey'd tongue, a heart of gall,
Is fancy's spring, but sorrow's fall.

Thy gown, thy shoes, thy beds of roses,
Thy cap, thy kirtle, and thy posies;
Soon break, soon wither, soon forgotten,
In folly ripe, in reason rotten.

Thy belt of straw, and ivy buds,
Thy coral clasps, and amber studs,
All these in me no means can move,
To come to thee, and be thy love.

But could youth last, and love still breed,
Had joys no date, and age no need;
Then these delights my mind might move,
To live with thee and be thy love.

SIR WALTER RALEIGH

Jenny to D. G. Rossetti

I wonder what you're thinking of – D.G.R. on Jenny

You think I'm sleeping, Mr R.
That only shows how wrong you are!
Not likely I'd drop off, myself,
Before your guinea's on the shelf.
A girl must live; and who's to blame
If there's no credit in this game?
Still writing? You're *that* kind of man?
Well, let's be cosy while we can.
Though I must say I do not care
For all these poets with long hair,
And painters with their rings and cloaks;
I never really like their jokes.
Look what they done to poor Miss S.
She's like a living ghost, I guess.
Just for a painting, so they say,
They lay her in her bath all day.
There's Mr Swinburne – well, you should see
The verses what he wrote for me.
They really are – well, not quite nice.
I wouldn't care to read them twice.
Some pictures I could take to. Once
I saw a show of Mr Hunt's.
And Mr Millais' and Rossetti's
At least aren't rude like Mr Etty's.
At last. He's closed his little book
I've half a mind to take a look.
What, going now?
                        Well, there's a ninny!
I never earned an easier guinea.

PONTIFEX

345

Cynara to Ernest Dowson

Yes, you forgot much, Poet! – even a woman's heart.
Riot and roses, mad music, and stronger wine –
Not those, O God! not those could rive us two apart,
Had you but sense to blur the shape of your new passion,
With cloudy words confused the stark outline,
You had been faithful to me, Poet, in *our* fashion.

But fool! oh fool! to dot the 'i's' and cross the 't's'!
With 'yesternight', 'her lips', and that warm heart that lay
Night-long within your arms; – did bought red mouths so please
Your night (night desolate and sick of an old passion)
That you must stamp their image on my day?
You have been faithless to me, Poet, in *my* fashion.

L . E . J O N E S

Lucasta to Richard Lovelace

Nay, love dwells in no nunnery;
    Nor think, with nicest art
Compounding Love and Chivalry,
    To gain a woman's heart.

'Not Honour's self' hadst thou but sworn
    'Shall woo me from her side!'
My love had grown to make reborn
    What in such passion died.

Love heeds the wild and broken cry,
    Not the well-turned conceit;
I could have loved thee more, had thy
    Professions been less neat.

L . E . J O N E S

The Fat White Woman to Frances Cornford

Why do you rush through the fields in trains,
Guessing so much and so much;
Why do you flash through the flowery meads,
Fat-headed poet whom nobody reads;
And how do you know such a frightful lot
About people in gloves as such?

And how the devil can you be sure,
Guessing so much and so much,
How do you know but what someone who loves
Always to see me in nice white gloves
At the end of the field you are rushing by,
Is waiting for his Old Dutch?

G. K. CHESTERTON

Nursery Rhymes Rewritten

Sing a Song of Sixpence

John Milton

O chant, ye Muses, some melodious lay
Of silvern tanner or a pouch of grain,
That tender nurslings of a summer's day,
Those heav'nly songsters, be incarcerate
Within the confines of a pasty shell!
See'st not the monarch, brooding o'er his gold,
The while his consort evilly placates
Her appetite, and she who doth but serve –

And yet doth wait the while – most horribly
(By such a tender minstrel of the air
As was aforesaid clapp'd beneath a crust)
Of her olfact'ry organ is deprived.

RHODA TUCK POOK

Little Jack Horner

Anthony Powell

Horner had got himself established as far as possible from the centre
of the room and I was suddenly made aware, as one often is by
actions which are in themselves quite commonplace, that he was
about to do something which would give him enormous satisfaction.
He had somehow acquired a large seasonal confection which he was
beginning to attack with a degree of enthusiasm I had not seen him
display since the midnight feasts we had enjoyed at school. Eschew-
ing the normal recourse to eating utensils, he plunged his hand
through the pastry and extracted an entire fruit, an achievement
which was accompanied by a cry of self-congratulation and a beatific
expression reminiscent of some of those on the faces one sees in the
more popular of the portraits.

ALAN ALEXANDER

Baa Baa Black Sheep

William Wordsworth

The skylark and the jay sang loud and long,
The sun was calm and bright, the air was sweet
When all at once I heard above the throng
Of jocund birds a single plaintive bleat.

And, turning, saw, as one sees in a dream
It was a Sheep had broke the moorland peace
With his sad cry, a creature who did seem
The blackest thing that ever wore a fleece.

I walked towards him on the stony track
And, pausing for a time between two crags,
I asked him: 'Have you wool upon your back?'
Thus he bespake: 'Enough to fill three bags.'

Most courteously, in measured tones he told
Who would receive each bag and where they dwelt;
And oft, now years have passed and I am old,
I recollect with joy that inky pelt.

WENDY COPE

Three Blind Mice

Gerard Manley Hopkins

Ah see, see! the sightless, the flight fleet
Of squealing squeakers, a wisp-whiskered trinity:
How needless, heedless of wife's knife's vicinity,
Throat-threatening, they run than rather retreat!
Now tails trimmed, a timorous trio's feet
Come tip-tumbling in marvellous, mewling affinity
Of mice! In a trice, with One-in-Three divinity,
They chase the chopper, which lightly lopped each seat!

And what harvester, reaper, weeps not at such horrible halving,
    When lengths, limp, lie strength-ended, and behind
Is bare, each stropped, stripped, cropped by her carving?

    How hard is the farm-mistress' arm to their harmless kind:
For the fast-footed, fated field-mice, parlour-bent, were starving,
    Thieving for cheese, for a rind, yet ah! were all blind!

BILL GREENWELL

349

Old King Cole

W. B. Yeats

The unpurged images of day unroll
All Dooney's drunken fiddlers are abed;
Only Old Cole is still awake, he calls
In the unhearing dark for pipe and bowl
And for the fiddling relics of the dead,
   Sang the ruined castle walls
     Fiddle-dee, fiddle-dee.

A silent fiddle is a paltry thing,
Catgut and wood; until a merry soul
Gives life to silence and adds flesh to bones,
Then mere complexities of bow and string
Yield to this midnight music's fol-de-rol,
   Sang the scattered castle stones
     Fiddle-dee, fiddle-dee.

GERARD BENSON

Ride a Cock-horse

T. S. Eliot

A slow coming we had of it,
Just at the worst time of the year:
In spring is the wintriest weather.
With the cock-horses fretful and wanting their sugar,
There were times when we began to wonder
If there was such a place as Banbury.
We would have abandoned the search
But for the promise of the Cross; so we continued
And arrived at evening, not a moment too soon,
Finding the lady;
It was (you may say) satisfactory.

Certainly there were bells on her feet, and such bells
Tinkling and partly tinkling,
And her fingers were heavy with many rings.
Had we been drawn here by memory before birth, or curiosity?
In our ignorance is our understanding.

E. O. PARROTT

The Grand Old Duke of York

J. D. Salinger

There was this goddam English duke for Chrissake – and boy wasn't
he just so damn grand and all. Anyway, this crazy sonuvabitch has
this bunch of ten thousand crumby West Point rejects who are
about as much use to him as a hole in the head. So this crazy duke
walks the ass off these jerks up and down this lousy goddam hill.
And these G Is work it out that when they reach the top of this hill
they're up for Chrissake and when they reach the bottom they're
down for Chrissake – which is a pretty big deal. Anyway there's this
real smart sonuvabitch and he blew everyone's goddam mind when
he says that halfway up is not up and not down neither. But you
know – I felt kinda sorry for the guy. I get like that sometimes – and
when he spoke, I was damn near bawling. I really was.

TIM HOPKINS

Little Boy Blue

Alexander Pope

Rise up, thou azured infant, to whose care
The plaintive flocks at eventide repair;
Thy woolly charges on lush pastures dine,
And round the wheatfield tramp the hungry kine.

Lest Nature fail, and Agriculture cease,
Send forth one blast, and all shall be at peace.
But where is he whom I have thus addressed,
Whose age is little, but whose skill's confessed?
This hand protruding from the harvest pile –
Can it be his? and do the heavens smile?
Yet Ceres loads her blessings on his chest;
Deep is his slumber, and serene his rest.
Leave one so young to err like any man,
And let the rest live better – if we can.

PAUL GRIFFIN

Jack Sprat

Ernest Hemingway

'Come in, Jack.'
  'I d'wanta come in.'
  'D'wanta come in, hell. Come in bright boy.'
  They went in.
  'I'll have eats now,' she said. She was fat and red.
  'I d'want nothing,' Jack said. He was thin and pale.
  'D'want nothin' hell. You have eats now, bright boy.'
  She called the waiter. 'Bud,' she said, 'gimme bacon and beans – twice.'
  Bud brought the bacon and beans.
  'I d'want bacon. It's too fat,' said Jack.
  'D'want bacon, hell. I'll eat the fat. You eat the lean. OK, big boy?'
  'OK,' Jack said.
  They had eats.
  'Now lick the plate clean,' she said.
  'Aw, honey,' said Jack, 'I aint gotta, do I?'
  'Yup,' she said. 'You gotta.'
  They both licked their plates clean.

HENRY HETHERINGTON

Solomon Grundy

P. G. Wodehouse

It's odd how Dame Fortune (whom I sometimes suspect of being Aunt Agatha in drag) takes the most frightful scunner to some chappies. Take the case of little Sol Grundy, prize Drone and no slouch when it came to the festive bread-bunging. No sooner does the poor mutt get himself under starter's orders for the Life Stakes (with yours truly standing sponsor at the font) than he's spliced to the most god-awful girl east of Esher. Then, before you can say 'Man Friday', he's wrapped his lungs round some bacillus of no fixed address, starts going downhill with the speed of a welshing bookie and – hey presto! – 24 hours later, he's shuffled off this mortal whatsit and is pushing up the dandelions. As Jeeves remarked: 'Here today – gone yesterday' – or words to that effect. Smart cove, Jeeves.

MARTIN FAGG

Little Miss Muffet

Stevie Smith

When I sat down beside her,
I'd no thought of harming
The poor little lass – I wanted to be
Not alarming but charming.

Come back to your tuffet, dear Miss Muffet,
I was sad when you didn't stay;
I only wanted to squat and watch
You eating your curds and whey.

I may look crawly and creepy,
But I'm really quite disarming,
A friendly arachnid who's trying to be
Calming – and not alarming.

MARTIN FAGG

353

Mary, Mary

William Shakespeare

Sweet coz, how contrary thy garden grows,
We have heard, and fain would learn the manner o't.

MARY

My liege, I may not speak with feigning lips
To say that this my garden is as those,
Which custom and dull usage have made stale
And hackneyed in the world's regard. For they
In flowers, shrubs, and bosky coppices
Abound, and arbours green-embowered.
But my poor plot teems with those tiny shells,
Which, clinging to the adamantine cliffs,
Beat back the envious ocean's boist'rous surge
In strong despite. And, when mild zephyrs breathe,
Sweet silvern bells hard by make melody.
And, in the stead of flowers, row on row
Of stateliest damsels, each one perfect bloom,
Make bright my borders. So my garden grows,
More stranger none.

We do believe it well.

G. F. FORREST

Hey Diddle Diddle

Robert Browning

Hey! Diddle diddle, t'employ a childhood phrase
And thus begin my tale (tale of a cat),
And where else, tell me masters, to begin
This rigmarole of puss and violin
Than here at top o' th' page? Then *Diddle*, I says

A feline fiddlist and a leaping cow,
You catch my drift? I thought not. Hold, I trow,
     Hold hard. A cat (hold on to that!)
     A fiddle, and a cow i' th' sky
     Over the moon! milk for the green cheese,
(A fancy but I set it down) and these
Occurrences watched by a Pekingese,
A pooch who laughs, though none knows how or why,
At plate and spoon eloping. Zooks! The moon's adaze!

                                   GERARD BENSON

Jack and Jill

William Wordsworth

Close by the cataract a widow dwelt
With but a son and daughter to beguile
Her failing years; her lad was christened Jack,
His sister, Jill. Once, in a time of drought,
Their well being dry, she sent her young ones off,
Bearing a bucket, to a wholesome tarn
High on the fell, to fetch some water home.
Descending, Jack, missing the sheep track, tripped
And in his headlong fall injured his pate;
His sister likewise tumbled after him.
With all convenient speed Jack trotted home,
Repaired his skull with rustic remedy,
Paper and vinegar – at which Jill scoffed
Invoking thus her beldam's violent rage.

                                   GERARD BENSON

Georgy Porgy

Lord Macaulay

Then up rose Gorgius Porgius
   Of pudding and of pie –
So stands it in the nursery book,
   To witness if I lie –
He marked the maidens' coming;
   Of no avail their tears;
He kissed them all both large and small,
   At least so it appears.

So there he stood triumphant,
   That wrought the deed of shame,
Thinking, no doubt, when they came out,
   He might repeat the game.
But, when the maidens later
   Came trooping forth to play,
'Twas then our hero's courage failed,
His previous boldness naught availed,
Before the advancing host he quailed,
   And turned, and fled away.

G. F. FORREST

Girls and Boys Come out to Play

Sir John Betjeman

Girls and boys, come out to play,
With Nigel, Lalage, Kirsten and me,
Where the conifers darken at close of day
The picture windows of SE3.

Come out, come out, for Daddy's away –
It's his Parents' Association day –
And Mummy's reporting on cut-price soup
To the Blackheath and Greenwich Consumer Group.

Come with a whoop and come with a call
Past Raggity Ann's to Foxes Dale;
A packet of twenty will serve for all
From the Player's machine in Tranquil Vale.

Then home at last to our Span maisonette
And Bournvita in front of the TV set,
Comfily perched on the Hille settee
Sit Nigel, Lalage, Kirsten and me.

HILARY

Rock-a-Bye, Baby

Alexander Pope

O undulate, thou innocent, and rest
Upon this arboraceous summit's breast.
When that the zephyrs rouse themselves irate,
Thy nest shall with like fervour oscillate;
And, when the branch by sudden blast be riven,
May watching cherubs waft thy soul to heaven.

RHODA TUCK POOK

Children's Books

Richmal Crompton: Just William

'To the woods!' said William.

'What for?' said Violet Elizabeth. 'Are you going to play with me?'

'We're going to rape you,' said William. 'Aren't we, Ginger?'

' 'Course,' said Ginger, dutifully.

'What's wape?' lisped Violet Elizabeth. Clearly, William had aroused her interest.

William hesitated. 'Well – er,' he said. 'Everyone knows what rape is, don't they, Ginger?'

' 'Course,' replied Ginger. 'Everyone knows that.'

He, William, wished he had been able to see what Robert and his latest girlfriend had actually been *doing* when he, William, watched them through the window of his, Robert's, car, parked in the drive the previous evening.

But Violet Elizabeth was having misgivings. 'I'll thcream and thcream till I'm thick,' she said. 'I *can*,' she added.

'How loud can you scream?' asked William.

Violet Elizabeth screamed, not very loudly.

'To the woods!' said William. 'C'mon, Ginger!'

'Crumbs!' said William. 'She *has* been "thick".'

TOM LAWRENCE

Lewis Carroll: Alice in Wonderland

'Off with her clothes!' roared the Queen.

'How very strange!' exclaimed Alice.

'Who is that impertinent young girl?' demanded the Queen, 'and why is she wearing so many clothes?'

'Chimneys are her thing,' leered the White Rabbbit, 'she likes putting her foot up them.'

'*Chacun à son flue*,' remarked the Queen, and began to do things with a hedgehog which Alice did not altogether like.

'What curious people!' Alice could not restrain herself from saying out loud. The King, who had been looking at Alice with vigorous interest since the White Rabbit's remark, murmured to her: 'I am a curious fellow. And while we're on the subject, how do you like the look of those soldiers over there?' Alice saw a soldier, doubled up, and moving his head against the midriff of another soldier.

'The croquet hoops have become tangled up!' said the King, and absently began to play croquet with himself . . .

J. Y. WATSON

Arthur Ransome: Swallows and Amazons

'Why are you and Peggy called the Amazons, Nancy?'

'Well, it certainly isn't because we've cut one breast off!' Nancy laughed merrily and continued to whittle her jibstay. 'Oh, I know *that*,' John said impatiently. 'Peggy showed me when you were caulking Captain Flint's bottom. She's the one who ought to be called Titty.'

'If it comes to that, why are you called the Swallows?'

'That was Susan's idea,' John admitted. 'It was after she saw some film that really impressed her – *Deep Boat* I think it was called.'

'Shiver my timbers! You're still a bit of a landlubber aren't you?' Nancy whacked John playfully with her jibstay. 'Look, let's pop into your tent and I'll show you what Susan really meant . . .'

A scream rent the air. 'But, Nancy,' John stammered. 'You are . . . you are . . . a *boy*!'

'Of course I am. Why do you think I'm called Nancy, duckie?'

J. M. CROOKS

Enid Blyton: Noddy

It had been reported that police advice had been given to students of Keele University who were said to have been practising nudity.

When Mr Plod the policeman heard from Little Noddy what the Naughty Students had done he was extremely cross. 'Now look, Mr Head Teacher,' he said, 'your boys and girls must be punished. Everyone who saw them with no clothes on was dreadfully shocked, and everyone who didn't see them is dreadfully angry too. We were *quite* annoyed when they marched about shouting "Be kind to Golliwogs!" though everybody knows that Golliwogs are bad because they have nasty black faces. And it wasn't very nice of them to throw petrol bombs and paint at people's houses, but boys and girls do get up to some mischievous little pranks. But taking all your clothes off isn't a prank – it's Wicked and Disgusting. Give them a good spanking and send them home to their Mummies and Daddies. Just think, Mr Head Teacher, if we stop students taking their clothes off, there may not be any one day. *Won't* that be lovely?'

J. M. CROOKS

Kenneth Grahame: The Wind in the Willows

They had settled in armchairs at each side of a cheerful fire, the Rat trying to find a rhyme for something or other and the Mole toasting muffins for tea. Suddenly, the half-finished verses slipping from his knee, the Rat reached to the corner cupboard and took a deep draught from a bottle which the Mole had not seen before. 'Mole, old chap,' he said, 'have you ever wondered why I invited you, a total stranger, to live here rent-free, using my boat, meeting my friends?' His eyes had a sinister glint, his snout seemed unexpectedly longer, his teeth more pointed.

'I know, Ratty, that you are the kindest . . .' Mole realized for the first time how much bigger Water Rats were than himself.

'Did I tell you before,' snarled Ratty, 'how much I've always fancied a moleskin smoking jacket?'

GEORGE VAN SCHAICK

Captain W. E. Johns: Biggles Battles On

The plane banked sharply to the left as we hurtled downwards, but the Fokker Wolf was still on our tail.

'A-a-a-a-a-a-a-zing,' went the twin cowl-mounted Mittelschmertz 25mm cannons.

'Peng!' it went, in German, as one of the shells bit into the sleek wooden fuselage.

'"Peng"?' cogitated Biggles. 'That's the German for "Bang!"'

'We've been hit,' volunteered Ginger grimly.

'Nothing,' said Biggles grimlier, as he slipped his leather-gloved hand over the by now moistened joystick. He pulled it back in a series of sharp jerks.

'Level off a mo,' put in Algy drily and through drawn lips stepped purposefully into the body of the aircraft, past the by now shapely nude lady navigator; and back into the rear of the plane. The door of the Gents Only Sauna hung precariously from one hinge. He slammed it shut with a haunting squawk, and fought his way past the two naked WAAFs wrestling in perfumed sump-oil. He erupted into the Aft Leather Room, to find Wingco still chained to a cross, wearing the by now familiar black hood bearing the also familiar Wing Commanderic braid.

'Have your way with me, you hunk of manhood,' he hinted coyly.

'What ho, old sport!' hazarded Algy gingerly. 'I say old man, the Group's a bit dashed worried – thinks you might have some kind of, well . . . you know, problem . . . you old bison . . .' He fingered his cigarette nervously.

'Don't worry about me, old tapir, I've pulled through a lot worse than this.'

The plane lurched suddenly as Biggles swerved to avoid a hail of bullets that pumped in spurts out of the penis-like nosecone of the pursuing Fokker. Algy rushed for'ard.

'Everything OK, Skipper?' he admitted.

'We haven't made it yet,' inserted Biggles, as he gritted his thighs and plunged his machine into a savage spin.

As they plunged downwards, the mighty engines throbbed and the well-lubricated pistons thrust themselves back and forth in their vice-like steel sheaths.

'You look a bit green around the gills, old eland,' observed Biggles smoothly.

'Never felt better,' puked Algy . . .

GRAHAM CHAPMAN

Frank Richards: Greyfriars

'Wharton!' boomed Mr Quelch. 'Wretched boy! You have been smoking!'

'No, sir,' Harry Wharton lied. 'It was those chaps who left as you came through the dorm, Cherry and Bull.' Quivering in his hiding place, Bunter gasped. Harry Wharton was a sneak!

'I had thought', observed Mr Quelch acidly, 'that I might have had to give you six of the best before you revealed the names of your friends. At least.'

'I didn't want to have to blub, sir. Besides, why should I suffer for those bounders?'

'See me in my study after Prep.,' said Mr Quelch, and departed.

'Now, Bunter,' said Harry Wharton, dragging the Owl of the Remove from behind the curtain, 'and take your bags down.'

'Ow! Urrrgh! Yaroo! You rotten beast!'

'As Coker said down at the pub today, there's a lot of things I've been missing at Greyfriars, up till now.'

E. O. PARROTT

Other Men's Muses

Geoffrey Chaucer Rewrites Sir John Betjeman

THE TALE OF MISS HUNTER DUNN

A MAYDE ther was, y-clept Joan Hunter Dunn,
In all of Surrie, comelier wench was none,
Yet wondrous greet of strength was she with-alle,
Ful lustily she smote the tenis-balle,
And whether lord or lady she wolde pleye,
With thirtie, fortie love wolde winne the day.
A SQUYER eke ther was, in horseless cariage,
And he wolde fayn have sought her hand in marriage,
Though he coude songes make, with mery rime,
At tennis she out-pleyed him every time;
To make her wyfe he saw but little chaunce,
But then be-thought to take her to a daunce
In gentil Camberlee, where after dark
They held long daliaunce in the cariage park;
Eftsoons, Cupide had the twain in thralle,
And this they found the beste game of alle.

STANLEY J. SHARPLESS

Sir William Empson Rewrites William Wordsworth

from INTIMATIONS OF IMMORTALITY (*Last Part*)

All photosynthesis must have a scheme;
No lover would prognosticate divorce.
Where water moves, projection is the theme.

When legs oblige big planets have a force.
White hairs grow solemn when the sun discards
Fallacious wisdom for a tribal source.

Ethnology or rumour? Yellow cards
For those rude sinners, trophies for the fit,
With whom must empathize reflective bards

Who learn, by cardiac measure or slow wit,
The differential of a chemic dream,
Small cells still to the fancy may transmit.

BASIL RANSOME-DAVIES

William McGonagall Rewrites Rupert Brooke

Oh! if by any unfortunate chance I should happen to die,
In a French field of turnips or radishes I'll lie.
But thinking of it as really Scottish all the time
Because my patriotic body will impart goodness to the slime.
For I've been brought up by the bonnie country of Scotland
Which I like very much indeed with its lochs and plots of land
And many other picturesque sites which any tourist can see
So long as he is able to pay British Rail the requisite fee.

And you might give a thought too to my decomposing body
As it lies, poor dead thing, under the frog soddy.
For it will be thinking too of my very nice home country
And its weather which is anything but sultry,
And all the exceedingly jocund times I enjoyed there
And frolicked when I was able to in the soggy Scottish air.

J. Y. WATSON

Sir John Betjeman Rewrites John Donne

When we played in the nursery till seven,
Drank cocoa, and fought and cried 'Pax',
Did we dream of this amorous heaven –
You in Arpège, and me in my Daks?
The world jets about in a hurry,
While pundits and media-men fuss.
Our Concorde's a bedroom in Surrey:
Very Sanderson, very us.
So pass the Rice Krispies, my honey,
And let's listen in to *Today*,
For our love is as solid as money
And sound as this egg on my tray.

BASIL RANSOME-DAVIES

Jane Austen Rewrites Dylan Thomas

MILK WOOD PARK

Llareggub was a name not to be found in any Baronetage; indeed its name was in itself a matter of some dispute; some authorities declaring, authoritatively, that its orthography was suspect. Whatever the spelling it was a fact that there was no Llareggub Hall on page or seafront; and money proved similarly scanty.

This had long been an annoyance to Captain Cat, who derived much pleasure from dreams of wealth and aristocracy. He was a man upon whom Nature had bestowed generous portions of Vanity; a talent he had repaid tenfold. His was a courtesy title given by his parents in the hope, which proved as vain as their offspring, that this would assist a suitable match. It had effected an introduction to Rosie, elder daughter of Mr and Mrs Probert; but nothing for Society to speak of had come from this union.

ROY KELLY

Dylan Thomas Rewrites Jane Austen

FIRST VOICE: It is night in the smug-as-a-bug-in-a-rug household of Mr and Mrs Dai Bennet and their simpering daughters – five breast-bobbing man-hungry titivators, innocent as ice-cream, panting for balls and matrimony.

MRS BENNET: Our new neighbour, Mr Darcy, quite tickles my fancy.

MR BENNET: Don't let him turn Lizzy's head Darcy-versy.

ELIZABETH: I shall wed whom I please.

FIRST VOICE: And busy Lizzy retires to her room with visions of bridling up the aisle to 'I will' with half-a-dozen demon lovers. She dreams of coaches and pairs and being a fine lady; dressing for dinner in a silken gown and undressing afterwards for heaven knows what in the saucy haven of a double bed; swoons, seductions and *sal volatile*; tears, tantrums and tedium; the pettish petticoquettish world of the country-house marriage-go-round from which she and her whinnying sisterhood can never hope to escape.

STANLEY J. SHARPLESS

Sir John Betjeman Rewrites William Wordsworth

METROLAND'S IMMORTALITY

Drinking fountains, fields for ponies,
  Surrey hills, suburban Groves,
How I love your courts for tennis,
Where each Doris had her Dennis
(Venus she, and he Adonis),
  Cocktail dresses, greens and mauves!

I love them still as in the Twenties,
  Nobody could love them more,
Life was absolutely topping –
We were reading without stopping
Percy Westermans and Hentys,
  No adventure seemed a bore.

Though I'm not completely sober
  And my meaning isn't clear,
I feel swamped by my own sweetness –
Sometimes I'd escape with fleetness,
Like a chocolate-enrober
  Rushing to the pub for beer!

Doris, you were young and tender,
  Lovely in your underwear,
You'd convert me more than Newman!
You're a flower, and I am human,
Lusting for your warm suspender,
  Keen to show you I still care!

GAVIN EWART

W. H. Auden Rewrites John Keats

ODE TO A NIGHTINGALE

'O how shall I reach you?' said bardie to birdie,
'A drink would be dandy to lift me aloft,
But since I am pintless the notion is pointless
And poetry's pinions are suitably soft.'

'O whom have you sung to?' said rhymer to roamer,
'You've booted no bucket, your cards are intact,
And Scrooges and Cratchits have suffered your crotchets
And spatial restrictions you've notably lacked.'

'O are you off now?' said tattler to tootler,
'Well, maybe it's time that our tongues were both tied –
A dream or a vision? You've all heard my version;
I'm off for that pint while the pundits decide.'

MARY HOLTBY

Daisy Ashford Rewrites Jane Austen

PRYDE AND PREDJUDISS

Lizzie thourght that Lady Kathareen de Burr was far too prowd and needed taking down a cupple of pegs.

'Our peddygree may not be so posh as yours,' she said, 'nor our country pile so sumshus, but we have the anshent pride of yomen, which is not to be sneezed at. Before accepting the hand of your neview, Darsey, and pledging my troth, I had already spurned the advances of another suetor, and, what is more, a clurgyman to boot.'

The Lady Kathareen was looking sumwhat insolent while Lizzie was torking and cried in a slitely snearing way: 'I am not the tinniest bit surprised, you pert and skeeming miss! A yung woman who uses red ruge and other abominashuns has probably whole strings of inamorartars!'

Lizzie bridled at the lofty scoff and said huffily: 'It is no cosmetick art that cullurs my check. It is my mayden blud stung to furry by your peevishness!'

The Lady Kathareen was crusshed.

MARTIN FAGG

Graham Greene Rewrites Charles Dickens

OLIVER TWIST

. . . Hunger nagged in his belly. He watched the master scooping the thin gruel from the copper, allotting it meagrely in the thick basins, passing it grudgingly down the shivering ranks of the foundlings.

Then the grace, a long, unctuous recital, as if, the boy thought bitterly, the Whole Mercy were being shared out.

Basins in their hands, the waifs lapped the gruel noisily like voracious dogs. The boy thought of the role he'd been diced into, and for once he swallowed the nauseous liquid with relish. The drained bowl was the cue. He waited until his companions had finished, savouring the histrionic pause like a gunman hesitating over his sights.

He heard the last basin thumped on a table behind him. Taking his own bowl, he walked with bony arrogance to where the master stood beside the copper. 'The same again,' he said. 'A double, this time, and make it quick.'

For a moment, the master wavered on his feet with surprise. Then, like a boxer coming off the ropes, he aimed viciously for the boy's jaw. Shifting his head with contemptuous nonchalance, the boy said, 'Maybe this'll persuade you,' and there was the glitter of a knife . . .

JOHN DIGBY

Edward Fitzgerald Rewrites T. S. Eliot

THE LOVE SONG OF J. OMAR KHAYYÁM

Awake! for Morning in the Pan of Night
Has dropped the Egg that puts bad Dreams to Flight;
And Newspapers and empty Bottles gleam
Encircled by a Hangman's Noose of Light.

I sometimes think there's none so red a Nose
As when some *fin-de-siècle* Poet goes;
That every Hyacinth the Garden wears
Through a blank Pair of female Sockets blows.

Come fill the Tea-cups and the Ices bring
So little time to hear the Mermaids sing,
The Footman waits already with my Hat;
I shall be Seventy in the Fire of Spring.

The Moving Finger writes; and, having writ,
Some other Finger comes to cancel it,
And out of a single word and half a line
Makes Verses of profundity and Wit.

ROY FULLER

INDEX OF AUTHORS
PARODIED

INDEX OF PARODISTS

SOURCES AND
ACKNOWLEDGEMENTS

Every effort has been made to trace copyright-holders. The publishers apologize for any omissions and would be grateful to be informed of corrections to be made in subsequent editions.

James Agate: for 'The Eumenides at Home', from *Modern Humour* (Dent).

Woody Allen: for 'Mr Big', from *Getting Even*, copyright © 1971 by Woody Allen. (Reprinted by permission of Random House Inc. and W. H. Allen and Co. Ltd.)

J. M. Barrie: for 'The Adventure of the Two Collaborators', from *Taking Off* (Methuen, London). (Reprinted by permission of Hodder & Stoughton Ltd.)

Michael Barsley: for 'Upon Julia's Clothes', from *Grabberwocky*. (Reprinted by permission of John Murray (Publishers) Ltd.)

William Bealby-Wright: for 'The Wordsworths'.

Sir Max Beerbohm: for Act II of 'Savanarola Brown', 'A Luncheon (Thomas Hardy Entertains the Prince of Wales)', 'The Guerdon' and 'Scruts'. (Reprinted by permission of Heinemann Ltd and Sir Rupert Hart-Davis.)

Robert Benchley: for 'Christmas Afternoon', from *A Benchley Round-Up*, © 1921 by Harper & Row, Publishers, Inc.; renewed 1949 by Gertrude D. Benchley. (Reprinted by permission of Harper & Row, Publishers, Inc.)

Alan Bennett: for 'Place Names of China'. (Reprinted by permission of A. D. Peters & Co. Ltd.)

Gerard Benson: for 'The Girl of So Ho', 'The Probatioun Officer's Tale', 'To his Coarse Mistress', 'Ben Barley', 'More Hard Times', 'My Garden', 'Initial Poem', 'Daddy's Not Taking You to the Zoo Tomorrow, Not If I Can Help It', 'Old King Cole', 'Hey Diddle Diddle' and 'Jack & Jill'.

Morris Bishop: for 'Ozymandias Revisited', from *The Best of Morris Bishop*. (Reprinted by permission of Putnam Inc.)

Edward Blishen: for 'My Mouse', 'The Morning's Journal', 'A Blurb for the Dustjacket of *The Turn of the Screw*'.

Malcolm Bradbury: for 'Voluptia', 'Last Things', 'The Sublime and the Ridiculous' and 'Room at the Bottom' (Secker & Warburg Ltd.)

Anthony Brode: for 'Breakfast with Gerard Manley Hopkins'. (Reprinted by permission of *Punch*.)

Charles Causley: for 'Betjeman, 1984', from *Collected Poems* (Macmillan Ltd). (Reprinted by permission of David Higham Associates Ltd.)

Graham Chapman: for 'Biggles Battles On', from *A Liar's Autobiography* (Methuen, London).

G. K. Chesterton: for 'From a Spanish Cloister', 'Old King Cole – Variations of an Air', 'The Fat White Woman to Frances Cornford' from *Collected Poems of G. K. Chesterton*. (Reprinted by permission of A. P. Watt Ltd on behalf of Miss D. E. Collins.)

Cyril Connolly: for 'Told in Gath', from *The Condemned Playground* (Hogarth Press), © the Estate of Cyril Connolly, and 'Bond Strikes Camp', from *Previous Convictions* (Hogarth Press), © the Estate of Cyril Connolly. (Reprinted by permission of Deborah Rogers Ltd.)

Wendy Cope: for 'Strugnell's Rubáiyát', 'A Policeman's Lot', 'Mr Strugnell', 'E Pericoloso Sporgersi', 'Budgie Finds His Voice', 'The Lavatory Attendant' and 'Baa Baa Black Sheep', from *Making Cocoa for Kingsley Amis*. (Reprinted by permission of Faber & Faber Ltd.)

Alan Coren: for 'The Gollies Karamazov', 'The Caretaker . . . or Private Life'. (Reprinted by permission of *Punch*.)

Sir Noël Coward: for 'Contours', 'Sunday Morning at Wiesbaden', from *A Withered Nosegay*. (Reprinted by permission of Methuen, London, and Michael Imison Playrights.)

Russell Davies: for 'Book Review'. (Reprinted by permission of A. D. Peters & Co. Ltd.)

Thomas Derrick: for 'The Sun It Shines', from *A Shropshire Racket*. (Reprinted by permission of Sheed & Ward Ltd.)

Peter De Vries: for 'Morning Disturbance', 'Poets', 'The Tents of Wickedness'. (Reprinted by permission of A. P. Watt Ltd.) For 'Requiem for a Noun, *or* Intruder in the Dust' from *Without a Stitch in Time*. (Reprinted by permission of Watkins/Loomis Agency, Inc.)

H. F. Ellis: for 'Sense and Centenaries' from *A Bee in the Bonnet* (Methuen, London.)

Sir William Empson: for 'Just a Smack at Auden' from *Collected Poems*. (Reprinted by permission of the author's estate and Chatto & Windus).

Gavin Ewart: for 'The Most Famous Poem of J. Strugnell', 'Sir John Betjeman rewrites Wordsworth'.

Martin Fagg: for 'Another Passionate Shepherd', 'To My Lady Nicotine', 'The Poet Sees Himself', 'Elegy', 'The Unexpurgated Water Babies', 'Transistors', 'Foes Beyond', 'The Importance of Being Ernestine', 'The Reunion Dinner', 'Cats!', 'Nunsmantle', 'Hound Puss', 'Nothing Succeeds like Failure', 'The Cloisters of Power', 'Lewis Eliot's Revolution Diary', 'Solomon Grundy', 'Little Miss Muffet', 'Daisy Ashford Rewrites Jane Austen'.

Colin Falck: for 'Keeping up with Kingsley'.

P. W. R. Foot: for 'Adventures in the Fur Game' from *Bindweed's Best Seller* (Pan). (Reprinted by permission of Mrs Foot.)

Michael Foster: for 'Recruiting Song'.

Iain Frazier: for 'LGA-ORD'. (Reprinted by permission of Farrar Straus & Giroux Inc.)

Roy Fuller: for 'Edward Fitzgerald rewrites T. S. Eliot'.

Stella Gibbons: for an excerpt from 'Cold Comfort Farm'. (Reprinted by permission of Curtis Brown Ltd, on behalf of the author.)

Harry Graham: for 'The Queys Are Mooping', from The Realms of Melody, Macmillan Publishers, 1931.

Graham Greene: for 'H. A. Baxter' parody of Graham Greene (*New Statesman*, 7 April 1961) from *Verse Autobiography*. (Reprinted by permission of Laurence Pollinger Ltd.)

Sir Hugh Greene ('Sebastian Eleigh'): for two parodies of Graham Greene: 'Biography of Hugh', 'Extract from an Imaginary Novel'.

Bill Greenwell: for 'Baked Beauty', 'Initial Poem', 'A Third World War Poem', 'Looking in the Mirror', 'A Bear Called Paddington', 'Birth', 'Birthday', 'The Pig on Ted Hughes', 'Three Blind Mice'.

Paul Griffin: for 'The Modern Brook', 'Off Wenlock Edge', 'New Tarantella', 'Porphyria to Robert Browning', 'Little Boy Blue'.

T. Griffiths: for 'My First Abstract', 'What Really Happened in the Malabar Caves'.

Arthur Guiterman: for 'Alibi', 'Sea-chill'. (Reprinted by permission of Louise H. Sclove.)

Lance Haward: for 'It's Those Daffodils Again'.

Mary Holtby: for 'W.S. at his Mirror', 'Last Poem', 'McQuiddity', 'The Fair Youth Responds to William Shakespeare', 'W. H. Auden Rewrites John Keats'.

Tim Hopkins: for 'I Am a Racist', 'Post-Natal Pome', 'The Grand Old Duke of York'.

A. E. Housman: for 'Fragment of a Greek Tragedy' from *Collected Poems*. (Reprinted by permission of The Society of Authors and Jonathan Cape Ltd.)

Clive James; for 'The Improved Version of Peregrine Prykke's Pilgrimage through the London Literary World'. (Reprinted by permission of the author.)

Joyce Johnson: for 'Ode to Conservation'.

L. E. Jones: for 'Our Head-waiter', 'The Charlady at Patterne Hall', 'On Jane Austen', 'The Death of King Edward VII', 'Cynara to Ernest Dowson', 'Lucasta to Richard Lovelace', from *A la Carte* (Secker & Warburg Ltd).

James Joyce: for 'A Letter to Harriet Weaver, in the Style of *The Waste Land*'. (Reprinted by permission of The Society of Authors as the Literary Representative of the Estate of James Joyce.)

Roy Kelly: for 'Jane Austen Rewrites Dylan Thomas'.

Hugh Kingsmill: for 'What, Still Alive at Twenty-two?', 'Summer Time on Bredon'. (Reprinted by permission of Lady Hopkinson.)

Rudyard Kipling: for 'The Muse among the Motorists', from *Collected Poems*. (Reprinted by permission of A. P. Watt Ltd.)

Ven. H. F. Kirkpatrick: for 'New Cautionary Tale'. (Reprinted by permission of Mrs Ann Draper.)

Allan M. Laing: for 'This Railway Station', 'Voyage to Cynosuria', 'The Charwoman', 'Shaw: Opening Paragraph of his Memoirs', 'Damon Runyon on Henry James', 'The Heavenly Fish Queue', from *Bank Holiday on Parnassus*. (Reprinted by permission of Allen & Unwin Ltd.)

Richard Le Gallienne: for 'A Melton Mowbray Pork Pie'. (Reprinted by permission of The Society of Authors as the Literary Representative of the Estate of Richard Le Gallienne, and Dodd, Mead & Co.)

Tom Lehrer: for 'I Hold Your Hand in Mine', from *Too Many Songs* (Methuen, London). (Reprinted by permission of the author.)

David Lodge: for 'A's Trial', 'The British Museum Reading Room' (Secker & Warburg Ltd).

Russell Lucas: for 'Boswell: from his *Life of Dr Johnson*', 'Bertie and Emma'.

Arthur Marshall: for 'On the Derationing of Sweets'.

Ronn Marvin: for 'When to the Sessions' (Owl Publishers).

George Moor: for 'The Lost Girl Trespasser', from *Bindweed's Best Seller*.

J. W. Morris: for 'What I Think of Hiawatha', from *Parodies*, ed. Dwight MacDonald (Faber & Faber Ltd).

J. B. Morton: for 'Kindness to the Starfish', 'A Spot of Verse', 'The Queen of Minikoi', 'Ezra Pound: Another Canto', 'When We Were Very Silly', from *Beachcomber* (Heinemann Ltd). (Reprinted by permission of A. D. Peters & Co. Ltd.)

John Julius Norwich: for 'On First Hearing that Wordsworth had an Illegitimate Child'.

L. A. Pavey: for 'First Person Circular'.

Noel Petty: for 'There's a Breathless Hush'.

Fiona Pitt-Kethley: for 'The Lamb on William Blake'.

Ezra Pound: for 'Ancient Music', 'The Charge of the Bread Brigade', from the poems of Alfred Venison from *Collected Shorter Poems*. (Reprinted by permission of Faber & Faber Ltd.)

Richard Quick: for 'Bank-holiday Fever', 'Under Broadcasting House'.

Basil Ransome-Davies: for 'Just a Few Friends', 'A Toad on Philip Larkin', 'Sir William Empson Rewrites William Wordsworth', 'Sir John Betjeman Rewrites John Donne'.

Henry Reed: for 'Chard Whitlow' from *A Map of Verona*. (Reprinted by permission of the author.)

Margaret Rogers: for 'Paradise Lost 2–0', 'Little Brothers and Sisters'.

Ken Rudge: for 'The Wind in the Willows'.

Sagittarius: for 'Once More Unto the Peace', 'The Hardened Brat', 'I Will Arise', from *Quiver's Choice*. (Reprinted by permission of the author.)

Sir Owen Seaman: for 'A Birthday Ode to Mr Alfred Austin' from *Owen Seaman. A Selection* (Methuen, London).

Walter C. Sellar & R. J. Yeatman: for 'How I Brought the Good News from Aix to Ghent, or Vice Versa', from *Horse Nonsense* (Methuen, London).

Stanley J. Sharpless: for 'King Canute', 'All's Well', 'Boswell: from his *Life of Dr Johnson*', 'Elizabeth Barrett Browning: Sonnet', 'Spring is Here', 'A Song Against Super-Markets', 'A Cricket Commentary', 'Autumn', 'At the Post Office', 'Remember Lot's Wife', 'Second-hand Car Dealer', 'Geoffrey Chaucer Rewrites Sir John Betjeman', 'Dylan Thomas Rewrites Jane Austen'.

Stanley Shaw: for 'Christopher Smart to His Mirror' (*New Statesman*).

Frank Sidgwick: for 'An Antient Poem', from *The Comic Muse*. (Reprinted by permission of William Collins Sons & Co. Ltd.)

Cornelia Otis Skinner: for 'For Whom the Gong Sounds'. (Reprinted by permission of *New Yorker* magazine and International Creative Management.)

Sir John Squire: for 'If Gray had had to write his Elegy in the Cemetery at Spoon River', 'The Little Commodore', 'At Martinmas', 'The Tales I Hear', 'When I Leapt over Tower Bridge', © Raglan Squire. (Reprinted by permission of Raglan Squire.)

Andrew Stibbs: for 'Ode to a Slug', 'Slug', 'Slug Resting'.

L. A. G. Strong: for 'A Memory'. (Reprinted by permission of A. D. Peters & Co. Ltd.)

John Stanley Sweetman: for 'On Herself'.

Kenneth Tynan: for 'Just Plain Folks'. (Reprinted by permission of the *Observer*.)

Peter Veale: for 'When Icicles', 'Memories of 1966', 'Christie's Minstrels', 'Nun-running'.

N. J. Warburton: for 'Peter Rabbit', 'The Famous Five Take Tea with Gaius Caesar Augustus Germanicus and Family', 'The Snake on D. H. Lawrence'.

W. F. N. Watson: for 'The Hicche-hykere', 'God Bless Nanny'.

E. B. White: for 'A Classic Waits for Me', from *The Second Tree from the Corner*, © 1944, 1954 by E. B. White. (Reprinted by permission of Harper & Row, Publishers, Inc.)

Katharine Whitehorn: for 'The Man Who Hangs Head Downwards', 'Mummy', from the *Observer*. (Reprinted by permission of A. D. Peters & Co. Ltd.)

Roger Woddis: for 'By All Accounts', 'Enter Puck', 'How They Brought the Bad News', 'The Bug-eyed Listeners', 'A Ticket-Collector's Love Song', '"Four-Feet" on Rudyard Kipling', from *Parodies* from *The Woddis Collection*. (Reprinted by permission of Century Hutchinson Ltd.)

FOR THE BEST IN PAPERBACKS, LOOK FOR THE 🐧

In every corner of the world, on every subject under the sun, Penguins represent quality and variety – the very best in publishing today.

For complete information about books available from Penguin and how to order them, write to us at the appropriate address below. Please note that for copyright reasons the selection of books varies from country to country.

In the United Kingdom: For a complete list of books available from Penguin in the U.K., please write to *Dept EP, Penguin Books Ltd, Harmondsworth, Middlesex, UB7 0DA*

In the United States: For a complete list of books available from Penguin in the U.S., please write to *Dept BA, Viking Penguin, 299 Murray Hill Parkway, East Rutherford, New Jersey 07073*

In Canada: For a complete list of books available from Penguin in Canada, please write to *Penguin Books Canada Limited, 2801 John Street, Markham, Ontario L3R 1B4*

In Australia: For a complete list of books available from Penguin in Australia, please write to the *Marketing Department, Penguin Books Australia Ltd, P.O. Box 257, Ringwood, Victoria 3134*

In New Zealand: For a complete list of books available from Penguin in New Zealand, please write to the *Marketing Department, Penguin Books (N.Z.) Ltd, Private Bag, Takapuna, Auckland 9*

In India: For a complete list of books available from Penguin in India, please write to *Penguin Overseas Ltd, 706 Eros Apartments, 56 Nehru Place, New Delhi 110019*

FOR THE BEST IN PAPERBACKS, LOOK FOR THE

A CHOICE OF PENGUINS

Castaway Lucy Irvine

'Writer seeks "wife" for a year on a tropical island.' This is the extraordinary, candid, sometimes shocking account of what happened when Lucy Irvine answered the advertisement, and found herself embroiled in what was not exactly a desert island dream. 'Fascinating' – *Daily Mail*

Out of Africa Karen Blixen (Isak Dinesen)

After the failure of her coffee-farm in Kenya, where she lived from 1913 to 1931, Karen Blixen went home to Denmark and wrote this unforgettable account of her experiences. 'No reader can put the book down without some share in the author's poignant farewell to her farm' – *Observer*

The Lisle Letters Edited by Muriel St Clare Byrne

An intimate, immediate and wholly fascinating picture of a family in the reign of Henry VIII. 'Remarkable . . . we can really hear the people of early Tudor England talking' – Keith Thomas in the *Sunday Times*. 'One of the most extraordinary works to be published this century' – J. H. Plumb

In My Wildest Dreams Leslie Thomas

The autobiography of Leslie Thomas, author of *The Magic Army* and *The Dearest and the Best*. From Barnardo boy to original virgin soldier, from apprentice journalist to famous novelist, it is an amazing story. 'Hugely enjoyable' – *Daily Express*

India: The Siege Within M. J. Akbar

'A thoughtful and well-researched history of the conflict, 2,500 years old, between centralizing and separatist forces in the sub-continent. And remarkably, for a work of this kind, it's concise, elegantly written and entertaining' – Zareer Masani in the *New Statesman*

The Winning Streak Walter Goldsmith and David Clutterbuck

Marks and Spencer, Saatchi and Saatchi, United Biscuits, G.E.C. . . . The U.K.'s top companies reveal their formulas for success, in an important and stimulating book that no British manager can afford to ignore.

A CHOICE OF PENGUINS

Adieux: A Farewell to Sartre   Simone de Beauvoir

A devastatingly frank account of the last years of Sartre's life, and his death, by the woman who for more than half a century shared that life. 'A true labour of love, there is about it a touching sadness, a mingling of the personal with the impersonal and timeless which Sartre himself would surely have liked and understood' – *Listener*

Business Wargames   James Barrie

How did BMW overtake Mercedes? Why did Laker crash? How did McDonalds grab the hamburger market? Drawing on the tragic mistakes and brilliant victories of military history, this remarkable book draws countless fascinating parallels with case histories from industry world-wide.

Metamagical Themas   Douglas R. Hofstadter

This astonishing sequel to the best-selling, Pulitzer Prize-winning *Gödel, Escher, Bach* swarms with 'extraordinary ideas, brilliant fables, deep philosophical questions and Carrollian word play' – Martin Gardner

Into the Heart of Borneo   Redmond O'Hanlon

'Perceptive, hilarious and at the same time a serious natural-history journey into one of the last remaining unspoilt paradises' – *New Statesman*. 'Consistently exciting, often funny and erudite without ever being overwhelming' – *Punch*

A Better Class of Person   John Osborne

The playwright's autobiography, 1929–56. 'Splendidly enjoyable' – John Mortimer. 'One of the best, richest and most bitterly truthful autobiographies that I have ever read' – Melvyn Bragg

The Secrets of a Woman's Heart   Hilary Spurling

The later life of Ivy Compton-Burnett, 1920–69. 'A biographical triumph . . . elegant, stylish, witty, tender, immensely acute – dazzles and exhilarates . . . a great achievement' – Kay Dick in the *Literary Review*. 'One of the most important literary biographies of the century' – *New Statesman*

FOR THE BEST IN PAPERBACKS, LOOK FOR THE 🐧

A CHOICE OF PENGUINS

An African Winter   Preston King   With an Introduction by Richard Leakey

This powerful and impassioned book offers a unique assessment of the interlocking factors which result in the famines of Africa and argues that there *are* solutions and we *can* learn from the mistakes of the past.

Jean Rhys: Letters 1931–66
Edited by Francis Wyndham and Diana Melly

'Eloquent and invaluable . . . her life emerges, and with it a portrait of an unexpectedly indomitable figure' – Marina Warner in the *Sunday Times*

Among the Russians   Colin Thubron

One man's solitary journey by car across Russia provides an enthralling and revealing account of the habits and idiosyncrasies of a fascinating people. 'He sees things with the freshness of an innocent and the erudition of a scholar' – *Daily Telegraph*

The Amateur Naturalist   Gerald Durrell with Lee Durrell

'Delight . . . on every page . . . packed with authoritative writing, learning without pomposity . . . it represents a real bargain' – *The Times Educational Supplement*. 'What treats are in store for the average British household' – *Books and Bookmen*

The Democratic Economy   Geoff Hodgson

Today, the political arena is divided as seldom before. In this exciting and original study, Geoff Hodgson carefully examines the claims of the rival doctrines and exposes some crucial flaws.

They Went to Portugal   Rose Macaulay

An exotic and entertaining account of travellers to Portugal from the pirate-crusaders, through poets, aesthetes and ambassadors, to the new wave of romantic travellers. A wonderful mixture of literature, history and adventure, by one of our most stylish and seductive writers.

FOR THE BEST IN PAPERBACKS, LOOK FOR THE

A CHOICE OF PENGUINS

The Book Quiz Book   Joseph Connolly

Who was literature's performing flea . . .? Who wrote 'Live Now, Pay Later . . .'? Keats and Cartland, Balzac and Braine, Coleridge conundrums, Eliot enigmas, Tolstoy teasers . . . all in this brilliant quiz book. You will be on the shelf without it . . .

Voyage through the Antarctic   Richard Adams and Ronald Lockley

Here is the true, authentic Antarctic of today, brought vividly to life by Richard Adams, author of *Watership Down*, and Ronald Lockley, the world-famous naturalist. 'A good adventure story, with a lot of information and a deal of enthusiasm for Antarctica and its animals' – *Nature*

Getting to Know the General   Graham Greene

'In August 1981 my bag was packed for my fifth visit to Panama when the news came to me over the telephone of the death of General Omar Torrijos Herrera, my friend and host . . .' 'Vigorous, deeply felt, at times funny, and for Greene surprisingly frank' – *Sunday Times*

Television Today and Tomorrow: Wall to Wall Dallas?
Christopher Dunkley

Virtually every British home has a television, nearly half now have two sets or more, and we are promised that before the end of the century there will be a vast expansion of television delivered via cable and satellite. How did television come to be so central to our lives? Is British television really the best in the world, as politicians like to assert?

Arabian Sands   Wilfred Thesiger

'In the tradition of Burton, Doughty, Lawrence, Philby and Thomas, it is, very likely, the book about Arabia to end all books about Arabia' – *Daily Telegraph*

When the Wind Blows   Raymond Briggs

'A visual parable against nuclear war: all the more chilling for being in the form of a strip cartoon' – *Sunday Times*. 'The most eloquent anti-Bomb statement you are likely to read' – *Daily Mail*

A CHOICE OF PENGUINS

A Fortunate Grandchild 'Miss Read'

Grandma Read in Lewisham and Grandma Shafe in Walton on the Naze were totally different in appearance and outlook, but united in their affection for their grand-daughter – who grew up to become the much-loved and popular novelist.

The Ultimate Trivia Quiz Game Book Maureen and Alan Hiron

If you are immersed in trivia, addicted to quiz games, endlessly nosey, then this is the book for you: over 10,000 pieces of utterly dispensable information!

The Diary of Virginia Woolf
Five volumes, edited by Quentin Bell and Anne Olivier Bell

'As an account of the intellectual and cultural life of our century, Virginia Woolf's diaries are invaluable; as the record of one bruised and unquiet mind, they are unique'– Peter Ackroyd in the *Sunday Times*

Voices of the Old Sea Norman Lewis

'I will wager that *Voices of the Old Sea* will be a classic in the literature about Spain' – *Mail on Sunday*. 'Limpidly and lovingly Norman Lewis has caught the helpless, unwitting, often foolish, but always hopeful village in its dying summers, and saved the tragedy with sublime comedy' – *Observer*

The First World War A. J. P. Taylor

In this superb illustrated history, A. J. P. Taylor 'manages to say almost everything that is important for an understanding and, indeed, intellectual digestion of that vast event . . . A special text . . . a remarkable collection of photographs' – *Observer*

Ninety-Two Days Evelyn Waugh

With characteristic honesty, Evelyn Waugh here debunks the romantic notions attached to rough travelling: his journey in Guiana and Brazil is difficult, dangerous and extremely uncomfortable, and his account of it is witty and unquestionably compelling.

FOR THE BEST IN PAPERBACKS, LOOK FOR THE

A CHOICE OF PENGUINS

The Big Red Train Ride   Eric Newby

From Moscow to the Pacific on the Trans-Siberian Railway is an eight-day journey of nearly six thousand miles through seven time zones. In 1977 Eric Newby set out with his wife, an official guide and a photographer on this journey. 'The best kind of travel book' – Paul Theroux

Star Wars   Edited by E. P. Thompson

With contributions from Rip Bulkeley, John Pike, Ben Thompson and E. P. Thompson, and with a Foreward by Dorothy Hodgkin, OM, this is a major book which assesses all the arguments for Star Wars and proceeds to make a powerful – indeed unanswerable – case against it.

Selected Letters of Malcolm Lowry
Edited by Harvey Breit and Margerie Bonner Lowry

Lowry emerges from these letters not only as an extremely interesting man, but also a lovable one' – Philip Toynbee

PENGUIN CLASSICS OF WORLD ART

Each volume presents the complete paintings of the artist and includes: an introduction by a distinguished art historian, critical comments on the painter from his own time to the present day, 64 pages of full-colour plates, a chronological survey of his life and work, a basic bibliography, a fully illustrated and annotated *catalogue raisonné*.

Titles already published or in preparation

Botticelli, Bruegel, Canaletto, Caravaggio, Cézanne, Dürer, Giorgione, Giotto, Leonardo da Vinci, Manet, Mantegna, Michelangelo, Picasso, Piero della Francesca, Raphael, Rembrandt, Toulouse-Lautrec, van Eyck, Vermeer, Watteau

Also compiled by E. O. Parrott

THE PENGUIN BOOK OF LIMERICKS

'Wit, sharp comment, mood music, landscape, philosophy; all of these are in Mr Parrott's fine selection. Nor does it neglect the Double Limerick, the limeraiku, the Reverse Limerick, Beheaded Limericks, though sportiness, naughtiness and all the traditional qualities are well and tastefully represented, in several shades of blue . . .' – Gavin Ewart in the *Guardian*

'He seems to have read not only every previous collection but also far-flung limerick competitions, as well as being the recipient of many an improper verse from proud authors' – R. G. G. Price in *Punch*

and

HOW TO BECOME WELL-READ
IN ONE EVENING

This superbly efficient book allows one to savour the wealth of great literature without the time-consuming tedium of having to read it. It contains some 150 succinct and entertaining encapsulations of the best-known books in the English language, including a few foreign works familiar to us in translation. Through them you will rapidly acquire nearly all that is worth knowing about the books.

'Very funny. Well calculated to put all teachers of English Literature in their places' – John Mortimer

'A box of bright little buttons, sharp and clever' – Frank Muir